S0-ADH-554

A BOOK OF ENGLISH ESSAYS

(1600–1900)

A BOOK OF ENGLISH ESSAYS

(1600-1900)

Selected by STANLEY V. MAKOWER and BASIL H. BLACKWELL

Essay Index Reprint Series

BOOKS FOR LIBRARIES PRESS
FREEPORT, NEW YORK

First Published 1912
Reprinted 1972

Library of Congress Cataloging in Publication Data

Makower, Stanley Victor, ed.
A book of English essays (1600-1900).

(Essay index reprint series)
Reprint of the 1912 ed., which was issued as no. 172 of The World's classics series.
1. English essays. I. Blackwell, Sir Basil, 1889- joint ed. II. Title.
PR1363.M3 1972 824'.008 73-37845
ISBN 0-8369-2609-9

PRINTED IN THE UNITED STATES OF AMERICA
BY
NEW WORLD BOOK MANUFACTURING CO., INC.
HALLANDALE, FLORIDA 33009

PREFACE

In selecting the following Essays we have been guided by a desire to secure variety, not only in the outlook and equipment of our authors, but also in the subjects by which we have chosen to represent them. It was our object to set before the reader a rich and entertaining banquet rather than to make a bid for the critic's recognition of the supreme merits of each dish. In other words, we have wanted the essays chosen to differ from one another as widely and in as great a variety of ways as was compatible with the resolution to maintain a high level of excellence throughout the book.

In conformity with this plan we have chosen relatively few essays on literary subjects. To be made acquainted with a master's thoughts on some common topic of daily life is to enjoy a rarer and a more profitable glimpse of his genius than we can get by reading his opinions on the work of a brother author. Bacon and Goldsmith, differing from each other so profoundly and in so many ways as to offer the best because the most widely divergent standards for the comparison and contrast of all other essays, agree in this, that they avoid writing on literary subjects. To all save the student of poetry Addison is less entertaining when he writes of Milton than when he writes of Popular Superstitions.

Of the word Essay it is necessary to say something, because at different times it has borne different meanings. Johnson's definition of it as a loose sally of the mind ; an irregular undigested piece', covered its employment by authors to excuse shortcomings, and to disarm the critic in his examination of a work which boasted of no pretence to literature. Some such idea of admitted or implied failure in a worthy experiment adhered to Montaigne's use of the word in those *Essais* which were published in 1580. But the decay of this sense began in fact with this publication, although the author expressed his apology for being 'something fantastical'. For that very wandering from point to point which in Montaigne was a habit of mind, was developed by the English essayists of the eighteenth century into a deliberate study. Out of what Montaigne would have been only too pleased to call 'irregularity and want of finish' they invented a literary quality which in Goldsmith rose to a perfection of carelessness in approaching and retreating from a subject.

It was in another direction from that taken by Montaigne and his followers that Bacon enlarged the meaning of the word essay in literature. He applied it to his pieces not in the sense of 'an experiment', but in the sense of 'a test or assay'. He weighed and examined his subjects one by one.

With the grip of his intellect he clung to each separate subject as to a rock while he treated of it, refusing to dip to the invading wave of kindred ideas by which it was surrounded. In the dedication of his second edition of pieces to Prince Henry of Wales in 1612 he wrote of them as 'brief notes, set down rather significantly than curiously, which I have called Essays. The word is late, but the thing is ancient'. And he went on to point out that Seneca's epistles to Lucilius were, if read aright, nothing but essays.

Informed by the spirit of this definition we should have found it no very difficult task to include in this collection a number of letters or lectures of which at least Addison or Steele would have been ready to admit that 'if one mark them well' they are but essays. With the aid of such freedom we should have been able to represent women writers much more adequately than by stricter adherence to a verbal distinction in nomenclature. By a slightly more reckless exercise of this freedom we could have included many a public discourse or many a chapter complete in itself from a work comprising a number of kindred subjects. We have preferred, however, to interpret our task in a narrower spirit, consoling ourselves with the reflection that the more we had widened our field (and most regretfully was Sterne excluded), the more arbitrary to many a reader must have appeared our selection.

We have in more than one instance chosen essays on subjects closely akin, in order to compare their treatment by contemporaries or men of different epochs.

Mr. Makower had not long been engaged on a selection of English essays, when his regretted death left this fruit of his taste and experience in the forming.

CONTENTS

FRANCIS BACON

VISCOUNT ST. ALBANS

1561–1626

I. OF MASQUES AND TRIUMPHS

THESE things are but toys to come amongst such serious observations; but yet, since princes will have such things, it is better they should be graced with elegancy, than daubed with cost. Dancing to song is a thing of great state and pleasure. I understand it that the song be in choir, placed aloft and accompanied with some broken music; and the ditty fitted to the device. Acting in song, especially in dialogues, hath an extreme good grace; I say acting, not dancing (for that is a mean and vulgar thing); and the voices of the dialogue would be strong and manly (a bass and a tenor, no treble), and the ditty high and tragical, not nice or dainty. Several choirs placed one over against another, and taking the voice by catches anthem-wise, give great pleasure. Turning dances into figure is a childish curiosity; and generally, let it be noted that those things which I here set down are such as do naturally take the sense, and not respect petty wonderments. It is true the alterations of scenes, so it be quietly and without noise, are things of great beauty and pleasure; for they feed and relieve the eye before it be full of the same object. Let the scenes abound with light specially coloured and varied; and let the masquers, or any other that are to come down from the scene, have some motions upon the scene itself before their coming down; for it draws the eye strangely, and makes it with great pleasure to desire to see that it cannot perfectly discern. Let the songs be loud and cheerful, and not chirpings or pulings: let the music likewise be sharp and loud and well placed. The colours that show best by candlelight are white, carnation, and a kind of seawater green; and oes or spangs, as they are of no great cost, so they are of most glory. As for rich embroidery, it is lost and not discerned. Let the suits of the masquers be graceful, and such as become the person when the vizors are off; not after examples of known attires, Turks, soldiers, mariners, and the like. Let antimasques not be long; they have been commonly of fools, satyrs, baboons, wild men, antics, beasts, sprites, witches, Ethiopes, pigmies, turquets, nymphs, rustics, Cupids, statuas moving, and the like. As for angels, it is not comical enough to put them in antimasques: and anything that is hideous, as devils, giants, is on the other side as unfit; but chiefly, let the music of them be recreative, and with some strange changes. Some sweet odours suddenly coming forth, without any drops falling, are, in such a company as there is steam and heat, things of great pleasure and refreshment. Double masques, one of men another of ladies, addeth state and variety; but all is nothing except the room be kept clear and neat.

For justs and tourneys and barriers, the glories

of them are chiefly in the chariots, wherein the challengers make their entry; especially if they be drawn with strange beasts, as lions, bears, camels, and the like; or in the devices of their entrance, or in the bravery of their liveries, or in the goodly furniture of their horses and armour. But enough of these toys.

II. OF SUPERSTITION

It were better to have no opinion of God at all than such an opinion as is unworthy of Him; for the one is unbelief, the other is contumely: and certainly superstition is the reproach of the Deity. Plutarch saith well to that purpose: *Surely*, saith he, *I had rather a great deal men should say there was no such man at all as Plutarch, than that they should say that there was one Plutarch that would eat his children as soon as they were born*; as the poets speak of Saturn. And, as the contumely is greater towards God, so the danger is greater towards men. Atheism leaves a man to sense, to philosophy, to natural piety, to laws, to reputation: all which may be guides to an outward moral virtue, though religion were not; but superstition dismounts all these, and erecteth an absolute monarchy in the minds of men. Therefore atheism did never perturb states; for it makes men wary of themselves, as looking no further; and we see the times inclined to atheism (as the time of Augustus Caesar) were civil times; but superstition hath been the confusion of many states, and bringeth in a new *primum mobile* that ravisheth all the spheres of government. The master of superstition is the people; and in all superstition wise men follow fools; and arguments are fitted to practice in a reversed order. It was gravely said by some of the prelates in the Council of Trent, where the doctrine of the schoolmen bare great sway, *that the schoolmen were like astronomers, which did feign eccentrics and epicycles, and such engines of orbs to save the phenomena, though they knew there were no such things*; and, in like manner, that the schoolmen had framed a number of subtile and intricate axioms and theorems, to save the practice of the Church. The causes of superstition are: pleasing and sensual rites and ceremonies; excess of outward and pharisaical holiness; over-great reverence of traditions, which cannot but load the Church; the stratagems of prelates for their own ambition and lucre; the favouring too much of good intentions, which openeth the gate to conceits and novelties; the taking an aim at divine matters by human, which cannot but breed mixture of imaginations; and, lastly, barbarous times, especially joined with calamities and disasters. Superstition, without a veil, is a deformed thing; for as it addeth deformity to an ape to be so like a man, so the similitude of superstition to religion makes it the more deformed: and as wholesome meat corrupteth to little worms, so good forms and orders corrupt into a number of petty observances. There is a superstition in avoiding superstition, when men think to do best if they go furthest from the superstition formerly received; therefore care would be had that (as it fareth in ill purgings) the good be not taken away with the bad, which commonly is done when the people is the reformer.

III. OF GREAT PLACE

Men in great place are thrice servants: servants of the sovereign or state, servants of fame, and servants of business; so as they have no freedom, neither in their persons, nor in their actions, nor in their times. It is a strange desire to seek power and to lose liberty; or to seek power over others, and to lose power over a man's self. The rising unto place is laborious, and by pains men come to greater pains; and it is sometimes base, and by indignities men come to dignities. The standing is slippery, and the regress is either a downfall, or at least an eclipse, which is a melancholy thing: *Cum non sis qui fueris, non esse cur velis vivere.* Nay, retire men cannot when they would, neither will they when it were reason; but are impatient of privateness even in age and sickness, which require the shadow; like old townsmen, that will be still sitting at their street-door, though thereby they offer age to scorn. Certainly, great persons had need to borrow other men's opinions to think themselves happy; for if they judge by their own feeling they cannot find it: but if they think with themselves what other men think of them, and that other men would fain be as they are, then they are happy as it were by report, when, perhaps, they find the contrary within; for they are the first that find their own griefs, though they be the last that find their own faults. Certainly, men in great fortunes are strangers to themselves, and while they are in the puzzle of business they have no time to tend their health either of body or mind. *Illi mors gravis incubat, qui notus nimis omnibus, ignotus moritur sibi.* In place there is licence to do good and evil; whereof the latter is a curse: for in evil the best condition is not to will, the second not to can. But power to do good is the true and lawful end of aspiring; for good thoughts (though God accept them) yet towards men are little better than good dreams, except they be put in act; and that cannot be without power and place, as the vantage and commanding ground. Merit and good works is the end of man's motion; and conscience of the same is the accomplishment of man's rest: for if a man can be partaker of God's theatre, he shall likewise be partaker of God's rest. *Et conversus Deus, ut aspiceret opera quae fecerunt manus suae, vidit quod omnia essent bona nimis*; and then the Sabbath.

In the discharge of thy place set before thee the best examples; for imitation is a globe of precepts; and after a time set before thee thine own example; and examine thyself strictly whether thou didst not best at first. Neglect not also the examples of those that have carried themselves ill in the same place; not to set off thyself by taxing their memory, but to direct thyself what to avoid. Reform, therefore, without bravery or scandal of former times and persons; but yet set it down to thyself, as well to create good precedents as to follow them. Reduce things to the first institution, and observe wherein and how they have degenerated; but yet ask counsel of both times; of the ancient time what is best, and of the latter time what is fittest. Seek to make thy course regular, that men may know beforehand what they may expect; but be not too positive and peremptory; and express thyself well when thou digressest from thy rule. Preserve the right of thy place, but stir not questions of jurisdiction; and rather assume thy right in silence and *de facto*, than voice it with claims and challenges. Preserve likewise the rights of inferior places; and think it more honour to direct in chief than to be busy in all. Embrace and invite helps and advices touching the execution of thy place; and do not drive away such as bring thee information as meddlers, but accept of them in good part.

The vices of authority are chiefly four: delays, corruption, roughness, and facility. For delays, give easy access; keep times appointed; go through with that which is in hand, and interlace not business but of necessity. For corruption, do not only bind thine own hands or thy servants' hands from taking, but bind the hands of suitors also from offering; for integrity used doth the one; but integrity professed, and with a manifest detestation of bribery, doth the other; and avoid not only the fault, but the suspicion. Whosoever is found variable, and changeth manifestly without manifest cause, giveth suspicion of corruption: therefore, always when thou changest thine opinion or course, profess it plainly and declare it, together with the reasons that move thee to change, and do not think to steal it. A servant or a favourite, if he be inward, and no other apparent cause of esteem, is commonly thought but a by-way to close corruption. For roughness, it is a needless cause of discontent: severity breedeth fear, but roughness breedeth hate. Even reproofs from authority ought to be grave, and not taunting. As for facility, it is worse than bribery; for bribes come but now and then; but if importunity or idle respects lead a man, he shall never be without;

as Salomon saith, *To respect persons is not good; for such a man will transgress for a piece of bread.*

It is most true that was anciently spoken; *A place showeth the man*; and it showeth some to the better and some to the worse: *Omnium consensu capax imperii, nisi imperasset,* saith Tacitus of Galba; but of Vespasian he saith, *Solus imperantium Vespasianus mutatus in melius*; though the one was meant of sufficiency, the other of manners and affection. It is an assured sign of a worthy and generous spirit, whom honour amends; for honour is or should be the place of virtue; and as in nature things move violently to their place and calmly in their place, so virtue in ambition is violent, in authority settled and calm. All rising to great place is by a winding stair; and if there be factions, it is good to side a man's self whilst he is in the rising, and to balance himself when he is placed. Use the memory of thy predecessor fairly and tenderly; for if thou dost not, it is a debt will sure be paid when thou art gone. If thou have colleagues, respect them; and rather call them when they look not for it, than exclude them when they have reason to look to be called. Be not too sensible or too remembering of thy place in conversation and private answers to suitors; but let it rather be said, *When he sits in place, he is another man.*

SIR THOMAS OVERBURY

1581–1613

A FRANKLIN

HIS outside is an ancient yeoman of England, though his inside may give arms (with the best gentlemen) and never see the herald. There is no truer servant in the house than himself. Though he be master, he says not to his servants, 'Go to field,' but, 'Let us go;' and with his own eye doth both fatten his flock and set forward all manner of husbandry. He is taught by nature to be contented with a little; his own fold yields him both food and raiment: he is pleased with any nourishment God sends, whilst curious gluttony ransacks, as it were, Noah's ark for food, only to feed the riot of one meal. He is never known to go to law; understanding to be law-bound among men is like to be hide-bound among his beasts; they thrive not under it: and that such men sleep as unquietly as if their pillows were stuffed with lawyers' penknives. When he builds, no poor tenant's cottage hinders his prospect: they are indeed his almshouses, though there be painted on them no such superscription: he never sits up late, but when he hunts the badger, the vowed foe of his lambs: nor uses he any cruelty, but when he hunts the hare, nor subtilty, but when he setteth snares for the snite or pitfalls for the blackbird; nor oppression, but when in the month of July he goes to the next river and shears his sheep. He allows of honest pastime, and thinks not the bones of the dead anything bruised, or the worse for it, though the country lasses dance in the churchyard after evensong. Rock Monday, and the wake in summer, shrovings, the wakeful catches on Christmas Eve, the hoky, or seed-cake, these he yearly keeps, yet holds them no relics of Popery. He is not so inquisitive after news derived from the privy closet, when the finding of an aerie of hawks in his own ground, or the foaling of a colt come of a good strain, are tidings more pleasant, more profitable. He is lord paramount within himself, though he hold by never so mean a tenure; and dies the more contentedly (though he leave his heir young), in regard he leaves him not liable to a covetous guardian. Lastly, to end him: he cares not when his end comes, he needs not fear his audit, for his quietus is in heaven.

11

JOHN EARLE

1601 (?)–1665

A YOUNG RAW PREACHER

Is a bird not yet fledged, that hath hopped out of his nest to be chirping on a hedge, and will be straggling abroad at what peril soever. His backwardness in the university hath set him thus forward; for had he not truanted there, he had not been so hasty a divine. His small standing, and time, hath made him a proficient only in boldness, out of which, and his table-book, he is furnished for a preacher. His collections of study are the notes of sermons, which, taken up at St. Mary's, he utters in the country: and if he write brachigraphy, his stock is so much the better. His writing is more than his reading, for he reads only what he gets without book. Thus accomplished he comes down to his friends, and his first salutation is grace and peace out of the pulpit. His prayer is conceited, and no man remembers his college more at large. The pace of his sermon is a full career, and he runs wildly over hill and dale, till the clock stop him. The labour of it is chiefly in his lungs; and the only thing he has made in it himself, is the faces. He takes on against the Pope without mercy, and has a jest still in lavender for Bellarmine: yet he preaches heresy, if it comes in his way, though with a mind, I must needs say, very orthodox. His action is all passion, and his speech interjections.

He has an excellent faculty in bemoaning the people, and spits with a very good grace. His style is compounded of twenty several men's, only his body imitates some one extraordinary. He will not draw his handkercher out of his place, nor blow his nose without discretion. His commendation is, that he never looks upon book ; and indeed, he was never used to it. He preaches but once a year, though twice on Sunday ; for the stuff is still the same, only the dressing a little altered. He has more tricks with a sermon, than a tailor with an old cloak, to turn it, and piece it, and at last quite disguise it with a new preface. If he have waded farther in his profession, and would shew reading of his own, his authors are postils, and his school-divinity a catechism. His fashion and demure habit gets him in with some town-precisian, and makes him a guest on Friday nights. You shall know him by his narrow velvet cape, and serge facing ; and his ruff, next his hair, the shortest thing about him. The companion of his walk is some zealous tradesman, whom he astonishes with strange points, which they both understand alike. His friends and much painfulness may prefer him to thirty pounds a year, and this means to a chamber-maid : with whom we leave him now in the bonds of wedlock. Next Sunday you shall have him again.

13

OWEN FELTHAM

1602 (?)–1668

OF DREAMS

DREAMS are notable means of discovering our own inclinations. The wise man learns to know himself as well by the night's black mantle, as the searching beams of day. In sleep, we have the naked and natural thoughts of our souls: outward objects interpose not, either to shuffle in occasional cogitations, or hale out the included fancy. The mind is then shut up in the Borough of the body; none of the *Cinque Ports* of the *Isle of Man*, are then open, to in-let any strange disturbers. Surely, how we fall to vice, or rise to virtue, we may by observation find in our dreams. It was the wise Zeno, that said, he could collect a man by his dreams. For then the soul stated in a deep repose, bewrayed her true affections: which, in the busy day, she would either not shew, or not note. It was a custom among the *Indians*, when their kings went to their sleep, to pray with piping acclamations, that they might have happy dreams; and withal consult well for their subjects' benefit: as if the night had been a time, wherein they might grow good, and wise. And certainly, the wise man is the wiser for his sleeping, if he can order well in the day, what the eyeless night presenteth him. Every dream is not to be counted of: nor yet are all to be cast away with contempt. I would neither be a *Stoic*, superstitious in all; nor yet an *Epicure*, considerate of none. If the *Physician* may by them judge of the disease of the body, I see not but the *Divine* may do so, concerning the soul. I doubt not but the genius of the soul is waking, and motive even in the fastest closures of the imprisoning eyelids. But to presage from these thoughts of sleep, is a wisdom that I would not reach to. [The best use we can make of dreams, is observation: and by that, our own correction, or encouragement. For 'tis not doubtable, but that the mind is working, in the dullest depth of sleep.] I am confirmed by *Claudian*,

Omnia quae sensu volvuntur vota diurno,
Tempore nocturno, reddit amica quies.
Venator defessa toro cum membra reponit,
Mens tamen ad silvas, et sua lustra redit.
Judicibus lites, aurigae somnia currus,
Vanaque nocturnis meta cavetur equis.
Furto gaudet amans; permutat navita Merces:
Et vigil elapsas quaerit avarus opes.
Blandaque largitur frustra sitientibus aegris
Irriguus gelido pocula fonte sopor.
Me quoque Musarum studium, sub nocte silenti,
Artibus assiduis, sollicitare solet.

Day thoughts, transwinged from th' industrious breast,
All seem re-acted in the night's dumb rest.
When the tired Huntsman, his repose begins,
Then flies his mind to woods, and wild beast dens.
Judges dream cases: Champions seem to run,
With their night Coursers, the vain bounds to shun.
Love hugs his rapes, the Merchant traffic minds.
The miser thinks he some lost treasure finds.
And to the thirsty sick, some potion cold,
Stiff flattering sleep, inanely seems to hold.
Yea, and in th' age of silent rest, even I,
Troubled with Art's deep musings, nightly lie.

Dreams do sometimes call us to a recognition of our inclinations, which print the deeper, in so undisturbed times. I could wish men to give them their consideration, but not to allow them their trust, though sometimes, 'tis easy to pick out a profitable moral. Antiquity had them in much more reverence, and did oft account them prophecies, as is easily found in the sacred volume: and among the *Heathen*, nothing was more frequent. *Astyages* had two, of his daughter *Mandana*, the vine and the flood. *Calphurnia* of her *Caesar*; *Hecuba* of *Paris*; and almost every prince among them, had his fate shewed in interpreted dreams. *Galen* tells of one, that dreamed his thigh was turned to stone, and soon after, it was struck with a dead palsy. The aptness of the humours to the like effects, might suggest something to the mind, then apt to receive. So that I doubt not but either to preserve health or amend the life, dreams may, to a wise observer, be of special benefit. I would neither depend upon any, to incur a prejudice, nor yet cast them all away in a prodigal neglect and scorn. I find it of one that having long been troubled with the paining spleen: that he dreamt, if he opened a certain vein, between two of his fingers, he should be cured: which he awaked, did, and mended. But, indeed I would rather believe this, than be drawn to practise after it. These plain predictions are more rare foretellings, used to be lapped in more obscure folds: and now that art lost, Christianity hath settled us to less inquisition; it is for a Roman soothsayer to read those darker spirits of the night, and tell that still Dictator, his dream of his mother, signified his subjecting the world to himself. 'Tis now so out of use, that I think it not to be recovered. And were it not for the power of the Gospel, in crying down the vanity of men, it would appear a wonder, how a science so pleasing to humanity, should fall so quite to ruin.

SIR THOMAS BROWNE

1605–1682

ON DREAMS

HALF our days we pass in the shadow of the earth; and the brother of death exacteth a third part of our lives. A good part of our sleep is pieced out with visions and fantastical objects, wherein we are confessedly deceived. The day supplieth us with truths; the night with fictions and falsehoods, which uncomfortably divide the natural account of our beings. And, therefore, having passed the day in sober labours and rational inquiries of truth, we are fain to betake ourselves unto such a state of being, wherein the soberest heads have acted all the monstrosities of melancholy, and which unto open eyes are no better than folly and madness.

Happy are they that go to bed with grand music, like Pythagoras, or have ways to compose the fantastical spirit, whose unruly wanderings take off inward sleep, filling our heads with St. Anthony's visions, and the dreams of Lipara in the sober chambers of rest.

Virtuous thoughts of the day lay up good treasures for the night; whereby the impressions of imaginary forms arise into sober similitudes, acceptable unto our slumbering selves and preparatory unto divine impressions. Hereby Solomon's sleep was happy. Thus prepared, Jacob might well dream of angels upon a pillow of stone. And the best sleep of Adam might be the best of any after.

That there should be divine dreams seems unreasonably doubted by Aristotle. That there are demoniacal dreams we have little reason to doubt. Why may there not be angelical? If there be guardian spirits, they may not be inactively about us in sleep; but may sometimes order our dreams; and many strange hints, instigations, or discourses, which are so amazing unto us, may arise from such foundations.

But the phantasms of sleep do commonly walk in the great road of natural and animal dreams, wherein the thoughts or actions of the day are acted over and echoed in the night. Who can therefore wonder that Chrysostom should dream of St. Paul, who daily read his Epistles; or that Cardan, whose head was so taken up about the stars, should dream that his soul was in the moon! Pious persons, whose thoughts are daily busied about heaven, and the blessed state thereof, can hardly escape the nightly phantasms of it, which though sometimes taken for illuminations, or divine dreams, yet rightly perpended may prove but animal visions, and natural night-scenes of their awaking contemplations.

Many dreams are made out by sagacious exposition, and from the signature of their subjects; carrying their interpretation in their fundamental sense and mystery of similitude, whereby, he that understands upon what natural fundamental every notional dependeth, may, by symbolical adaptation, hold a ready way to read the characters of Morpheus. In dreams of such a nature, Artemidorus

Achmet, and Astrampsichus, from Greek, Egyptian, and Arabian oneiro-criticism, may hint some interpretation: who, while we read of a ladder in Jacob's dream, will tell us that ladders and scalary ascents signify preferment; and while we consider the dream of Pharaoh, do teach us that rivers overflowing speak plenty, lean oxen, famine and scarcity; and therefore it was but reasonable in Pharaoh to demand the interpretation from his magicians, who, being Egyptians, should have been well versed in symbols and the hieroglyphical notions of things. The greatest tyrant in such divinations was Nabuchodonosor, while, besides the interpretation, he demanded the dream itself; which being probably determined by divine immission, might escape the common road of phantasms, that might have been traced by Satan.

When Alexander, going to besiege Tyre, dreamt of a satyr, it was no hard exposition for a Grecian to say, 'Tyre will be thine.' He that dreamed that he saw his father washed by Jupiter and anointed by the sun, had cause to fear that he might be crucified, whereby his body would be washed by the rain, and drop by the heat of the sun. The dream of Vespasian was of harder exposition; as also that of the emperor Mauritius, concerning his successor Phocas. And a man might have been hard put to it, to interpret the language of Aesculapius, when to a consumptive person he held forth his fingers; implying thereby that his cure lay in dates, from the homonomy of the Greek, which signifies dates and fingers.

We owe unto dreams that Galen was a physician, Dion an historian, and that the world hath seen some notable pieces of Cardan; yet, he that should order his affairs by dreams, or make the night a rule unto the day, might be ridiculously deluded; wherein Cicero is much to be pitied, who having excellently discoursed of the vanity of dreams, was yet undone by the flattery of his own, which urged him to apply himself unto Augustus.

However dreams may be fallacious concerning outward events, yet may they be truly significant at home; and whereby we may more sensibly understand ourselves. Men act in sleep with some conformity unto their awaked senses; and consolations or discouragements may be drawn from dreams which intimately tell us ourselves. Luther was not like to fear a spirit in the night, when such an apparition would not terrify him in the day. Alexander would hardly have run away in the sharpest combats of sleep, nor Demosthenes have stood stoutly to it, who was scarce able to do it in his prepared senses. Persons of radical integrity will not easily be perverted in their dreams, nor noble minds do pitifully things in sleep. Crassus would have hardly been bountiful in a dream, whose fist was so close awake. But a man might have lived all his life upon the sleeping hand of Antonius.

There is an art to make dreams, as well as their interpretations; and physicians will tell us that some food makes turbulent, some gives quiet, dreams. Cato, who doted upon cabbage, might find the crude effects thereof in his sleep; wherein the Egyptians might find some advantage by their superstitious abstinence from onions. Pythagoras might have calmer sleeps, if he totally abstained from beans. Even Daniel, the great interpreter of dreams, in his leguminous diet, seems to have chosen no advantageous food for quiet sleeps, according to Grecian physic.

To add unto the delusion of dreams, the fantastical objects seem greater than they are; and being beheld in the vaporous state of sleep, enlarge their diameters unto us; whereby it may prove more easy to dream of giants than pigmies. Democritus might seldom dream of atoms, who so often thought of them. Helmont might dream himself a bubble extending unto the eighth sphere. A little water makes a sea; a small puff of wind a tempest. A grain of sulphur kindled in the blood may make a flame like Ætna; and a small spark in the bowels of Olympias a lightning over all the chamber.

But, beside these innocent delusions, there is a sinful state of dreams. Death alone, not sleep, is able to put an end unto sin; and there may be a night-book of our iniquities; for beside the transgressions of the day, casuists will tell us of mortal sins in dreams, arising from evil precogitations; meanwhile human law regards not noctambulos; and if a night-walker should break his neck, or kill a man, takes no notice of it.

Dionysius was absurdly tyrannical to kill a man for dreaming that he had killed him; and really to take away his life, who had but fantastically taken away his. Lamia was ridiculously unjust to sue a young man for a reward, who had confessed that pleasure from her in a dream which she had denied unto his awaking senses: conceiving that she had merited somewhat from his fantastical fruition and shadow of herself. If there be such debts, we owe deeply unto sympathies; but the common spirit of the world must be judge in such arrearages.

If some have swooned, they may have also died in dreams, since death is but a confirmed swooning. Whether Plato died in a dream, as some deliver, he must rise again to inform us. That some have never dreamed, is as improbable as that some have never laughed. That children dream not the first half-year; that men dream not in some countries, with many more, are unto me sick men's dreams; dreams out of the ivory gate, and visions before midnight.

THOMAS FULLER

1608–1661

THE GOOD SEA CAPTAIN

CONCEIVE him now in a man-of-war, with his letters of mart, well armed, victualled, and appointed, and see how he acquits himself.

The more power he hath, the more careful he is not to abuse it. Indeed, a sea captain is a king in the island of a ship, supreme judge, above appeal, in causes civil and criminal, and is seldom brought to an account in courts of justice on land for injuries done to his own men at sea.

He is careful in observing of the Lord's day. He hath a watch in his heart, though no bells in a steeple to proclaim that day by ringing to prayers.

He is as pious and thankful when a tempest is past, as devout when it is present: not clamorous to receive mercies, and tongue-tied to return thanks.

Escaping many dangers makes him not presumptuous to run into them.

In taking a prize he most prizeth the men's lives whom he takes; though some of them may chance to be negroes or savages. It is the custom of some to cast them overboard, and there is an end of them: for the dumb fishes will tell no tales. But the murder is not so soon drowned as the men. What! is a brother by half-blood no kin? A savage hath God to his father by creation, though not the church to his mother, and God will revenge his innocent blood. But our captain counts the image of God nevertheless his image cut in ebony as if done in ivory, and in the blackest Moors he sees the representation of the King of heaven.

In dividing the gains he wrongs none who took pains to get them. Not shifting off his poor mariners with nothing, or giving them only the garbage of the prize, and keeping all the flesh to himself. In time of peace he quietly returns home, and turns not to the trade of pirates, who are the worst sea vermin, and the devil's water-rats.

His voyages are not only for profit, but some for honour and knowledge; to make discoveries of new countries, imitating the worthy Christopher Columbus.

Our sea captain is likewise ambitious to perfect what the other began. He counts it a disgrace, seeing all mankind is one family, sundry countries but several rooms, that we who dwell in the parlour (so he counts Europe) should not know the out-lodgings of the same house, and the world be scarce acquainted with itself before it be dissolved from itself at the day of judgement.

He daily sees and duly considers God's wonders in the deep.

EDWARD HYDE

FIRST EARL OF CLARENDON

1609–1674

OF WAR

Montpellier, 1670.

As the plague in the body drives all persons away but such who live by it, searchers, and those who are to bury the corpse, who are as ready to strangle those who do not die soon enough, as to bury them; and they who recover are very long tried with the malignity, and remain longer deserted by their neighbours and friends out of fear of infection; so war in a state makes all men abandon it but those who are to live by the blood of it, and who have the pillaging of the living as well as of the dead; and if it recover, and the war be extinguished, there remains such a weakness and paleness, so many ghastly marks of the distemper, that men remain long frighted from their old familiarity, from the confidence they formerly had of their own security, and of the justice of that state, the war leaving still an ill odour behind it, and much infection in the nature and manners of those who are delighted with it. Of all the punishments and judgements that the provoked anger of the Divine Providence can pour out upon a nation full of transgressions, there is none so terrible and destroying as that of war. David knew he did wisely when he preferred and chose the plague before either of the other judgements that he was to undergo for numbering the people, though it cost him no less than seventy thousand subjects; so vast a number that three months' progress of the most victorious and triumphant enemy could hardly have consumed; and the one had been as much the hand of the Lord as the other, and could as easily have been restrained, or bound by his power: the arrow of pestilence was shot out of his own bow, and did all its execution without making the pride or malice of man instrumental in it; the insolence whereof is a great aggravation of any judgement that is laid upon us, and health is restored in the same moment the contagion ceaseth; whereas in war, the confidence and the courage which a victorious army contracts by notable successes, and the dejection of spirit and the consternation which a subdued party undergoes by frequent defeats, is not at an end when the war is determined, but hath its effects very long after; and the tenderness of nature, and the integrity of manners, which are driven away, or powerfully discountenanced by the corruption of war, are not quickly recovered; but instead thereof a roughness, jealousy, and distrust introduced, that makes conversation unpleasant and uneasy, and the weeds which grow up in the shortest war can hardly be pulled up and extirpated without a long and unsuspected peace. When God pleases to send this heavy calamity upon us, we cannot avoid it; but why we should be solicitous to embark ourselves in this leaky vessel, why our own anger, and ambition, and emulation, should engage us in unreasonable and unjust wars, nay, why, without any of these provocations, we should be disposed to run to war, and *periclitari periculi causa*, will require better reason to justify us, than most that are concerned in it are furnished with. *Iugulantur homines ne nihil agatur*, was the complaint and amazement of a philosopher, who knew of none of those restraints which Christianity hath laid upon mankind. That men should kill one another for want of something else to do (which is the case of all volunteers in war) seems to be so horrible to humanity, that there needs no divinity to control it. It was a divine contemplation of the same philosopher, that when Providence had so well provided for, and secured the peace between nations, by putting the sea between, that it might not be in their power to be ill neighbours, mankind should be so mad as to devise shipping, to affect death so much *sine spe sepulturae*; and when they are safe on land, to commit themselves to the waves and the fierce winds, *quorum felicitas est ad bella perferri*; and that those winds which God had created, *ad custodiendam cœli terrarumque temperiem*, and to cherish the fruits and trees of the earth, should be made use of so contrary to his intentions, *ut legiones, equitemque gestarent*, and bring people (whom he had placed at that distance) together, to imbrue their hands in each other's blood; indeed it must be a very savage appetite, that engages men to take so much pains, and to run so many and great hazards, only to be cruel to those whom they are able to oppress.

They who allow no war at all to be lawful, have consulted both nature and religion much better than they who think it may be entered into to comply with the ambition, covetousness, or revenge of the greatest princes and monarchs upon earth:

as if God had only inhibited single murders, and left mankind to be massacred according to the humour and appetite of unjust and unreasonable men, of what degree or quality soever. They who think it most unlawful, know well that force may be repelled with force; and that no man makes war who doth only defend what is his own from an attempt of violence; he who kills another that he may not be killed himself by him who attempts it, is not guilty of murder by the law of God or man. And truly, they who are the cause and authors of any war that can justly and safely be avoided, have great reason to fear that they shall be accountable before the Supreme Judge for all the rapine and devastation, all the ruin and damage, as well as the blood, that is the consequence of that war. War is a licence to kill and slay all those who inhabit that land, which is therefore called the enemy's, because he who makes the war hath a mind to possess it; and must there not many of the laws of God, as well as of man, be cancelled and abolished, before a man can honestly execute or take such a licence? What have the poor inhabitants of that land done that they must be destroyed for cultivating their own land, in the country where they were born? and can any king believe that the names of those are left out of the records of God's creation, and that the injuries done to them shall not be considered? War is a depopulation, defaces all that art and industry hath produced, destroys all plantations, burns churches and palaces, and mingles them in the same ashes with the cottages of the peasant and the labourer; it distinguishes not of age, or sex, or dignity, but exposes all things and persons, sacred and profane, to the same contempt and confusion; and reduces all that blessed order and harmony, which hath been the product of peace and religion, into the chaos it was first in; as if it would contend with the Almighty in uncreating what He so wonderfully created, and since polished. And is it not a most detestable thing to open a gap to let this wild boar enter into the garden of Christians, and to make all this havöc and devastation in countries planted and watered by the equal Redeemer of mankind, and whose ears are open to the complaints of the meanest person who is oppressed? It is no answer to say that this universal suffering, and even the desolation that attends it, are the inevitable consequences and events of war, how warrantably soever entered into, but rather an argument, that no war can be warrantably entered into, that may produce such intolerable mischiefs; at least if the ground be not notoriously just and necessary, and like to introduce as much benefit to the world as damage and inconvenience to a part of it; and as much care taken as is possible to suppress that rage and licence, which is the wanton cause of half the destruction.

It may be, upon a strict survey and disquisition into the elements and injunctions of Christian religion, no war will be found justifiable, but as it is the process that the law of nature allows and prescribes for justice sake, to compel those to abstain from doing wrong, or to repair the wrong they have done, who can by no other way be induced to do either; as when one sovereign prince doth an injury to another, or suffers his subjects to do it without control or punishment; in either of which cases, the injured prince in his own right, or the rights of his subjects, is to demand justice from the other, and to endeavour to obtain it by all the peaceable means that can be used; and then if there be an absolute refusal to give satisfaction, or such a delay, as in the inconvenience amounts to a refusal, there is no remedy left, but the last process, which is force; since nothing can be in itself more odious, or more against the nature and institution of sovereign power, than to do wrong, and to refuse to administer justice; and, therefore, the mischiefs which attend, and which cannot but fall upon the persons and fortunes of those who are least guilty of the injury and injustice, because the damage can very hardly reach the prince, but in his subjects, will be by the supreme Judge cast upon his account who is the original cause and author of the first transgression. And if it be very difficult to find any other just cause to warrant so savage a proceeding as all war produces, what can we think of most of that war which for some hundred of years has infested the Christian world, so much to the dishonour of Christianity, and in which the lives of more men have been lost than might have served to have driven infidelity out of the world, and to have peopled all those parts which yet remain without inhabitants? Can we believe that all those lives are forgotten, and that no account shall be rendered of them? If the saving the life of any single person who is in danger to perish, hath much of merit in it, though it be a duty incumbent to humanity, with what detestation and horror must we look upon those, who upon deliberation are solicitous to bring millions of men together to no other purpose than to kill and destroy; and they who survive are conducted as soon as may be to another butchery, to another opportunity to kill more men, whom they know not, and with whom they are not so much as angry. The grammarians have too much reason to derive *bellum, a belluis*; all war hath much of the beast in it; *immane quiddam et belluarum simile*; very much of the man must be put off that there may be enough of the beast: princes must be obeyed, and because they may have just cause of war, their subjects must obey and serve them in it, without taking upon them to examine whether it be just or no, *Servi tua est conditio, ratio ad te nihil*; they have no liberty to doubt when their duty is clear to obey; but where there is none of that obligation, it is wonderful, and an unnatural appetite that disposes men to be soldiers, that they may know how to live, as if the understanding the advantage how to kill most men together were a commendable science to raise their fortune; and what reputation soever it may have in politics, it can have none in religion, to say, that the art and conduct of a soldier is not infused by nature, but by study, experience, and observation; and therefore that men are to learn it, in order to serve their own prince and country, which may be assaulted and invaded by a skilful enemy, and hardly defended by ignorant and unskilful officers; when, in truth, the man who conscientiously weighs this common argument, will find that it is made by appetite to excuse, and not by reason to support, an ill custom; since the guilt contracted by shedding the blood of one single innocent man, is too dear a price to pay for all the skill that is to be learned in that devouring profession; and that all the science that is necessary for a just defence may be attained without contracting a guilt, which is like to make the defence the more difficult. And we have instances enough of the most brave and effectual defences made upon the advantage of innocence, against the boldest, skilful, and injurious aggressor, whose guilt often makes his understanding too weak to go through an unjust attempt, against a resolute though less experienced defender.

It must seem strange to any one, who considers that Christian religion, that is founded upon love, and charity, and humility, should not only not extinguish this unruly appetite to war, but make the prosecution of it the more fierce and cruel; there having scarce been so much rage and inhumanity practised in any war, as in that between Christians. The ancient Romans, who for some ages arrived to the greatest perfection in the observations of the obligations of honour, justice, and humanity, of all men who had no light from religion, instituted a particular triumph for those their generals who returned with victory without the slaughter of men. It were to be wished that the modern Christian Romans were endued with the same blessed spirit, and that they believed that the voice of blood is loud and importunate; they would not then think it their office and duty, so far to kindle this firebrand war, and to nourish all occasions to inflame it, as to obstruct and divert all overtures of extinguishing it; and to curse and excommunicate all those who shall consent or submit to such overtures, when they are wearied, tired, and even consumed with weltering in each other's blood, and have scarce blood enough left to give them strength to enjoy the blessings of peace. What can be more unmerciful, more unworthy of the title of Christians, than such an aversion from stopping those issues of blood, and from binding up those wounds which have been bleeding so long? and yet we have seen those inhuman bulls let loose by two popes, who would be thought to have the sole power committed to them by Christ, to inform the world of his will and pleasure; the one against the peace of Germany, and the other against that with the Low Countries; by both which these his vicars-general absolve all men from observing it, though they are bound by their oaths never to swerve from it. We may piously believe that all the princes of the world, who have wantonly, or without just and manifest provocation, obliged their subjects to serve them in a war, by which millions of men have been exposed to slaughter, fire, and famine, will sooner find remission of all the other sins they have committed, than for that obstinate outrage against the life of man, and the murders which have been committed by their authority.

33

ABRAHAM COWLEY

1618–1667

THE DANGERS OF AN HONEST MAN IN MUCH COMPANY

If twenty thousand naked Americans were not able to resist the assaults of but twenty well-armed Spaniards, I see little possibility for one honest man to defend himself against twenty thousand knaves who are all furnished *cap-à-pie*, with the defensive arms of worldly prudence, and the offensive too of craft and malice. He will find no less odds than this against him, if he have much to do in human affairs. The only advice therefore which I can give him is, to be sure not to venture his person any longer in the open campaign, to retreat and entrench himself, to stop up all avenues, and draw up all bridges against so numerous an enemy.

The truth of it is, that a man in much business must either make himself a knave, or else the world will make him a fool: and, if the injury went no farther than the being laughed at, a wise man would content himself with the revenge of retaliation; but the case is much worse, for these civil cannibals too, as well as the wild ones, not only dance about such a taken stranger, but at last devour him. A sober man cannot get too soon out of drunken company, though they be never so kind and merry among themselves; it is not unpleasant only, but dangerous, to him.

Do ye wonder that a virtuous man should love to be alone? It is hard for him to be otherwise; he is so, when he is among ten thousand: neither is the solitude so uncomfortable to be alone without any other creature, as it is to be alone in the midst of wild beasts. Man is to man all kind of beasts; a fawning dog, a roaring lion, a thieving fox, a robbing wolf, a dissembling crocodile, a treacherous decoy, and a rapacious vulture. The civilest, methinks, of all nations, are those whom we account the most barbarous; there is some moderation and good nature in the Toupinambaltians, who eat no men but their enemies, whilst we learned and polite and Christian Europeans, like so many pikes and sharks, prey upon everything that we can swallow. It is the great boast of eloquence and philosophy, that they first congregated men dispersed, united them into societies, and built up the houses and the walls of cities. I wish they could unravel all they had woven; that we might have our woods and our innocence again, instead of our castles and our policies. They have assembled many thousands of scattered people into one body: it is true, they have done so; they have brought them together into cities to cozen, and into armies to murder, one another: they found them hunters and fishers of wild creatures: they have made them hunters and fishers of their brethren: they boast to have reduced them to a state of peace, when the truth is, they have only taught them an art of war; they have framed, I must confess, wholesome laws for the restraint of vice, but they raised first that devil, which now they conjure and cannot bind: though there were before no punishments for wickedness, yet there was less committed, because there were no rewards for it.

But the men, who praise philosophy from this topic, are much deceived: let oratory answer for itself, the tinkling perhaps of that may unite a swarm; it never was the work of philosophy to assemble multitudes, but to regulate only, and govern them, when they were assembled; to make the best of an evil, and bring them, as much as is possible, to unity again. Avarice and ambition only were the first builders of towns, and founders of empire; they said, 'Go to, let us build us a city and a tower whose top may reach unto Heaven, and let us make us a name, lest we be scattered abroad upon the face of the earth.'[1] What was the beginning of Rome, the metropolis of all the world? what was it, but a concourse of thieves, and a sanctuary of criminals? It was justly named by the augury of no less than twelve vultures, and the founder cemented his walls with the blood of his brother. Not unlike to this was the beginning even of the first town too in the world, and such is the original sin of most cities: their actual increase daily with their age and growth; the more people, the more wicked all of them; every one brings in his part to inflame the contagion: which becomes at last so universal and so strong, that no precepts can be sufficient preservatives, nor anything secure our safety, but flight from among the infected.

We ought, in the choice of a situation, to regard above all things the healthfulness of the place, and the healthfulness of it for the mind, rather than for the body. But suppose (which is hardly to

[1] Gen. xi. 4.

be supposed) we had antidote enough against this poison; nay, suppose further, we were always and at all pieces armed and provided, both against the assaults of hostility, and the mines of treachery, it will yet be but an uncomfortable life to be ever in alarms; though we were compassed round with fire, to defend ourselves from wild beasts, the lodging would be unpleasant, because we must always be obliged to watch that fire, and to fear no less the defects of our guard, than the diligences of our enemy. The sum of this is, that a virtuous man is in danger to be trod upon and destroyed in the crowd of his contraries, nay, which is worse, to be changed and corrupted by them; and that it is impossible to escape both these inconveniences without so much caution as will take away the whole quiet, that is the happiness, of his life.

Ye see then, what he may lose; but, I pray, what can he get there?

Quid Romae faciam? Mentiri nescio.[1]

What should a man of truth and honesty do at Rome? He can neither understand nor speak the language of the place; a naked man may swim in the sea, but it is not the way to catch fish there; they are likelier to devour him, than he them, if he bring no nets, and use no deceits. I think, therefore, it was wise and friendly advice, which Martial gave to Fabian,[2] when he met him newly arrived at Rome:

Honest and poor, faithful in word and thought;
What has thee, Fabian, to the city brought?
Thou neither the buffoon nor bawd canst play,
Nor with false whispers th' innocent betray;

[1] Juv. *Sat.* iii. 41. [2] Mart. iv. *Ep.* 5.

Nor corrupt wives, nor from rich beldames get
A living by thy industry and sweat;
Nor with vain promises and projects cheat,
Nor bribe or flatter any of the great.
But you're a man of learning, prudent, just;
A man of courage, firm, and fit for trust.
Why you may stay, and live unenvied here;
But (faith) go back, and keep you where you were.

Nay, if nothing of all this were in the case, yet the very sight of uncleanness is loathsome to the cleanly; the sight of folly and impiety, vexatious to the wise and pious.

Lucretius,[1] by his favour, though a good poet, was but an ill-natured man, when he said, it was delightful to see other men in a great storm, and no less ill-natured should I think Democritus, who laughed at all the world, but that he retired himself so much out of it, that we may perceive he took no great pleasure in that kind of mirth. I have been drawn twice or thrice by company to go to Bedlam, and have seen others very much delighted with the fantastical extravagancy of so many various madnesses; which upon me wrought so contrary an effect, that I always returned, not only melancholy, but even sick with the sight. My compassion there was perhaps too tender, for I meet a thousand madmen abroad, without any perturbation; though, to weigh the matter justly, the total loss of reason is less deplorable than the total depravation of it. An exact judge of human blessings, of riches, honours, beauty, even of wit itself, should pity the abuse of them, more than the want.

Briefly, though a wise man could pass never so securely through the great roads of human life, yet

[1] Lucr., lib. ii. 1.

he will meet perpetually with so many objects and occasions of compassion, grief, shame, anger, hatred, indignation, and all passions but envy (for he will find nothing to deserve that), that he had better strike into some private path; nay, go so far, if he could, out of the common way, 'ut nec facta audiat Pelopidarum,' that he might not so much as hear of the actions of the sons of Adam. But, whither shall we fly then? into the deserts, like the ancient hermits?

> *—Qua terra patet, fera regnat Erinnys,*
> *In facinus iurasse putes.*[1]

One would think that all mankind had bound themselves by an oath to do all the wickedness they can; that they had all (as the Scripture speaks) 'sold themselves to sin': the difference only is, that some are a little more crafty (and but a little, God knows) in making of the bargain. I thought, when I went first to dwell in the country, that without doubt I should have met there with the simplicity of the old poetical golden age; I thought to have found no inhabitants there, but such as the shepherds of Sir Philip Sidney in Arcadia, or of Monsieur d'Urfé upon the banks of Lignon; and began to consider with myself, which way I might recommend no less to posterity the happiness and innocence of the men of Chertsea: but to confess the truth, I perceived quickly, by infallible demonstrations, that I was still in Old England, and not in Arcadia or La Forrest; that, if I could not content myself with anything less than exact fidelity in human conversation, I had almost as good go back and seek for it in the

[1] Ovid, *Metam.* i. 241.

Court, or the Exchange, or Westminster Hall. I ask again, then, whither shall we fly, or what shall we do? The world may so come in a man's way, that he cannot choose but salute it; he must take heed, though, not to go a whoring after it. If, by any lawful vocation, or just necessity, men happen to be married to it, I can only give them St. Paul's advice: 'Brethren, the time is short; it remains, that they that have wives be as though they had none.—But I would that all men were even as I myself.'[1]

In all cases, they must be sure, that they do *mundum ducere*, and not *mundo nubere*. They must retain the superiority and headship over it: happy are they, who can get out of the sight of this deceitful beauty, that they may not be led so much as into temptation; who have not only quitted the metropolis, but can abstain from ever seeing the next market-town of their country.

[1] 1 Cor. vii. 29.

JOHN DRYDEN

1631–1700

CHARACTER OF M. ST. EVREMONT

I KNOW how nice an undertaking it is to write of a living author: yet the example of Father Bouhours has somewhat encouraged me in this attempt. Had not Monsieur St. Evremont been very considerable in his own country, that famous Jesuit would not have ventured to praise a person in disgrace with the government of France, and living here in banishment. Yet in his *Pensées Ingénieuses*, he has often cited our author's thoughts and his expressions, as the standard of judicious thinking, and graceful speaking: an undoubted sign that his merit was sufficiently established, when the disfavour of the court could not prevail against it. There is not only a justness in his conceptions, which is the foundation of good writing, but also a purity of language, and a beautiful turn of words, so little understood by modern writers; and which indeed was found at Rome but at the latter end of the Commonwealth, and ended with Petronius, under the Monarchy.

If I durst extend my judgement to particulars, I would say that our author has determined very nicely in his opinion of Epicurus, and that what he has said of his morals, is according to nature, and reason.

It is true, that as I am a religious admirer of Virgil, I could wish that he had not discovered our father's nakedness.[1] But after all, we must confess that Aeneas was none of the greatest heroes, and that Virgil was sensible of it himself. But what could he do? the Trojan on whom he was to build the Roman Empire had been already vanquished; he had lost his country, and was a fugitive. Nay more, he had fought unsuccessfully with Diomedes, and was only preserved from death by his mother goddess, who received a wound in his defence. So that Virgil, bound as he was to follow the footsteps of Homer, who had thus described him, could not reasonably have altered his character, and raised him in Italy to a much greater height of prowess than he found him formerly in Troy. Since therefore he could make no more of him in valour, he resolved not to give him that virtue, as his principal; but chose another, which was piety. It is true, this latter, in the composition of a hero, was not altogether so shining as the former; but it entitled him more to the favour of the gods, and their protection, in all his undertakings; and, which was the poet's chiefest aim, made a nearer resemblance betwixt Aeneas and his patron, Augustus Caesar, who, above all things, loved to be flattered for being pious, both to the gods and his relations. And that very piety, or gratitude, (call it which you please,) to the memory of his

[1] In his *Reflections on Segrais' Translation of Virgil.*

uncle, Julius, gave him the preference, amongst the soldiers, to Mark Antony; and consequently raised him to the empire. As for personal courage, that of Augustus was not pushing;[1] and the poet, who was not ignorant of that defect, for that reason durst not ascribe it, in the supreme degree, to him who was to represent his Emperor under another name: which was managed by him with the most imaginable fineness; for had valour been set uppermost, Augustus must have yielded to Agrippa. After all, this is rather to defend the courtier, than the poet; and to make his hero escape again, under the covert of a cloud. Only we may add, what I think Bossu says, that the Roman Commonwealth being now changed into a monarchy, Virgil was helping to that design; by insinuating into the people the piety of their new conqueror, to make them the better brook this innovation, which was brought on them by a man who was favoured by the gods.—Yet we may observe, that Virgil forgot not, upon occasion, to speak honourably of Aeneas, in point of courage, and that particularly in the person of him by whom he was overcome. For Diomedes compares him with Hector, and even with advantage:

Quicquid apud durae cessatum est moenia Troiae
Hectoris Aeneaeque manu victoria Graium
Haesit, et in decimum vestigia rettulit annum:
Ambo animis, ambo insignes praestantibus armis;
Hic pietate prior.

As for that particular passage, cited by Monsieur

[1] At the battle of Philippi he is supposed to have feigned sickness, to avoid taking a part in the engagement; and almost all his subsequent victories were obtained by Agrippa, and the other generals whom he employed.

St. Evremont, where Aeneas shows the utmost fear, in the beginning of a tempest,

Extemplo Aeneae solvuntur frigore membra, &c.

why may it not be supposed, that having been long at sea, he might be well acquainted with the nature of a storm; and, by the rough beginning, foresee the increase and danger of it? at least, as a father of his people, his concernment might be greater for them than for himself; and if so, what the poet takes from the merit of his courage, is added to the prime virtue of his character, which was his piety. Be this said with all manner of respect and deference to the opinion of Monsieur St. Evremont; amongst whose admirable talents, that of penetration is not the least. He generally dives into the very bottom of his authors; searches into the inmost recesses of their souls, and brings up with him those hidden treasures which had escaped the diligence of others. His examination of the *Grand Alexandre*,[1] in my opinion, is an admirable piece of criticism; and I doubt not but that his observations on the English theatre had been as absolute in their kind, had he seen with his own eyes, and not with those of other men. But conversing in a manner wholly with the court, which is not always the truest judge, he has been unavoidably led into mistakes, and given to some of our coarsest poets a reputation abroad, which they never had at home. Had his conversation in the town been more general, he had certainly received other ideas on that subject; and not transmitted those names into his own country, which will be forgotten by posterity in ours.

[1] A French tragedy.

Thus I have contracted my thoughts on a large subject: for whatever has been said falls short of the true character of Monsieur St. Evremont and his writings: and if the translation you are about to read does not everywhere come up to the original, the translator desires you to believe, that it is only because that he has failed in his undertaking.

45

JONATHAN SWIFT

1667–1745

HINTS TOWARD AN ESSAY ON CONVERSATION

I HAVE observed few obvious subjects to have been so seldom, or at least so slightly, handled as this; and indeed I know few so difficult to be treated as it ought, nor yet, upon which there seems so much to be said.

Most things pursued by men for the happiness of public or private life, our wit or folly have so refined, that they seldom subsist but in idea; a true friend, a good marriage, a perfect form of government, with some others, require so many ingredients, so good in their several kinds, and so much niceness in mixing them, that for some thousands of years men have despaired of reducing their schemes to perfection: but, in conversation, it is, or might be otherwise; for here we are only to avoid a multitude of errors, which, although a matter of some difficulty, may be in every man's power, for want of which it remains as mere an idea as the other. Therefore it seems to me, that the truest way to understand conversation, is to know the faults and errors to which it is subject, and from thence every man to form maxims to himself whereby it may be regulated, because it requires few talents to which most men are not born, or at least may not acquire, without any great genius or study. For nature has left every man a capacity of being agreeable, though not of shining in company; and there are a hundred men sufficiently qualified for both, who, by a very few faults, that they might correct in half an hour, are not so much as tolerable.

I was prompted to write my thoughts upon this subject by mere indignation, to reflect that so useful and innocent a pleasure, so fitted for every period and condition of life, and so much in all men's power, should be so much neglected and abused.

And in this discourse it will be necessary to note those errors that are obvious, as well as others which are seldomer observed, since there are few so obvious, or acknowledged, into which most men, some time or other, are not apt to run.

For instance: nothing is more generally exploded than the folly of talking too much; yet I rarely remember to have seen five people together, where some one among them has not been predominant in that kind, to the great constraint and disgust of all the rest. But among such as deal in multitudes of words, none are comparable to the sober deliberate talker, who proceeds with much thought and caution, makes his preface, branches out into several digressions, finds a hint that puts him in mind of another story, which he promises to tell you when this is done; comes back regularly to his subject, cannot readily call to mind some person's name, holding his head, complains of his memory; the whole company all this while in suspense; at length says, it is no matter, and so goes on. And, to crown the business, it perhaps proves at last a story the company has heard fifty times before; or, at best, some insipid adventure of the relater.

Another general fault in conversation, is that

of those who affect to talk of themselves; some, without any ceremony, will run over the history of their lives; will relate the annals of their diseases, with the several symptoms and circumstances of them; will enumerate the hardships and injustice they have suffered in court, in parliament, in love, or in law. Others are more dexterous, and with great art will lie on the watch to hook in their own praise; they will call a witness to remember they always foretold what would happen in such a case, but none would believe them; they advised such a man from the beginning, and told him the consequences, just as they happened; but he would have his own way. Others make a vanity of telling their faults; they are the strangest men in the world; they cannot dissemble; they own it is a folly; they have lost abundance of advantages by it; but if you would give them the world, they cannot help it; there is something in their nature that abhors insincerity and constraint; with many other insufferable topics of the same altitude.

Of such mighty importance every man is to himself, and ready to think he is so to others; without once making this easy and obvious reflection, that his affairs can have no more weight with other men, than theirs have with him; and how little that is, he is sensible enough.

Where a company has met, I often have observed two persons discover, by some accident, that they were bred together at the same school or university; after which the rest are condemned to silence, and to listen while these two are refreshing each other's memory, with the arch tricks and passages of themselves and their comrades.

I know a great officer of the army, who will sit for some time with a supercilious and impatient silence, full of anger and contempt for those who are talking; at length, of a sudden, demanding audience, decide the matter in a short dogmatical way; then withdraw within himself again, and vouchsafe to talk no more, until his spirits circulate again to the same point.

There are some faults in conversation, which none are so subject to as the men of wit, nor ever so much as when they are with each other. If they have opened their mouths, without endeavouring to say a witty thing, they think it is so many words lost: it is a torment to the hearers, as much as to themselves, to see them upon the rack for invention, and in perpetual constraint, with so little success. They must do something extraordinary, in order to acquit themselves, and answer their character, else the standers-by may be disappointed, and be apt to think them only like the rest of mortals. I have known two men of wit industriously brought together, in order to entertain the company, where they have made a very ridiculous figure, and provided all the mirth at their own expense.

I know a man of wit, who is never easy but where he can be allowed to dictate and preside: he neither expects to be informed or entertained, but to display his own talents. His business is to be good company, and not good conversation; and therefore he chooses to frequent those who are content to listen, and profess themselves his admirers. And, indeed, the worst conversation I ever remember to have heard in my life, was that at Will's coffee-house, where the wits (as they were called) used formerly to assemble; that is to say, five or six men who had writ plays, or at least prologues, or had share in a miscellany, came thither, and entertained one another with their trifling composures, in so important an air, as if they had been the noblest efforts of human nature, or that the fate of kingdoms depended on them; and they were usually attended with an humble audience of young students from the inns of court, or the universities; who, at due distance, listened to these oracles, and returned home with great contempt for their law and philosophy, their heads filled with trash, under the name of politeness, criticism, and *belles lettres*.

By these means, the poets, for many years past, were all overrun with pedantry. For, as I take it, the word is not properly used; because pedantry is the too frequent or unseasonable obtruding our own knowledge in common discourse, and placing too great a value upon it; by which definition, men of the court, or the army, may be as guilty of pedantry, as a philosopher or a divine; and it is the same vice in women, when they are over copious upon the subject of their petticoats, or their fans, or their china. For which reason, although it be a piece of prudence, as well as good manners, to put men upon talking on subjects they are best versed in, yet that is a liberty a wise man could hardly take; because, beside the imputation of pedantry, it is what he would never improve by.

The great town is usually provided with some player, mimic, or buffoon, who has a general reception at the good tables; familiar and domestic with persons of the first quality, and usually sent for at every meeting to divert the company;

against which I have no objection. You go there as to a farce or a puppet-show; your business is only to laugh in season, either out of inclination or civility, while this merry companion is acting his part. It is a business he has undertaken, and we are to suppose he is paid for his day's work. I only quarrel, when, in select and private meetings, where men of wit and learning are invited to pass an evening, this jester should be admitted to run over his circle of tricks, and make the whole company unfit for any other conversation, beside the indignity of confounding men's talents at so shameful a rate.

Raillery is the finest part of conversation; but, as it is our usual custom to counterfeit and adulterate whatever is too dear for us, so we have done with this, and turned it all into what is generally called repartee, or being smart; just as when an expensive fashion comes up, those who are not able to reach it, content themselves with some paltry imitation. It now passes for raillery to run a man down in discourse, to put him out of countenance, and make him ridiculous; sometimes to expose the defects of his person or understanding; on all which occasions, he is obliged not to be angry, to avoid the imputation of not being able to take a jest. It is admirable to observe one who is dexterous at this art, singling out a weak adversary, getting the laugh on his side, and then carrying all before him. The French, from whence we borrow the word, have a quite different idea of the thing, and so had we in the politer age of our fathers. Raillery, was to say something that at first appeared a reproach or reflection, but, by some turn of wit, unexpected and surprising, ended always in a compliment, and to the advantage of the person it was addressed to. And surely one of the best rules in conversation is, never to say a thing which any of the company can reasonably wish we had rather left unsaid; nor can there anything be well more contrary to the ends for which people meet together, than to part unsatisfied with each other or themselves.

There are two faults in conversation, which appear very different, yet arise from the same root, and are equally blameable; I mean an impatience to interrupt others; and the uneasiness of being interrupted ourselves. The two chief ends of conversation are to entertain and improve those we are among, or to receive those benefits ourselves; which whoever will consider, cannot easily run into either of these two errors; because, when any man speaks in company, it is to be supposed he does it for his hearers' sake, and not his own; so that common discretion will teach us not to force their attention, if they are not willing to lend it; nor, on the other side, to interrupt him who is in possession, because that is in the grossest manner to give the preference to our own good sense.

There are some people, whose good manners will not suffer them to interrupt you, but, what is almost as bad, will discover abundance of impatience, and lie upon the watch until you have done, because they have started something in their own thoughts, which they long to be delivered of. Meantime, they are so far from regarding what passes, that their imaginations are wholly turned upon what they have in reserve, for fear it should slip out of their memory; and thus they confine their invention, which might otherwise range over a hundred things full as good, and that might be much more naturally introduced.

There is a sort of rude familiarity, which some people, by practising among their intimates, have introduced into their general conversation, and would have it pass for innocent freedom or humour; which is a dangerous experiment in our northern climate, where all the little decorum and politeness we have, are purely forced by art, and are so ready to lapse into barbarity. This, among the Romans, was the raillery of slaves, of which we have many instances in Plautus. It seems to have been introduced among us by Cromwell, who, by preferring the scum of the people, made it a court entertainment, of which I have heard many particulars; and, considering all things were turned upside down, it was reasonable and judicious: although it was a piece of policy found out to ridicule a point of honour in the other extreme, when the smallest word misplaced among gentlemen ended in a duel.

There are some men excellent at telling a story, and provided with a plentiful stock of them, which they can draw out upon occasion in all companies; and, considering how low conversation runs now among us, it is not altogether a contemptible talent; however, it is subject to two unavoidable defects, frequent repetition, and being soon exhausted; so that, whoever values this gift in himself, has need of a good memory, and ought frequently to shift his company, that he may not discover the weakness of his fund; for those who are thus endued have seldom any other revenue, but live upon the main stock.

Great speakers in public are seldom agreeable in private conversation, whether their faculty be natural, or acquired by practice, and often venturing. Natural elocution, although it may seem a paradox, usually springs from a barrenness of invention, and of words; by which men who have only one stock of notions upon every subject, and one set of phrases to express them in, they swim upon the superficies, and offer themselves on every occasion; therefore, men of much learning, and who know the compass of a language, are generally the worst talkers on a sudden, until much practice has inured and emboldened them; because they are confounded with plenty of matter, variety of notions and of words, which they cannot readily choose, but are perplexed and entangled by too great a choice; which is no disadvantage in private conversation; where, on the other side, the talent of haranguing is, of all others, most unsupportable.

Nothing has spoiled men more for conversation, than the character of being wits; to support which, they never fail of encouraging a number of followers and admirers, who list themselves in their service, wherein they find their accounts on both sides by pleasing their mutual vanity. This has given the former such an air of superiority, and made the latter so pragmatical, that neither of them are well to be endured. I say nothing here of the itch of dispute and contradiction, telling of lies, or of those who are troubled with the disease called the wandering of the thoughts, so that they are never present in mind at what passes in discourse; for whoever labours under any of these possessions, is as unfit for conversation as a madman in Bedlam.

I think I have gone over most of the errors in

conversation that have fallen under my notice or memory, except some that are merely personal, and others too gross to need exploding; such as lewd or profane talk; but I pretend only to treat the errors of conversation in general, and not the several subjects of discourse, which would be infinite. Thus we see how human nature is most debased, by the abuse of that faculty which is held the great distinction between men and brutes: and how little advantage we make of that, which might be the greatest, the most lasting, and the most innocent, as well as useful pleasure of life: in default of which, we are forced to take up with those poor amusements of dress and visiting, or the more pernicious ones of play, drink, and vicious amours; whereby the nobility and gentry of both sexes are entirely corrupted both in body and mind, and have lost all notions of love, honour, friendship, generosity; which, under the name of fopperies, have been for some time laughed out of doors.

This degeneracy of conversation, with the pernicious consequences thereof upon our humours and dispositions, has been owing, among other causes, to the custom arisen, for some time past, of excluding women from any share in our society, farther than in parties at play, or dancing, or in the pursuit of an amour. I take the highest period of politeness in England (and it is of the same date in France) to have been the peaceable part of King Charles the First's reign; and from what we read of those times, as well as from the accounts I have formerly met with from some who lived in that court, the methods then used for raising and cultivating conversation were altogether different from ours: several ladies, whom we find celebrated by the poets of that age, had assemblies at their houses, where persons of the best understanding, and of both sexes, met to pass the evenings in discoursing upon whatever agreeable subjects were occasionally started; and although we are apt to ridicule the sublime platonic notions they had, or personated, in love and friendship, I conceive their refinements were grounded upon reason, and that a little grain of the romance is no ill ingredient to preserve and exalt the dignity of human nature, without which it is apt to degenerate into everything that is sordid, vicious, and low. If there were no other use in the conversation of ladies, it is sufficient that it would lay a restraint upon those odious topics of immodesty and indecencies, into which the rudeness of our northern genius is so apt to fall. And, therefore, it is observable in those sprightly gentlemen about the town, who are so very dexterous at entertaining a vizard mask in the park or the playhouse, that in the company of ladies of virtue and honour they are silent and disconcerted, and out of their element.

There are some people who think they sufficiently acquit themselves, and entertain their company, with relating facts of no consequence, nor at all out of the road of such common incidents as happen every day; and this I have observed more frequently among the Scots than any other nation, who are very careful not to omit the minutest circumstances of time or place; which kind of discourse, if it were not a little relieved by the uncouth terms and phrases, as well as accent and gesture, peculiar to that country, would be hardly tolerable. It is not a fault in company to talk much ; but to continue it long is certainly one ; for, if the majority of those who are got together be naturally silent or cautious, the conversation will flag, unless it be often renewed by one among them, who can start new subjects (provided he does not dwell upon them,) that leave room for answers and replies.

SIR RICHARD STEELE

1672–1729

AUTOCRATS AT A COFFEE-HOUSE

Hominem pagina nostra sapit.—MARTIAL.
Men and their manners I describe.

It is very natural for a man who is not turned for mirthful meetings of men, or assemblies of the fair sex, to delight in that sort of conversation which we find in coffee-houses. Here a man of my temper is in his element; for if he cannot talk, he can still be more agreeable to his company, as well as pleased in himself, in being only a hearer. It is a secret known but to few, yet of no small use in the conduct of life, that when you fall into a man's conversation, the first thing you should consider is, whether he has a greater inclination to hear you, or that you should hear him. The latter is the more general desire, and I know very able flatterers that never speak a word in praise of the persons from whom they obtain daily favours, but still practise a skilful attention to whatever is uttered by those with whom they converse. We are very curious to observe the behaviour of great men and their clients; but the same passions and interests move men in lower spheres; and I (that have nothing else to do but make observations) see in every parish, street, lane, and alley, of this populous city, a little potentate that has his court and his flatterers, who lay snares for his affection and favour, by the same arts that are practised upon men in higher stations.

In the place I most usually frequent, men differ rather in the time of day in which they make a figure, than in any real greatness above one another. I, who am at the coffee-house at six in a morning, know that my friend Beaver, the haberdasher, has a levee of more undissembled friends and admirers, than most of the courtiers or generals of Great Britain. Every man about him has, perhaps, a newspaper in his hand; but none can pretend to guess what step will be taken in any one court of Europe, till Mr. Beaver has thrown down his pipe, and declares what measures the allies must enter into upon this new posture of affairs. Our coffee-house is near one of the inns of court, and Beaver has the audience and admiration of his neighbours from six till within a quarter of eight, at which time he is interrupted by the students of the house; some of whom are ready dressed for Westminster at eight in a morning, with faces as busy as if they were retained in every cause there; and others come in their night-gowns to saunter away their time, as if they never designed to go thither. I do not know that I meet in any of my walks, objects which move both my spleen and laughter so effectually, as those young fellows at the Grecian, Squire's, Searle's, and all other coffee-houses adjacent to the law, who rise early for no other purpose but to publish their laziness. One would think these young virtuosos take a gay cap and slippers, with a scarf and party-coloured gown, to be ensigns of dignity; for the vain things approach each other with an air, which shows they regard one another for their vestments. I have observed that the superiority among these proceeds from an opinion of gallantry and fashion. The gentleman in the strawberry sash, who presides so much over the rest, has, it seems, subscribed to every opera this last winter, and is supposed to receive favours from one of the actresses.

When the day grows too busy for these gentlemen to enjoy any longer the pleasures of their deshabille with any manner of confidence, they give place to men who have business or good sense in their faces, and come to the coffee-house either to transact affairs, or enjoy conversation. The persons to whose behaviour and discourse I have most regard, are such as are between these two sorts of men ; such as have not spirits too active to be happy and well pleased in a private condition, nor complexions too warm to make them neglect the duties and relations of life. Of these sort of men consist the worthier part of mankind ; of these are all good fathers, generous brothers, sincere friends, and faithful subjects. Their entertainments are derived rather from reason than imagination ; which is the cause that there is no impatience or instability in their speech or action. You see in their countenances they are at home, and in quiet possession of their present instant as it passes, without desiring to quicken it by gratifying any passion, or prosecuting any new design. These are the men formed for society, and those little communities which we express by the word neighbourhood.

The coffee-house is the place of rendezvous to all that live near it, who are thus turned to relish calm and ordinary life. Eubulus presides over the middle hours of the day, when this assembly of men meet together. He enjoys a great fortune handsomely, without launching into expense; and exerts many noble and useful qualities, without appearing in any public employment. His wisdom and knowledge are serviceable to all that think fit to make use of them; and he does the office of a counsel, a judge, an executor, and a friend to all his acquaintance, not only without the profits which attend such offices, but also without the deference and homage which are usually paid to them. The giving of thanks is displeasing to him. The greatest gratitude you can show him, is to let him see you are the better man for his services; and that you are as ready to oblige others, as he is to oblige you.

In the private exigencies of his friends, he lends at legal value considerable sums which he might highly increase by rolling in the public stocks. He does not consider in whose hands his money will improve most, but where it will do most good.

Eubulus has so great an authority in his little diurnal audience, that when he shakes his head at any piece of public news, they all of them appear dejected; and on the contrary, go home to their dinners with a good stomach and cheerful aspect when Eubulus seems to intimate that things go well. Nay their veneration towards him is so great, that when they are in other company they speak and act after him; are wise in his sentences, and are no sooner sat down at their own tables, but they hope or fear, rejoice or despond, as they saw him do at the coffee-house. In a word, every man is Eubulus as soon as his back is turned.

Having here given an account of the several reigns that succeed each other from daybreak till dinner-time, I shall mention the monarchs of the afternoon on another occasion, and shut up the whole series of them with the history of Tom the Tyrant; who, as first minister of the coffee-house, takes the government upon him between the hours of eleven and twelve at night, and gives his orders in the most arbitrary manner to the servants below him, as to the disposition of liquors, coal, and cinders.

ON CONVERSATIONAL TALENT

Quid voveat dulci nutricula maius alumno,
Quam sapere, et fari ut possit quae sentiat?
HOR. 1. *Ep.* iv. 8.

What can the fondest mother wish for more,
E'en for her darling son, than solid sense,
Perceptions clear, and flowing eloquence?
R. WYNNE.

IT is no easy matter, when people are advancing in anything, to prevent their going too fast for want of patience. This happens in nothing more frequently than in the prosecution of studies. Hence it is, that we meet crowds who attempt to be eloquent before they can speak. They affect the flowers of rhetoric before they understand the parts of speech. In the ordinary conversation of this town, there are so many who can, as they call it, talk well, that there is not one in twenty that talks to be understood. This proceeds from an ambition to excel, or, as the term is, to shine in company. The matter is not to make themselves understood, but admired. They come together with a certain emulation, rather than benevolence.

When you fall among such companions, the safe way is to give yourself up, and let the orators declaim for your esteem, and trouble yourself no further. It is said, that a poet must be born so; but I think it may be much better said of an orator, especially when we talk of our town poets and orators; but the town poets are full of rules and laws; the town orators go through thick and thin, and are, forsooth, persons of such eminent natural parts, and knowledge of the world, that they despise all men as unexperienced scholastics, who wait for an occasion before they speak, or who speak no more than is necessary. They had half persuaded me to go to the tavern the other night, but that a gentleman whispered me, 'Pr'ythee, Isaac, go with us; there is Tom Varnish will be there, and he is a fellow that talks as well as any man in England.'

I must confess, when a man expresses himself well upon any occasion, and his falling into an account of any subject arises from a desire to oblige the company, or from fullness of the circumstance itself, so that his speaking of it at large is occasioned only by the openness of a companion; I say, in such a case as this, it is not only pardonable, but agreeable, when a man takes the discourse to himself; but when you see a fellow watch for opportunities for being copious, it is excessively troublesome. A man that stammers, if he has understanding, is to be attended with patience and good nature; but he that speaks more than he need, has no right to such an indulgence. The man who has a defect in his speech takes pains to come to you, while a man of weak capacity, with fluency of speech, triumphs in outrunning you.

The stammerer strives to be fit for your company; the loquacious man endeavours to show you, you are not fit for his.

With thoughts of this kind do I always enter into that man's company who is recommended as a person that talks well; but if I were to choose the people with whom I would spend my hours of conversation, they should be certainly such as laboured no further than to make themselves readily and clearly apprehended, and would have patience and curiosity to understand me. To have good sense, and ability to express it, are the most essential and necessary qualities in companions. When thoughts rise in us fit to utter, among familiar friends there needs but very little care in clothing them.

Urbanus is, I take it, a man one might live with whole years, and enjoy all the freedom and improvement imaginable, and yet be insensible of a contradiction to you in all the mistakes you can be guilty of. His great goodwill to his friends has produced in him such a general deference in his discourse, that if he differs from you in his sense of anything, he introduces his own thoughts by some agreeable circumlocution; or, 'he has often observed such and such a circumstance that made him of another opinion.' Again, where another would be apt to say, 'This I am confident of, I may pretend to judge of this matter as well as anybody'; Urbanus says, 'I am verily persuaded; I believe one may conclude.' In a word, there is no man more clear in his thoughts and expressions than he is, or speaks with greater diffidence. You shall hardly find one man of any consideration, but you shall observe one of less consequence form himself after him. This happens to Urbanus; but the man who steals from him almost every sentiment he utters in a whole week, disguises the theft by carrying it with quite a different air. Umbratilis knows Urbanus's doubtful way of speaking proceeds from good nature and good breeding, and not from uncertainty in his opinions. Umbratilis, therefore, has no more to do but repeat the thoughts of Urbanus in a positive manner and appear to the undiscerning a wiser man than the person from whom he borrows: but those who know him, can see the servant in his master's habit; and the more he struts, the less do his clothes appear his own.

In conversation, the medium is neither to affect silence or eloquence; not to value our approbation, and to endeavour to excel us who are of your company, are equal injuries. The great enemies therefore to good company, and those who transgress most against the laws of equality, which is the life of it, are, the clown, the wit, and the pedant. A clown, when he has sense, is conscious of his want of education, and with an awkward bluntness hopes to keep himself in countenance by overthrowing the use of all polite behaviour. He takes advantage of the restraint good breeding lays upon others not to offend him, to trespass against them, and is under the man's own shelter while he intrudes upon him. The fellows of this class are very frequent in the repetition of the words *rough* and *manly*. When these people happen to be by their fortunes of the rank of gentlemen, they defend their other absurdities by an impertinent courage; and, to help out the defect of their behaviour, add their being dangerous to their being disagreeable. This gentleman (though he displeases, professes to do so; and knowing that, dares still go on to do so) is not so painful a companion, as he who will please you against your will, and resolves to be a wit.

This man, upon all occasions, and whoever he falls in company with, talks in the same circle, and in the same round of chat which he has learned at one of the tables of this coffee-house. As poetry is in itself an elevation above ordinary and common sentiments; so there is no fop so very near a madman in indifferent company as a poetical one. He is not apprehensive that the generality of the world are intent upon the business of their own fortune and profession, and have as little capacity as curiosity to enter into matters of ornament or speculation. I remember at a full table in the city, one of these ubiquitary wits was entertaining the company with a soliloquy, for so I call it when a man talks to those who do not understand him, concerning wit and humour. An honest gentleman who sat next to me, and was worth half a plum,[1] stared at him, and observing there was some sense, as he thought, mixed with his impertinence, whispered me, 'Take my word for it, this fellow is more knave than fool.' This was all my good friend's applause of the wittiest man of talk that I was ever present at, which wanted nothing to make it excellent, but that there was no occasion for it.

The pedant is so obvious to ridicule, that it would be to be one to offer to explain him. He is a gentleman so well known, that there is none but those of his own class who do not laugh at and

[1] Fifty thousand pounds.

avoid him. Pedantry proceeds from much reading and little understanding. A pedant among men of learning and sense, is like an ignorant servant giving an account of a polite conversation. You may find he has brought with him more than could have entered into his head without being there, but still that he is not a bit wiser than if he had not been there at all.

JOSEPH ADDISON

1672–1719

THE VISION OF MIRZA

Omnem, quae nunc obducta tuenti
Mortales hebetat visus tibi, et humida circum
Caligat, nubem eripiam.—VIRG. *Aen.* ii. 604.

The cloud, which, intercepting the clear light,
Hangs o'er thy eyes, and blunts thy mortal sight,
I will remove.

WHEN I was at Grand Cairo, I picked up several Oriental manuscripts, which I have still by me. Among others I met with one entitled, The Visions of Mirza, which I have read over with great pleasure. I intend to give it to the public when I have no other entertainment for them; and shall begin with the first vision, which I have translated word for word as follows:

'On the fifth day of the moon, which, according to the custom of my forefathers I always keep holy, after having washed myself, and offered up my morning devotions, I ascended the high hills of Bagdad, in order to pass the rest of the day in meditation and prayer. As I was here airing myself on the tops of the mountains, I fell into a profound contemplation on the vanity of human life; and passing from one thought to another, "Surely," said I, "man is but a shadow, and life a dream." Whilst I was thus musing, I cast my eyes towards the summit of a rock that was not far from me, where I discovered one in the habit of a shepherd, with a little musical instrument in his hand. As I looked upon him he applied it to his lips, and began to play upon it.—The sound of it was exceeding sweet, and wrought into a variety of tunes that were inexpressibly melodious, and altogether different from anything I had ever heard. They put me in mind of those heavenly airs that are played to the departed souls of good men upon their first arrival in Paradise, to wear out the impressions of their last agonies, and qualify them for the pleasures of that happy place. My heart melted away in secret raptures.

'I had been often told that the rock before me was the haunt of a genius; and that several had been entertained with music who had passed by it, but never heard that the musician had before made himself visible. When he had raised my thoughts by those transporting airs which he played, to taste the pleasures of his conversation, as I looked upon him like one astonished, he beckoned to me, and by the waving of his hand, directed me to approach the place where he sat. I drew near with that reverence which is due to a superior nature; and as my heart was entirely subdued by the captivating strains I had heard, I fell down at his feet and wept. The genius smiled upon me with a look of compassion and affability that familiarized him to my imagination, and at once dispelled all the fears and apprehensions with which I approached him. He lifted me from the ground, and taking me by the hand, "Mirza," said he, "I have heard thee in thy soliloquies; follow me."

'He then led me to the highest pinnacle of the rock, and placing me on the top of it—"Cast thy eyes eastward," said he, "and tell me what thou seest." "I see," said I, "a huge valley, and a prodigious tide of water rolling through it." "The valley that thou seest," said he, "is the Vale of Misery, and the tide of water that thou seest is part of the great tide of Eternity." "What is the reason," said I, "that the tide I see rises out of a thick mist at one end, and again loses itself in a thick mist at the other?" "What thou seest," said he, "is that portion of Eternity which is called Time, measured out by the sun, and reaching from the beginning of the world to its consummation. Examine now," said he, "this sea that is thus bounded with darkness at both ends, and tell me what thou discoverest in it." "I see a bridge," said I, "standing in the midst of the tide." "The bridge thou seest," said he, "is human Life; consider it attentively." Upon a more leisurely survey of it, I found that it consisted of threescore and ten entire arches, with several broken arches, which, added to those that were entire, made up the number about an hundred. As I was counting the arches, the genius told me that this bridge consisted at first of a thousand arches: but that a great flood swept away the rest, and left the bridge in the ruinous condition I now beheld it. "But tell me further," said he, "what thou discoverest on it." "I see multitudes of people passing over it," said I, "and a black cloud hanging on each end of it." As I looked more attentively, I saw several of the passengers dropping through the bridge into the great tide that flowed underneath it; and, upon further examination, perceived there were innumerable trap-doors that lay concealed in the bridge, which the passengers no sooner trod upon, but they fell through them into the tide, and immediately disappeared. These hidden pit-falls were set very thick at the entrance of the bridge, so that throngs of people no sooner broke through the cloud but many of them fell into them. They grew thinner towards the middle, but multiplied and lay closer together towards the end of the arches that were entire.

'There were indeed some persons, but their number was very small, that continued a kind of hobbling march on the broken arches, but fell through one after another, being quite tired and spent with so long a walk.

'I passed some time in the contemplation of this wonderful structure, and the great variety of objects which it presented. My heart was filled with a deep melancholy to see several dropping unexpectedly in the midst of mirth and jollity, and catching at everything that stood by them to save themselves. Some were looking up towards the heavens in a thoughtful posture, and in the midst of a speculation stumbled and fell out of sight. Multitudes were very busy in the pursuit of bubbles that glittered in their eyes and danced before them; but often when they thought themselves within the reach of them, their footing failed, and down they sunk. In this confusion of objects, I observed some with scimitars in their hands, who ran to and fro upon the bridge, thrusting several persons on trap-doors which did not seem to lie in their way, and which they might have escaped had they not been forced upon them.

'The genius seeing me indulge myself in this melancholy prospect, told me I had dwelt long enough upon it. "Take thine eyes off the bridge," said he, "and tell me if thou yet seest anything thou dost not comprehend." Upon looking up, "what mean," said I, "those great flights of birds that are perpetually hovering about the bridge, and settling upon it from time to time? I see vultures, harpies, ravens, cormorants, and among many other feathered creatures several little winged boys, that perch in great numbers upon the middle arches." "These," said the genius, "are Envy, Avarice, Superstition, Despair, Love, with the like cares and passions that infest human life."

'I here fetched a deep sigh. "Alas," said I, "man was made in vain! how is he given away to misery and mortality! tortured in life, and swallowed up in death!" The genius being moved with compassion towards me, bid me quit so uncomfortable a prospect. "Look no more," said he, "on man in the first stage of his existence, in his setting out for eternity; but cast thine eye on that thick mist into which the tide bears the several generations of mortals that fall into it." I directed my sight as I was ordered, and (whether or no the good genius strengthened it with any supernatural force, or dissipated part of the mist that was before too thick for the eye to penetrate) I saw the valley opening at the further end, and spreading forth into an immense ocean, that had a huge rock of adamant running through the midst of it, and dividing it into two equal parts. The clouds still rested on one half of it, insomuch that I could discover nothing in it; but the other appeared to me a vast ocean planted with innumerable islands, that were covered with fruits and flowers, and interwoven with a thousand little shining seas that ran among them. I could see persons dressed in glorious habits with garlands upon their heads, passing among the trees, lying down by the sides of fountains, or resting on beds of flowers; and could hear a confused harmony of singing birds, falling waters, human voices, and musical instruments. Gladness grew in me upon the discovery of so delightful a scene. I wished for the wings of an eagle, that I might fly away to those happy seats; but the genius told me there was no passage to them, except through the gates of death that I saw opening every moment upon the bridge. "The islands," said he, "that lie so fresh and green before thee, and with which the whole face of the ocean appears spotted as far as thou canst see, are more in number than the sands on the sea-shore: there are myriads of islands behind those which thou here discoverest, reaching further than thine eye, or even thine imagination, can extend itself. These are the mansions of good men after death, who, according to the degree and kinds of virtue in which they excelled, are distributed among these several islands, which abound with pleasures of different kinds and degrees, suitable to the relishes and perfections of those who are settled in them; every island is a paradise accommodated to its respective inhabitants. Are not these, O Mirza, habitations worth contending for? Does life appear miserable that gives thee opportunities of earning such a reward? Is death to be feared, that will convey thee to so happy an existence? Think not man was made in vain, who has such an Eternity reserved for him." I gazed with inexpressible pleasure on these happy islands. At length, said I, "Show me now, I beseech thee, the secrets that lie hid under those dark clouds which cover the ocean on the other side of the rock of adamant." The genius making me no answer, I turned about to address myself to him a second time, but I found that he had left me; I then turned again to the vision which I had been so long contemplating: but instead of the rolling tide, the arched bridge, and the happy islands, I saw nothing but the long hollow valley of Bagdad, with oxen, sheep, and camels grazing upon the sides of it.'

POPULAR SUPERSTITIONS

Somnia, terrores magicos, miracula, sagas,
Nocturnos lemures, portentaque Thessala rides?

HOR., 2 *Ep.* ii. 208.

Visions and magic spells, can you despise,
And laugh at witches, ghosts, and prodigies?

GOING yesterday to dine with an old acquaintance, I had the misfortune to find his whole family very much dejected. Upon asking him the occasion of it, he told me that his wife had dreamt a strange dream the night before, which they were afraid portended some misfortune to themselves or to their children. At her coming into the room, I observed a settled melancholy in her countenance, which I should have been troubled for, had I not heard from whence it proceeded. We were no sooner sat down, but, after having looked upon me a little while, 'My dear,' says she, turning to her husband, 'you may now see the stranger that was in the candle last night.' Soon after this, as they began to talk of family affairs, a little boy at the lower end of the table told her that he was to go into join-hand on Thursday. 'Thursday!'

says she. 'No, child; if it please God, you shall not begin upon Childermas-day; tell your writing-master that Friday will be soon enough.' I was reflecting with myself on the oddness of her fancy, and wondering that anybody would establish it as a rule, to lose a day in every week. In the midst of these my musings, she desired me to reach her a little salt upon the point of my knife, which I did in such a trepidation and hurry of obedience, that I let it drop by the way; at which she immediately startled, and said it fell towards her. Upon this I looked very blank; and observing the concern of the whole table, began to consider myself, with some confusion, as a person that had brought a disaster upon the family. The lady, however, recovering herself after a little space, said to her husband with a sigh, 'My dear, misfortunes never come single.' My friend, I found, acted but an under part at his table, and, being a man of more good nature than understanding, thinks himself obliged to fall in with all the passions and humours of his yoke-fellow. 'Do not you remember, child,' says she, 'that the pigeon-house fell the very afternoon that our careless wench spilt the salt upon the table?'—'Yes,' says he, 'my dear, and the next post brought us an account of the battle of Almanza.' The reader may guess at the figure I made, after having done all this mischief. I dispatched my dinner as soon as I could, with my usual taciturnity; when to my utter confusion, the lady seeing me quitting my knife and fork, and laying them across one another upon my plate, desired me that I would humour her so far as to take them out of that figure, and place them side by side. What the absurdity was which I had committed I did not know, but I suppose there was some traditionary superstition in it; and therefore, in obedience to the lady of the house, I disposed of my knife and fork in two parallel lines, which is the figure I shall always lay them in for the future, though I do not know any reason for it.

It is not difficult for a man to see that a person has conceived an aversion to him. For my own part, I quickly found, by the lady's looks, that she regarded me as a very odd kind of fellow, with an unfortunate aspect. For which reason I took my leave immediately after dinner, and withdrew to my own lodgings. Upon my return home, I fell into a profound contemplation on the evils that attend these superstitious follies of mankind; how they subject us to imaginary afflictions, and additional sorrows, that do not properly come within our lot. As if the natural calamities of life were not sufficient for it, we turn the most indifferent circumstances into misfortunes, and suffer as much from trifling accidents as from real evils. I have known the shooting of a star spoil a night's rest; and have seen a man in love grow pale, and lose his appetite, upon the plucking of a merry-thought. A screech-owl at midnight has alarmed a family more than a band of robbers; nay, the voice of a cricket hath struck more terror than the roaring of a lion. There is nothing so inconsiderable which may not appear dreadful to an imagination that is filled with omens and prognostics. A rusty nail, or a crooked pin, shoot up into prodigies.

An old maid that is troubled with the vapours produces infinite disturbances of this kind, among her friends and neighbours. I know a maiden aunt of a great family, who is one of these antiquated Sibyls, that forebodes and prophesies from one end of the year to the other. She is always seeing apparitions, and hearing death-watches; and was the other day almost frighted out of her wits by the great house-dog that howled in the stable, at a time when she lay ill of the toothache. Such an extravagant cast of mind engages multitudes of people not only in impertinent terrors, but in supernumerary duties of life; and arises from that fear and ignorance which are natural to the soul of man. The horror with which we entertain the thoughts of death (or indeed of any future evil), and the uncertainty of its approach, fill a melancholy mind with innumerable apprehensions and suspicions, and consequently dispose it to the observation of such groundless prodigies and predictions. For as it is the chief concern of wise men to retrench the evils of life by the reasonings of philosophy; it is the employment of fools to multiply them by the sentiments of superstition.

For my own part, I should be very much troubled were I endowed with this divining quality, though it should inform me truly of everything that can befall me. I would not anticipate the relish of any happiness, nor feel the weight of any misery, before it actually arrives.

I know but one way of fortifying my soul against these gloomy presages and terrors of mind, and that is, by securing to myself the friendship and protection of that Being who disposes of events and governs futurity. He sees, at one view, the whole thread of my existence, not only that part of it which I have already passed through, but that which runs forward into all the depths of eternity. When I lay me down to sleep, I recommend myself to His care; when I awake, I give myself up to His direction. Amidst all the evils that threaten me, I will look up to Him for help, and question not but He will either avert them, or turn them to my advantage. Though I know neither the time nor the manner of the death I am to die, I am not at all solicitous about it; because I am sure that He knows them both, and that He will not fail to comfort and support me under them.

HENRY FIELDING

1707–1754

AN ESSAY ON NOTHING

The Introduction

It is surprising that, while such trifling matters employ the masterly pens of the present age, the great and noble subject of this essay should have passed totally neglected; and the rather, as it is a subject to which the genius of many of those writers who have unsuccessfully applied themselves to politics, religion, &c., is most peculiarly adapted.

Perhaps their unwillingness to handle what is of such importance may not improperly be ascribed to their modesty; though they may not be remarkably addicted to this vice on every occasion. Indeed I have heard it predicated of some, whose assurance in treating other subjects hath been sufficiently notable, that they have blushed at this. For such is the awe with which this Nothing inspires mankind, that I believe it is generally apprehended of many persons of very high character among us, that were title, power, or riches to allure them, they would stick at it.

But, whatever be the reason, certain it is, that except a hardy wit in the reign of Charles II, none ever hath dared to write on this subject: I mean openly and avowedly; for it must be confessed that most of our modern authors, however foreign the matter which they endeavour to treat may seem at their first setting out, they generally bring the work to this in the end. I hope, however, this attempt will not be imputed to me as an act of immodesty; since I am convinced there are many persons in this kingdom who are persuaded of my fitness for what I have undertaken. But as talking of a man's self is generally suspected to arise from vanity, I shall, without any more excuse or preface, proceed to my essay.

Section I

OF THE ANTIQUITY OF NOTHING

There is nothing falser than that old proverb which (like many other falsehoods) is in every one's mouth:

Ex nihilo nihil fit.

Thus translated by Shakespeare, in *Lear*:

Nothing can come of nothing.

Whereas, in fact, from Nothing proceeds everything. And this is a truth confessed by the philosophers of all sects: the only point in controversy between them being, whether Something made the world out of Nothing, or Nothing out of Something. A matter not much worth debating at present, since either will equally serve our turn. Indeed the wits of all ages seem to have ranged themselves on each side of this question, as their genius tended more or less to the spiritual or material substance. For those of the more spiritual species have inclined to the former, and those whose genius hath partaken more of the chief properties of matter, such as solidity, thickness, &c., have embraced the latter.

But whether Nothing was the *artifex* or *materies* only, it is plain in either case, it will have a right to claim to itself the origination of all things.

And farther, the great antiquity of Nothing is apparent from its being so visible in the account we have of the beginning of every nation. This is very plainly to be discovered in the first pages, and sometimes books, of all general historians; and, indeed, the study of this important subject fills up the whole life of an antiquary, it being always at the bottom of his inquiry, and is commonly at last discovered by him with infinite labour and pains.

Section II

OF THE NATURE OF NOTHING

Another falsehood which we must detect in the pursuit of this essay is an assertion, 'That no one can have an idea of Nothing': but men who thus confidently deny us this idea either grossly deceive themselves, or would impose a downright cheat on the world: for, so far from having none, I believe there are few who have not many ideas of it; though perhaps they may mistake them for the idea of Something.

For instance, is there any one who hath not an idea of immaterial substance?[1] Now what is immaterial substance, more than Nothing? But here we are artfully deceived by the use of words:

[1] The Author would not be here understood to speak against the doctrine of immateriality, to which he is a hearty well-wisher; but to point at the stupidity of those who, instead of immaterial *essence*, which would convey a rational meaning, have substituted immaterial *substance*, which is a contradiction in terms.

for, were we to ask another what idea he had of immaterial matter, or unsubstantial substance, the absurdity of affirming it to be Something would shock him, and he would immediately reply, it was Nothing.

Some persons perhaps will say, ' Then we have no idea of it ' ; but, as I can support the contrary by such undoubted authority, I shall, instead of trying to confute such idle opinions, proceed to show ; first, what Nothing is ; secondly, I shall disclose the various kinds of Nothing ; and, lastly shall prove its great dignity, and that it is the end of everything.

As it is extremely hard to define Nothing in positive terms, I shall therefore do it in negative. Nothing then is not Something. And here I must object to a third error concerning it, which is, that it is in no place ; which is an indirect way of depriving it of its existence ; whereas indeed it possesses the greatest and noblest place on this earth, viz. the human brain. But indeed this mistake had been sufficiently refuted by many very wise men ; who, having spent their whole lives in contemplation and pursuit of Nothing, have at last gravely concluded—*that there is Nothing in this world.*

Farther, as Nothing is not Something, so everything which is not Something is Nothing ; and wherever Something is not Nothing is : a very large allowance in its favour, as must appear to persons well skilled in human affairs.

For instance, when a bladder is full of wind, it is full of something ; but when that is let out, we aptly say, there is nothing in it.

The same may be as justly asserted of a man as

of a bladder. However well he may be bedaubed with lace, or with title, yet, if he have not something in him, we may predicate the same of him as of an empty bladder.

But if we cannot reach an adequate knowledge of the true essence of Nothing, no more than we can of matter, let us, in imitation of the experimental philosophers, examine some of its properties or accidents.

And here we shall see the infinite advantages which Nothing hath over Something; for, while the latter is confined to one sense, or two perhaps at the most, Nothing is the object of them all.

For, first, Nothing may be seen, as is plain from the relation of persons who have recovered from high fevers, and perhaps may be suspected from some (at least) of those who have seen apparitions, both on earth and in the clouds. Nay, I have often heard it confessed by men, when asked what they saw at such a place and time, that they saw Nothing. Admitting then there are two sights, viz. a first and second sight, according to the firm belief of some, Nothing must be allowed to have a very large share of the first, and as to the second, it hath it all entirely to itself.

Secondly, Nothing may be heard, of which the same proofs may be given as of the foregoing. The Argive mentioned by Horace is a strong instance of this:

Fuit haud ignobilis Argis,
Qui se credebat miros audire tragœdos,
In vacuo laetus sessor plausorque theatro.

That Nothing may be tasted and smelt is not only known to persons of delicate palates and nostrils. How commonly do we hear that such a thing smells or tastes of nothing! The latter I have heard asserted of a dish compounded of five or six savoury ingredients. And as to the former, I remember an elderly gentlewoman who had a great antipathy to the smell of apples, who, upon discovering that an idle boy had fastened some mellow apple to her tail, contracted a habit of smelling them whenever that boy came within her sight, though there were then none within a mile of her.

Lastly, feeling: and sure if any sense seems more particularly the object of matter only, which must be allowed to be Something, this doth Nay, I have heard it asserted, and with a colour of truth, of several persons, that they can feel nothing but a cudgel. Notwithstanding which, some have felt the motions of the spirit, and others have felt very bitterly the misfortunes of their friends, without endeavouring to relieve them. Now these seem two plain instances that Nothing is an object of this sense. Nay, I have heard a surgeon declare, while he was cutting off a patient's leg, that *he was sure he felt Nothing.*

Nothing is as well the object of our passions as our senses. Thus there are many who love Nothing, some who hate Nothing, and some who fear Nothing, &c.

We have already mentioned three of the properties of a noun to belong to Nothing; we shall find the fourth likewise to be as justly claimed by it, and that Nothing is as often the object of the understanding as of the senses.

Indeed some have imagined that knowledge, with the adjective *human* placed before it, is another word for Nothing. And one of the wisest men in the world declared he knew Nothing.

But, without carrying it so far, this I believe may be allowed, that it is at least possible for a man to know Nothing. And whoever hath read over many works of our ingenious moderns, with proper attention and emolument, will, I believe, confess that, if he understand them right, he understands Nothing.

This is a secret not known to all readers, and want of this knowledge hath occasioned much puzzling; for where a book or chapter or paragraph hath seemed to the reader to contain Nothing, his modesty hath sometimes persuaded him that the true meaning of the author hath escaped him, instead of concluding, as in reality the fact was, that the author in the said book, &c., did truly and bona fide mean Nothing. I remember once, at the table of a person of great eminence, and one no less distinguished by superiority of wit than fortune, when a very dark passage was read out of a poet famous for being so sublime that he is often out of the sight of his reader, some persons present declared they did not understand the meaning. The gentleman himself, casting his eye over the performance, testified a surprise at the dullness of his company, seeing Nothing could, he said, possibly be plainer than the meaning of the passage which they stuck at. This set all of us to puzzling again, but with like success; we frankly owned we could not find it out, and desired he would explain it. 'Explain it!' said the gentleman, 'why, he means Nothing.'

In fact, this mistake arises from a too vulgar error among persons unacquainted with the mystery of writing, who imagine it impossible that a man should sit down to write without any meaning at all! whereas, in reality, nothing is more common: for, not to instance in myself, who have confessedly set down to write this essay with Nothing in my head, or, which is much the same thing, to write about Nothing, it may be incontestably proved, *ab effectu*, that Nothing is commoner among the moderns. The inimitable author of a preface to the Posthumous Eclogues of a late ingenious young gentleman, says, 'There are men who sit down to write what they think, and others to think what they shall write.' But indeed there is a third and much more numerous sort, who never think either before they sit down or afterwards, and who, when they produce on paper what was before in their heads, are sure to produce Nothing.

Thus we have endeavoured to demonstrate the nature of Nothing, by showing first, definitively, *what it is not*; and, secondly, by describing *what it is*. The next thing therefore proposed is to show its various kinds.

Now some imagine these several kinds differ in name only. But, without endeavouring to confute so absurd an opinion, especially as these different kinds of Nothing occur frequently in the best authors, I shall content myself with setting them down, and leave it to the determination of the distinguished reader, whether it is probable, or indeed possible, that they should all convey one and the same meaning.

These are, Nothing *per se* Nothing; Nothing at all; Nothing in the least; Nothing in nature; Nothing in the world; Nothing in the whole world; Nothing in the whole universal world. And perhaps many other of which we say—Nothing.

Section III

OF THE DIGNITY OF NOTHING ; AND AN ENDEAVOUR TO PROVE THAT IT IS THE END AS WELL AS BEGINNING OF ALL THINGS.

Nothing contains so much dignity as Nothing. Ask an infamous worthless nobleman (if any such be) in what his dignity consists? It may not be perhaps consistent with his dignity to give you an answer, but suppose he should be willing to condescend so far, what could he in effect say? Should he say he had it from his ancestors, I apprehend a lawyer would oblige him to prove that the virtues to which his dignity was annexed descended to him. If he claims it as inherent in the title, might he not be told, that a title originally implied dignity, as it implied the presence of those virtues to which dignity is inseparably annexed; but that no implication will fly in the face of downright positive proof to the contrary. In short, to examine no farther, since his endeavour to derive it from any other fountain would be equally impotent, his dignity arises from Nothing, and in reality is Nothing. Yet, that this dignity really exists, that it glares in the eyes of men, and produces much good to the person who wears it, is, I believe, incontestable.

Perhaps this may appear in the following syllogism.

The respect paid to men on account of their titles is paid at least to the supposal of their superior virtues and abilities, or it is paid to Nothing.

But when a man is a notorious knave or fool it is impossible there should be any such supposal.

The conclusion is apparent.

Now, that no man is ashamed of either paying or receiving this respect I wonder not, since the great importance of Nothing seems, I think, to be pretty apparent: but that they should deny the Deity worshipped, and endeavour to represent Nothing as Something, is more worthy reprehension. This is a fallacy extremely common. I have seen a fellow, whom all the world knew to have Nothing in him, not only pretend to Something himself, but supported in that pretension by others who have been less liable to be deceived. Now whence can this proceed but from their being ashamed of Nothing? A modesty very peculiar to this age.

But, notwithstanding all such disguises and deceit, a man must have very little discernment who can live very long in courts, or populous cities, without being convinced of the great dignity of Nothing; and though he should, through corruption or necessity, comply with the vulgar worship and adulation, he will know to what it is paid; namely, to Nothing.

The most astonishing instance of this respect, so frequently paid to Nothing, is when it is paid (if I may so express myself) to something less than Nothing; when the person who receives it is not only void of the quality for which he is respected, but is in reality notoriously guilty of the vices directly opposite to the virtues whose applause he receives. This is, indeed, the highest degree of Nothing, or (if I may be allowed the word), the Nothingest of all Nothings.

Here it is to be known, that respect may be aimed at Something and really light on Nothing. For instance, when mistaking certain things called gravity, canting, blustering, ostentation, pomp, and such like, for wisdom, piety, magnanimity, charity, true greatness, &c., we give to the former the honour and reverence due to the latter. Not that I would be understood so far to discredit my subject as to insinuate that gravity, canting, &c., are really Nothing; on the contrary, there is much more reason to suspect (if we judge from the practice of the world) that wisdom, piety, and other virtues, have a good title to that name. But we do not, in fact, pay our respect to the former, but to the latter: in other words, we pay it to that which is not, and consequently pay it to Nothing.

So far then for the dignity of the subject on which I am treating. I am now to show, that Nothing is the end as well as beginning of all things.

That everything is resolvable, and will be resolved into its first principles, will be, I believe, readily acknowledged by all philosophers. As, therefore, we have sufficiently proved the world came from Nothing, it follows that it will likewise end in the same: but as I am writing to a nation of Christians, I have no need to be prolix on this head; since every one of my readers, by his faith, acknowledges that the world is to have an end, i. e. is to come to Nothing.

And, as Nothing is the end of the world, so is it of everything in the world. Ambition, the greatest, highest, noblest, finest, most heroic and godlike of all passions, what doth it end in?—Nothing. What did Alexander, Caesar, and all the rest of that heroic band, who have plundered and massacred so many millions, obtain by all their care, labour, pain, fatigue, and danger?—Could they speak for themselves must they not own, that the end of all their pursuit was Nothing? Nor is this the end of private ambition only. What is become of that proud mistress of the world—the *Caput triumphati orbis*—that Rome of which her own flatterers so liberally prophesied the immortality? In what hath all her glory ended? Surely in Nothing.

Again, what is the end of avarice? Not power, or pleasure, as some think, for the miser will part with a shilling for neither: not ease or happiness; for the more he attains of what he desires, the more uneasy and miserable he is. If every good in this world was put to him, he could not say he pursued one. Shall we say then he pursues misery only? That surely would be contradictory to the first principles of human nature. May we not therefore, nay, must we not confess, that he aims at Nothing? especially if he be himself unable to tell us what is the end of all this bustle and hurry, this watching and toiling, this self-denial and self-constraint?

It will not, I apprehend, be sufficient for him to plead that his design is to amass a large fortune, which he never can nor will use himself, nor would willingly quit to any other person: unless he can show us some substantial good which this fortune is to produce, we shall certainly be justified in concluding that his end is the same with that of ambition.

The great Mr. Hobbes so plainly saw this, that as he was an enemy to that notable immaterial substance which we have here handled, and therefore unwilling to allow it the large province we have contended for, he advanced a very strange doctrine and asserted truly,—That in all these grand pursuits the means themselves were the end proposed, viz. to ambition—plotting, fighting, danger, difficulty, and such like: to avarice—

cheating, starving, watching, and the numberless painful arts by which this passion proceeds.

However easy it may be to demonstrate the absurdity of this opinion it will be needless to my purpose, since, if we are driven to confess that the means are the only end attained, I think we must likewise confess that the end proposed is absolutely Nothing.

As I have shown the end of our two greatest and noblest pursuits, one or other of which engages almost every individual of the busy part of mankind, I shall not tire the reader with carrying him through all the rest, since I believe the same conclusion may be easily drawn from them all.

I shall therefore finish this Essay with an inference, which aptly enough suggests itself from what hath been said: seeing that such is its dignity and importance, and that it is really the end of all those things which are supported with so much pomp and solemnity, and looked on with such respect and esteem, surely it becomes a wise man to regard Nothing with the utmost awe and adoration; to pursue it with all his parts and pains; and to sacrifice to it his ease, his innocence, and his present happiness. To which noble pursuit we have this great incitement, that we may assure ourselves of never being cheated or deceived in the end proposed. The virtuous, wise, and learned may then be unconcerned at all the changes of ministries and of government; since they may be well satisfied, that while ministers of state are rogues themselves, and have inferior knavish tools to bribe and reward, true virtue, wisdom, learning, wit, and integrity, will most certainly bring their possessors—Nothing.

91

SAMUEL JOHNSON

1709–1784

THE ADVANTAGES OF LIVING IN A GARRET

Ὄσσαν ἐπ' Οὐλύμπῳ μέμασαν θέμεν· αὐτὰρ ἐπ' Ὄσσῃ
Πήλιον εἰνοσίφυλλον, ἵν' οὐρανὸς ἀμβατὸς εἴη.—Hom.

The Gods they challenge, and affect the skies:
Heav'd on *Olympus* tottering *Ossa* stood;
On *Ossa*, *Pelion* nods with all his wood.—Pope.

To the Rambler.

Sir,

Nothing has more retarded the advancement of learning than the disposition of vulgar minds to ridicule and vilify what they cannot comprehend. All industry must be excited by hope; and as the student often proposes no other reward to himself than praise, he is easily discouraged by contempt and insult. He who brings with him into a clamorous multitude the timidity of recluse speculation, and has never hardened his front in public life, or accustomed his passions to the vicissitudes and accidents, the triumphs and defeats of mixed conversation, will blush at the stare of petulant incredulity, and suffer himself to be driven by a burst of laughter, from the fortresses of demonstration. The mechanist will be afraid to assert before hardy contradiction, the possibility of tearing down bulwarks with a silkworm's thread; and the astronomer of relating the rapidity of light, the distance of the fixed stars, and the height of the lunar mountains.

If I could by any efforts have shaken off this cowardice, I had not sheltered myself under a borrowed name, nor applied to you for the means of communicating to the public the theory of a garret; a subject which, except some slight and transient strictures, has been hitherto neglected by those who were best qualified to adorn it, either for want of leisure to prosecute the various researches in which a nice discussion must engage them, or because it requires such diversity of knowledge, and such extent of curiosity, as is scarcely to be found in any single intellect: or perhaps others foresaw the tumults which would be raised against them, and confined their knowledge to their own breasts, and abandoned prejudice and folly to the direction of chance.

That the professors of literature generally reside in the highest stories, has been immemorially observed. The wisdom of the ancients was well acquainted with the intellectual advantages of an elevated situation: why else were the *Muses* stationed on *Olympus* or *Parnassus* by those who could with equal right have raised them bowers in the vale of *Tempe*, or erected their altars among the flexures of *Meander*? Why was *Jove* himself nursed upon a mountain? or why did the goddesses, when the prize of beauty was contested, try the cause upon the top of *Ida*? Such were the fictions by which the great masters of the earlier ages endeavoured to inculcate to posterity the importance of a garret, which, though they had been long obscured by the negligence and ignorance of succeeding times, were well enforced by the celebrated symbol of *Pythagoras*, ἀνέμων πνεόντων τὴν ἠχὼ προσκύνει, 'when the wind blows, worship its echo.' This could not but be understood by his disciples as an inviolable injunction to live in a garret, which I have found frequently visited by the echo and the wind. Nor was the tradition wholely obliterated in the age of *Augustus*, for *Tibullus* evidently congratulates himself upon his garret, not without some allusion to the *Pythagorean* precept.

> Quam iuvat immites ventos audire cubantem—
> Aut, gelidas hibernus aquas cum fuderit Auster,
> Securum somnos imbre iuvante sequi!
>
> How sweet in sleep to pass the careless hours,
> Lull'd by the beating winds and dashing show'rs!

And it is impossible not to discover the fondness of *Lucretius*, an earlier writer, for a garret, in his description of the lofty towers of serene learning, and of the pleasure with which a wise man looks down upon the confused and erratic state of the world moving below him.

> Sed nil dulcius est, bene quam munita tenere
> Edita doctrina sapientum templa serena,
> Despicere unde queas alios passimque videre
> Errare atque viam palantis quaerere vitae.
>
> —'Tis sweet thy lab'ring steps to guide
> To virtue's heights, with wisdom well supply'd,
> And all the magazines of learning fortify'd:
> From thence to look below on human kind,
> Bewilder'd in the maze of life, and blind.
>
> DRYDEN.

The institution has, indeed, continued to our own time; the garret is still the usual receptacle of the philosopher and poet; but this, like many ancient customs, is perpetuated only by an accidental imitation, without knowledge of the original reason for which it was established.

> Causa latet; res est notissima.
>
> The cause is secret, but th' effect is known.
>
> ADDISON.

Conjectures have, indeed, been advanced concerning these habitations of literature, but without much satisfaction to the judicious inquirer. Some have imagined, that the garret is generally chosen by the wits, as most easily rented; and concluded that no man rejoices in his aerial abode, but on the days of payment. Others suspect that a garret is chiefly convenient, as it is remoter than any other part of the house from the outer door, which is often observed to be infested by visitants, who talk incessantly of beer, or linen, or a coat, and repeat the same sounds every morning, and sometimes again in the afternoon, without any variation, except that they grow daily more importunate and clamorous, and raise their voices in time from mournful murmurs to raging vociferations. This eternal monotony is always detestable to a man whose chief pleasure is to enlarge his knowledge and vary his ideas. Others talk of freedom from noise, and abstraction from common business or amusements; and some, yet more visionary, tell us, that the faculties are enlarged by open prospects, and that the fancy is more at liberty when the eye ranges without confinement.

These conveniences may perhaps all be found in a well-chosen garret; but surely they cannot be supposed sufficiently important to have operated unvariably upon different climates, distant ages, and separate nations. Of a universal practice, there must still be presumed a universal cause, which however recondite and abstruse, may be perhaps reserved to make me illustrious by its discovery, and you by its promulgation.

It is universally known that the faculties of the mind are invigorated or weakened by the state of the body, and that the body is in a great measure regulated by the various compressions of the ambient element. The effects of the air in the production or cure of corporeal maladies have been acknowledged from the time of *Hippocrates*; but no man has yet sufficiently considered how far it may influence the operations of the genius, though every day affords instances of local understanding, of wits and reasoners, whose faculties are adapted to some single spot, and who, when they are removed to any other place, sink at once into silence and stupidity. I have discovered, by a long series of observations, that invention and elocution suffer great impediments from dense and impure vapours, and that the tenuity of a defecated air at a proper distance from the surface of the earth, accelerates the fancy, and sets at liberty those intellectual powers which were before shackled by too strong attraction, and unable to expand themselves under the pressure of a gross atmosphere. I have found dullness to quicken into sentiment in a thin ether, as water, though not very hot, boils in a receiver partly exhausted; and heads, in appearance empty, have teemed with notions upon rising ground, as the flaccid sides of a football would have swelled out into stiffness and extension.

For this reason I never think myself qualified to judge decisively of any man's faculties, whom I have only known in one degree of elevation; but take some opportunity of attending him from the cellar to the garret, and try upon him all the various degrees of rarefaction and condensation, tension and laxity. If he is neither vivacious aloft, nor serious below, I then consider him as hopeless; but as it seldom happens that I do not find the temper to which the texture of his brain is fitted, I accommodate him in time with a tube of mercury, first marking the point most favourable to his intellects, according to rules which I have long studied, and which I may, perhaps, reveal to mankind in a complete treatise of barometrical pneumatology.

Another cause of the gaiety and sprightliness of the dwellers in garrets is probably the increase of that vertiginous motion, with which we are carried round by the diurnal revolution of the earth. The power of agitation upon the spirits is well known; every man has felt his heart lightened in a rapid vehicle, or on a galloping horse; and nothing is plainer, than that he who towers to the fifth story, is whirled through more space by every circumrotation, than another that grovels upon the ground-floor. The nations between the tropics are known to be fiery, inconstant, inventive, and fanciful; because, living at the utmost length of the earth's diameter, they are carried about with more swiftness than those whom nature has placed nearer to the poles; and therefore, as it becomes a wise man to struggle with the inconveniences of his country, whenever celerity and acuteness are requisite, we must acuate our languor by taking a few turns round the centre in a garret.

If you imagine that I ascribe to air and motion effects which they cannot produce, I desire you to consult your own memory, and consider whether you have never known a man acquire reputation in his garret, which, when fortune or a patron had placed him upon the first floor, he was unable to maintain; and who never recovered his former vigour of understanding, till he was restored to his original situation. That a garret will make every man a wit, I am very far from supposing; I know there are some who would continue blockheads even on the summit of the *Andes*, or on the peak of *Teneriffe*. But let not any man be considered as unimproveable till this potent remedy has been tried; for perhaps he was formed to be great only in a garret, as the joiner of *Aretaeus* was rational in no other place but his own shop.

I think a frequent removal to various distances from the centre, so necessary to a just estimate of intellectual abilities, and consequently of so great use in education, that if I hoped that the public could be persuaded to so expensive an experiment, I would propose, that there should be a cavern dug, and a tower erected, like those which *Bacon* describes in *Solomon's* house, for the expansion and concentration of understanding, according to the exigence of different employments, or constitutions. Perhaps some that fume away in meditations upon time and space in the tower, might compose tables of interest at a certain depth; and he that upon level ground stagnates in silence, or creeps in narrative, might, at the height of half a mile, ferment into merriment, sparkle with repartee, and froth with declamation.

Addiso.. observes that we may find the heat of *Virgil's* climate, in some lines of his *Georgic*: so, when I read a composition, I immediately determine the height of the author's habitation. As an elaborate performance is commonly said to smell of the lamp, my commendation of a noble thought, a sprightly sally, or a bold figure, is to pronounce it fresh from the garret; an expression which would break from me upon the perusal of most of your papers, did I not believe, that you sometimes quit the garret, and ascend into the cock-loft.

HYPERTATUS

ON SORROW

Quanquam his solatiis acquiescam, debilitor et frangor eadem illa humanitate quae me, ut hoc ipsum permitterem, induxit. Non ideo tamen velim durior fieri: nec ignoro alios huiusmodi casus nihil amplius vocare quam damnum; eoque sibi magnos homines et sapientes videri. Qui an magni sapientesque sint, nescio: homines non sunt. Hominis est enim affici dolore, sentire: resistere tamen, et solatia admittere; non solatiis non egere.

PLINY.

These proceedings have afforded me some comfort in my distress; notwithstanding which, I am still dispirited and unhinged by the same motives of humanity that induced me to grant such indulgences. However, I by no means wish to become less susceptible of tenderness. I know these kind of misfortunes would be estimated by other persons only as common losses, and from such sensations they would conceive themselves great and wise men. I shall not determine either their greatness or their wisdom; but I am certain they have no humanity. It is the part of a man to be affected with grief; to feel sorrow, at the same time that he is to resist it, and to admit of comfort.

EARL OF ORRERY.

OF the passions with which the mind of man is agitated, it may be observed, that they naturally hasten towards their own extinction, by inciting and quickening the attainment of their objects. Thus fear urges our flight, and desire animates our progress; and if there are some which perhaps may be indulged till they outgrow the good appropriated to their satisfaction, as it is frequently observed of avarice and ambition, yet their immediate tendency is to some means of happiness really existing, and generally within the prospect. The miser always imagines that there is a certain sum that will fill his heart to the brim; and every ambitious man, like King Pyrrhus, has an acquisition in his thoughts that is to terminate his labours, after which he shall pass the rest of his life in ease or gaiety, in repose or devotion.

Sorrow is perhaps the only affection of the breast that can be excepted from this general remark, and it therefore deserves the particular attention of those who have assumed the arduous province of preserving the balance of the mental constitution. The other passions are diseases indeed, but they necessarily direct us to their proper cure. A man at once feels the pain, and knows the medicine, to which he is carried with greater haste as the evil which requires it is more excruciating, and cures himself by unerring instinct, as the wounded stags of Crete are related by Aelian to have recourse to vulnerary herbs. But for sorrow there is no remedy provided by nature; it is often occasioned by accidents irreparable, and dwells upon objects that have lost or changed their existence; it requires what it cannot hope, that the laws of the universe should be repealed; that the dead should return, or the past should be recalled.

Sorrow is not that regret for negligence or error which may animate us to future care or activity, or that repentance of crimes for which, however irrevocable, our Creator has promised to accept it as an atonement; the pain which arises from these causes has very salutary effects, and is every hour extenuating itself by the reparation of those miscarriages that produce it. Sorrow is properly that state of the mind in which our desires are fixed upon the past, without looking forward to the future, an incessant wish that something were otherwise than it has been, a tormenting and harassing want of some enjoyment or possession which we have lost, and which no endeavours can possibly regain. Into such anguish many have sunk upon some sudden diminution of their fortune, an unexpected blast of their reputation, or the loss of children or of friends. They have suffered all sensibility of pleasure to be destroyed by a single blow, have given up for ever the hopes of substituting any other object in the room of that which they lament, resigned their lives to gloom and despondency, and worn themselves out in unavailing misery.

Yet so much is this passion the natural consequence of tenderness and endearment, that, however painful and however useless, it is justly reproachful not to feel it on some occasions; and so widely and constantly has it always prevailed, that the laws of some nations, and the customs of others, have limited a time for the external appearances of grief caused by the dissolution of close alliances, and the breach of domestic union.

It seems determined, by the general suffrage of mankind, that sorrow is to a certain point laudable, as the offspring of love, or at least pardonable, as the effect of weakness; but that it ought not to be suffered to increase by indulgence, but must give way, after a stated time, to social duties, and the common avocations of life. It is at first unavoidable, and therefore must be allowed, whether with or without our choice; it may afterwards be admitted as a decent and affectionate testimony of kindness and esteem; something will be extorted by nature, and something may be given to the world. But all beyond the bursts of passion, or the forms of solemnity, is not only useless, but culpable; for we have no right to sacrifice, to the vain longings of affection, that time which providence allows us for the task of our station.

Yet it too often happens that sorrow, thus lawfully entering, gains such a firm possession of the mind, that it is not afterwards to be ejected; the mournful ideas, first violently impressed, and afterwards willingly received, so much engross the attention, as to predominate in every thought, to darken gaiety, and perplex ratiocination. An habitual sadness seizes upon the soul, and the faculties are chained to a single object, which can never be contemplated but with hopeless uneasiness.

From this state of dejection it is very difficult to rise to cheerfulness and alacrity, and therefore many who have laid down rules of intellectual health, think preservatives easier than remedies, and teach us not to trust ourselves with favourite enjoyments, not to indulge the luxury of fondness, but to keep our minds always suspended in such indifference, that we may change the objects about us without inconvenience or emotion.

An exact compliance with this rule might, perhaps, contribute to tranquillity, but surely it would never produce happiness. He that regards none so much as to be afraid of losing them, must live for ever without the gentle pleasures of sympathy and confidence; he must feel no melting fondness, no warmth of benevolence, nor any of those honest joys which nature annexes to the power of pleasing. And as no man can justly claim more tenderness than he pays, he must forfeit his share in that officious and watchful kindness which love only can dictate, and those lenient endearments by which love only can soften life. He may justly be overlooked and neglected by such as have more warmth in their heart; for who would be the friend of him, whom, with whatever assiduity he may be courted, and with whatever services obliged, his principles will not suffer to make equal returns, and who, when you have exhausted all the instances of goodwill, can only be prevailed on not to be an enemy?

An attempt to preserve life in a state of neutrality and indifference, is unreasonable and vain. If by excluding joy we could shut out grief, the scheme would deserve very serious attention; but since, however we may debar ourselves from happiness, misery will find its way at many inlets, and the assaults of pain will force our regard, though we may withhold it from the invitations of pleasure, we may surely endeavour to raise life above the middle point of apathy at one time, since it will necessarily sink below it at another.

But though it cannot be reasonable not to gain happiness for fear of losing it, yet it must be confessed, that in proportion to the pleasure of possession, will be for some time our sorrow for the loss; it is therefore the province of the moralist to inquire whether such pains may not quickly give way to mitigation. Some have thought that the most certain way to clear the heart from its embarrassment is to drag it by force into scenes of merriment. Others imagine, that such a transition is too violent, and recommend rather to soothe it into tranquillity, by making it acquainted with miseries more dreadful and afflictive, and diverting to the calamities of others the regards which we are inclined to fix too closely upon our own misfortunes.

It may be doubted whether either of those

remedies will be sufficiently powerful. The efficacy of mirth it is not always easy to try, and the indulgence of melancholy may be suspected to be one of those medicines, which will destroy, if it happens not to cure.

The safe and general antidote against sorrow, is employment. It is commonly observed, that among soldiers and seamen, though there is much kindness, there is little grief; they see their friend fall without any of that lamentation which is indulged in security and idleness, because they have no leisure to spare from the care of themselves; and whoever shall keep his thoughts equally busy, will find himself equally unaffected with irretrievable losses.

Time is observed generally to wear out sorrow, and its effects might doubtless be accelerated by quickening the succession and enlarging the variety of objects.

Si tempore longo
Leniri poterit luctus, tu sperne morari,
Qui sapiet sibi tempus erit.—Grotius.

'Tis long ere time can mitigate your grief;
To wisdom fly, she quickly brings relief.
F. Lewis.

Sorrow is a kind of rust of the soul, which every new idea contributes in its passage to scour away. It is the putrefaction of stagnant life, and is remedied by exercise and motion.

DAVID HUME

1711–1776

OF THE DIGNITY OR MEANNESS OF HUMAN NATURE

There are certain sects which secretly form themselves in the learned world, as well as factions in the political; and though sometimes they come not to an open rupture, they give a different turn to the ways of thinking of those who have taken part on either side. The most remarkable of this kind are the sects founded on the different sentiments with regard to the *dignity of human nature*; which is a point that seems to have divided philosophers and poets, as well as divines, from the beginning of the world to this day. Some exalt our species to the skies, and represent man as a kind of human demigod, who derives his origin from heaven, and retains evident marks of his lineage and descent. Others insist upon the blind sides of human nature, and can discover nothing, except vanity, in which man surpasses the other animals, whom he affects so much to despise. If an author possess the talent of rhetoric and declamation, he commonly takes part with the former: if his turn lie towards irony and ridicule, he naturally throws himself into the other extreme.

I am far from thinking that all those who have depreciated our species have been enemies to virtue, and have exposed the frailties of their fellow creatures with any bad intention. On the contrary, I am sensible that a delicate sense of morals, especially when attended with a splenetic temper, is apt to give a man a disgust of the world, and to make him consider the common course of human affairs with too much indignation. I must, however, be of opinion, that the sentiments of those who are inclined to think favourably of mankind, are more advantageous to virtue than the contrary principles, which give us a mean opinion of our nature. When a man is prepossessed with a high notion of his rank and character in the creation, he will naturally endeavour to act up to it, and will scorn to do a base or vicious action which might sink him below that figure which he makes in his own imagination. Accordingly we find, that all our polite and fashionable moralists insist upon this topic, and endeavour to represent vice unworthy of man, as well as odious in itself.[1]

We find few disputes that are not founded on some ambiguity in the expression; and I am persuaded that the present dispute, concerning the dignity or meanness of human nature, is not more exempt from it than any other. It may therefore be worth while to consider what is real, and what is only verbal, in this controversy.

That there is a natural difference between merit and demerit, virtue and vice, wisdom and folly, no reasonable man will deny: yet it is evident that, in affixing the term, which denotes either our approbation or blame, we are commonly more influenced by comparison than by any fixed unalterable standard in the nature of things. In like manner, quantity, and extension, and bulk,

[1] Women are generally much more flattered in their youth than men, which may proceed from this reason among others, that their chief point of honour is considered as much more difficult than ours, and requires to be supported by all that decent pride which can be instilled into them.

are by every one acknowledged to be real things: but when we call any animal *great* or *little*, we always form a secret comparison between that animal and others of the same species; and it is that comparison which regulates our judgement concerning its greatness. A dog and a horse may be of the very same size, while the one is admired for the greatness of its bulk, and the other for the smallness. When I am present, therefore, at any dispute, I always consider with myself whether it be a question of comparison or not that is the subject of controversy; and if it be, whether the disputants compare the same objects together, or talk of things that are widely different.

In forming our notions of human nature, we are apt to make a comparison between men and animals, the only creatures endowed with thought that fall under our senses. Certainly this comparison is favourable to mankind. On the one hand, we see a creature whose thoughts are not limited by any narrow bounds, either of place or time; who carries his researches into the most distant regions of this globe, and beyond this globe, to the planets and heavenly bodies; looks backward to consider the first origin, at least the history of the human race; casts his eye forward to see the influence of his actions upon posterity, and the judgements which will be formed of his character a thousand years hence; a creature, who traces causes and effects to a great length and intricacy; extracts general principles from particular appearances; improves upon his discoveries; corrects his mistakes; and makes his very errors profitable. On the other hand, we are presented with a creature the very reverse of this;

limited in its observations and reasonings to a few sensible objects which surround it; without curiosity, without foresight; blindly conducted by instinct, and attaining, in a short time, its utmost perfection, beyond which it is never able to advance a single step. What a wide difference is there between these creatures! And how exalted a notion must we entertain of the former, in comparison of the latter.

There are two means commonly employed to destroy this conclusion: *First*, By making an unfair representation of the case, and insisting only upon the weakness of human nature. And, *secondly*, By forming a new and secret comparison between man and beings of the most perfect wisdom. Among the other excellences of man, this is one, that he can form an idea of perfections much beyond what he has experience of in himself; and is not limited in his conception of wisdom and virtue. He can easily exalt his notions, and conceive a degree of knowledge, which, when compared to his own, will make the latter appear very contemptible, and will cause the difference between that and the sagacity of animals, in a manner, to disappear and vanish. Now this being a point in which all the world is agreed, that human understanding falls infinitely short of perfect wisdom, it is proper we should know when this comparison takes place, that we may not dispute where there is no real difference in our sentiments. Man falls much more short of perfect wisdom, and even of his own ideas of perfect wisdom, than animals do of man; yet the latter difference is so considerable, that nothing but a comparison with the former can make it appear of little moment.

It is also usual to *compare* one man with another; and finding very few whom we can call *wise* or *virtuous*, we are apt to entertain a contemptible notion of our species in general. That we may be sensible of the fallacy of this way of reasoning, we may observe, that the honourable appellations of wise and virtuous are not annexed to any particular degree of those qualities of *wisdom* and *virtue*, but arise altogether from the comparison we make between one man and another. When we find a man who arrives at such a pitch of wisdom as is very uncommon, we pronounce him a wise man: so that to say there are few wise men in the world, is really to say nothing; since it is only by their scarcity that they merit that appellation. Were the lowest of our species as wise as Tully or Lord Bacon, we should still have reason to say that there are few wise men. For in that case we should exalt our notions of wisdom, and should not pay a singular homage to any one who was not singularly distinguished by his talents. In like manner, I have heard it observed by thoughtless people, that there are few women possessed of beauty in comparison of those who want it; not considering that we bestow the epithet of *beautiful* only on such as possess a degree of beauty that is common to them with a few. The same degree of beauty in a woman is called deformity, which is treated as real beauty in one of our sex.

As it is usual, in forming a notion of our species, to *compare* it with the other species above or below it, or to compare the individuals of the species among themselves; so we often compare together the different motives or actuating principles of human nature, in order to regulate our judgement concerning it. And, indeed, this is the only kind of comparison which is worth our attention, or decides anything in the present question. Were our selfish and vicious principles so much predominant above our social and virtuous, as is asserted by some philosophers, we ought undoubtedly to entertain a contemptible notion of human nature.[1]

There is much of a dispute of words in all this controversy. When a man denies the sincerity of all public spirit or affection to a country and community, I am at a loss what to think of him. Perhaps he never felt this passion in so clear and distinct a manner as to remove all his doubts concerning its force and reality. But when he proceeds afterwards to reject all private friendship, if no interest or self-love intermix itself; I am then confident that he abuses terms, and confounds the ideas of things; since it is impossible for any one to be so selfish, or rather so stupid, as to make no difference between one man and another, and give no preference to qualities which engage his approbation and esteem. Is he also, say I, as insensible to anger as he pretends to be to friendship? And does injury and wrong no more affect him than kindness or benefits? Impossible: he does not know himself: he has forgotten the movements

[1] I may perhaps treat more fully of this subject in some future Essay. In the meantime I shall observe, what has been proved beyond question by several great moralists of the present age, that the social passions are by far the most powerful of any, and that even all the other passions receive from them their chief force and influence. Whoever desires to see this question treated at large, with the greatest force of argument and eloquence, may consult my Lord Shaftesbury's Inquiry concerning Virtue.

of his heart; or rather, he makes use of a different language from the rest of his countrymen, and calls not things by their proper names. What say you of natural affection? (I subjoin), Is that also a species of self-love? Yes; all is self-love. *Your* children are loved only because they are yours: *your* friend for a like reason: and *your* country engages you only so far as it has a connexion with *yourself*. Were the idea of self removed, nothing would affect you: you would be altogether unactive and insensible: or, if you ever give yourself any movement, it would only be from vanity, and a desire of fame and reputation to this same self. I am willing, reply I, to receive your interpretation of human actions, provided you admit the facts. That species of self-love which displays itself in kindness to others, you must allow to have great influence over human actions, and even greater, on many occasions, than that which remains in its original shape and form. For how few are there, having a family, children, and relations, who do not spend more on the maintenance and education of these than on their own pleasures? This, indeed, you justly observe, may proceed from their self-love, since the prosperity of their family and friends is one, or the chief, of their pleasures, as well as their chief honour. Be you also one of these selfish men, and you are sure of every one's good opinion and goodwill; or, not to shock your ears with these expressions, the self-love of every one, and mine among the rest, will then incline us to serve you, and speak well of you.

In my opinion, there are two things which have led astray those philosophers that have insisted so much on the selfishness of man. In the *first* place, they found that every act of virtue or friendship was attended with a secret pleasure; whence they concluded, that friendship and virtue could not be disinterested. But the fallacy of this is obvious. The virtuous sentiment or passion produces the pleasure, and does not arise from it. I feel a pleasure in doing good to my friend, because I love him; but do not love him for the sake of that pleasure.

In the *second* place, it has always been found, that the virtuous are far from being indifferent to praise; and therefore they have been represented as a set of vainglorious men, who had nothing in view but the applauses of others. But this also is a fallacy. It is very unjust in the world, when they find any tincture of vanity in a laudable action, to depreciate it upon that account, or ascribe it entirely to that motive. The case is not the same with vanity, as with other passions. Where avarice or revenge enters into any seemingly virtuous action, it is difficult for us to determine how far it enters, and it is natural to suppose it the sole actuating principle. But vanity is so closely allied to virtue, and to love the fame of laudable actions approaches so near the love of laudable actions for their own sake, that these passions are more capable of mixture, than any other kinds of affection; and it is almost impossible to have the latter without some degree of the former. Accordingly we find, that this passion for glory is always warped and varied according to the particular taste or disposition of the mind on which it falls. Nero had the same vanity in driving a chariot, that Trajan had in governing the empire with justice and ability. To love the glory of virtuous deeds is a sure proof of the love of virtue.

OLIVER GOLDSMITH

1728–1774

HAPPINESS IN A GREAT MEASURE DEPENDENT ON CONSTITUTION

When I reflect on the unambitious retirement in which I passed the earlier part of my life in the country, I cannot avoid feeling some pain in thinking that those happy days are never to return. In that retreat all nature seemed capable of affording pleasure; I then made no refinements on happiness, but could be pleased with the most awkward efforts of rustic mirth; thought cross purposes the highest stretch of human wit, and questions and commands the most rational amusement for spending the evening. Happy could so charming an illusion still continue! I find age and knowledge only contribute to sour our dispositions. My present enjoyments may be more refined, but they are infinitely less pleasing. The pleasure Garrick gives can no way compare to that I have received from a country wag, who imitated a Quaker's sermon. The music of Mattei is dissonance to what I felt when our old dairymaid sung me into tears with Johnny Armstrong's Last Good Night, or the Cruelty of Barbara Allen.

Writers of every age have endeavoured to show that pleasure is in us, and not in the objects offered for our amusement. If the soul be happily disposed, everything becomes a subject of entertainment, and distress will almost want a name.

Every occurrence passes in review like the figures of a procession: some may be awkward, others ill dressed; but none but a fool is for this enraged with the master of the ceremonies.

I remember to have once seen a slave in a fortification in Flanders, who appeared no way touched with his situation. He was maimed, deformed, and chained; obliged to toil from the appearance of day till nightfall, and condemned to this for life; yet, with all these circumstances of apparent wretchedness, he sung, would have danced, but that he wanted a leg, and appeared the merriest. happiest man of all the garrison. What a practical philosopher was here! A happy constitution supplied philosophy, and though seemingly destitute of wisdom, he was really wise. No reading or study had contributed to disenchant the fairy-land around him. Everything furnished him with an opportunity of mirth; and though some thought him from his insensibility a fool, he was such an idiot as philosophers might wish in vain to imitate.

They who, like him, can place themselves on that side of the world in which everything appears in a ridiculous or pleasing light, will find something in every occurrence to excite their good humour. The most calamitous events, either to themselves or others, can bring no new affliction; the whole world is to them a theatre, on which comedies only are acted. All the bustle of heroism or the rants of ambition serve only to heighten the absurdity of the scene, and make the humour more poignant. They feel, in short, as little anguish at their own distress, or the complaints of others, as the undertaker, though dressed in black, feels sorrow at a funeral.

Of all the men I ever read of, the famous Cardinal de Retz possessed this happiness of temper in the highest degree. As he was a man of gallantry, and despised all that wore the pedantic appearance of philosophy, wherever pleasure was to be sold, he was generally foremost to raise the auction. Being an universal admirer of the fair sex, when he found one lady cruel, he generally fell in love with another, from whom he expected a more favourable reception; if she too rejected his addresses, he never thought of retiring into deserts, or pining in hopeless distress. He persuaded himself, that instead of loving the lady, he only fancied he had loved her, and so all was well again. When Fortune wore her angriest look, when he at last fell into the power of his most deadly enemy, Cardinal Mazarine, and was confined a close prisoner in the Castle of Valenciennes, he never attempted to support his distress by wisdom or philosophy, for he pretended to neither. He laughed at himself and his persecutor, and seemed infinitely pleased at his new situation. In this mansion of distress, though secluded from his friends, though denied all the amusements and even the conveniences of life, teased every hour by the impertinence of wretches who were employed to guard him, he still retained his good humour, laughed at all their little spite, and carried the jest so far as to be revenged, by writing the life of his jailer.

All that the wisdom of the proud can teach is to be stubborn or sullen under misfortunes. The Cardinal's example will instruct us to be merry in circumstances of the highest affliction. It matters not whether our good humour be construed by others into insensibility, or even idiotism; it is happiness to ourselves, and none but a fool would measure his satisfaction by what the world thinks of it.

Dick Wildgoose was one of the happiest silly fellows I ever knew. He was of the number of those good-natured creatures that are said to do no harm to any but themselves. Whenever Dick fell into any misery, he usually called it *seeing life*. If his head was broke by a chairman, or his pocket picked by a sharper, he comforted himself by imitating the Hibernian dialect of the one, or the more fashionable cant of the other. Nothing came amiss to Dick. His inattention to money matters had incensed his father to such a degree, that all the intercession of friends in his favour was fruitless. The old gentleman was on his deathbed. The whole family, and Dick among the number, gathered round him. 'I leave my second son Andrew,' said the expiring miser, 'my whole estate, and desire him to be frugal.' Andrew, in a sorrowful tone, as is usual on these occasions, 'prayed Heaven to prolong his life and health to enjoy it himself.' 'I recommend Simon, my third son, to the care of his elder brother, and leave him beside four thousand pounds.' 'Ah! father,' cried Simon (in great affliction to be sure), 'may Heaven give you life and health to enjoy it yourself!' At last, turning to poor Dick; 'as for you, you have always been a sad dog, you'll never come to good, you'll never be rich, I'll leave you a shilling to buy a halter.' 'Ah! father,' cries Dick, without any emotion, 'may Heaven give you life and health to enjoy it yourself!' This was all the trouble the loss of fortune gave this thoughtless imprudent creature. However, the tenderness of an uncle recompensed the neglect of a father; and Dick is not only excessively good-humoured, but competently rich.

The world, in short, may cry out at a bankrupt who appears at a ball; at an author who laughs at the public which pronounces him a dunce; at a general who smiles at the reproach of the vulgar, or the lady who keeps her good humour in spite of scandal; but such is the wisest behaviour they can possibly assume; it is certainly a better way to oppose calamity by dissipation, than to take up the arms of reason or resolution to oppose it: by the first method we forget our miseries, by the last we only conceal them from others; by struggling with misfortunes we are sure to receive some wounds in the conflict. The only method to come off victorious is by running away.

ASEM; OR VINDICATION OF THE WISDOM OF PROVIDENCE IN THE MORAL GOVERNMENT OF THE WORLD. AN EASTERN TALE

Where Tauris lifts its head above the storm, and presents nothing to the sight of the distant traveller but a prospect of nodding rocks, falling torrents, and all the variety of tremendous nature; on the bleak bosom of this frightful mountain, secluded from society, and detesting the ways of men, lived Asem the Man-hater.

Asem had spent his youth with men, had shared in their amusements, and had been taught to love his fellow creatures with the most ardent affection; but, from the tenderness of his disposition, he exhausted all his fortune in relieving the wants of the distressed. The petitioner never sued in vain; the weary traveller never passed his door; he only desisted from doing good when he had no longer the power of relieving.

For a fortune thus spent in benevolence he expected a grateful return from those he had formerly relieved, and made his application with confidence of redress: the ungrateful world soon grew weary of his importunity; for pity is but a short-lived passion. He soon, therefore, began to view mankind in a very different light from that in which he had before beheld them; he perceived a thousand vices he had never before suspected to exist; wherever he turned, ingratitude, dissimulation, and treachery, contributed to increase his detestation of them. Resolved therefore to continue no longer in a world which he hated, and which repaid his detestation with contempt, he retired to this region of sterility, in order to brood over his resentment in solitude, and converse with the only honest heart he knew; namely, with his own.

A cave was his only shelter from the inclemency of the weather; fruits gathered with difficulty from the mountain's side his only food; and his drink was fetched with danger and toil from the headlong torrent. In this manner he lived, sequestered from society, passing the hours in meditation, and sometimes exulting that he was able to live independent of his fellow creatures.

At the foot of the mountain an extensive lake displayed its glassy bosom, reflecting on its broad surface the impending horrors of the mountain. To this capacious mirror he would sometimes descend, and, reclining on its steep banks, cast an eager look on the smooth expanse that lay before him. 'How beautiful,' he often cried, 'is Nature! how lovely even in her wildest scenes! How finely contrasted is the level plain that lies beneath me, with yon awful pile that hides its tremendous head in clouds! But the beauty of these scenes is no way comparable with their utility: from hence an hundred rivers are supplied, which distribute health and verdure to the various countries through which they flow. Every part of the universe is beautiful, just, and wise, but man; vile man is a solecism in nature, the only monster in the creation. Tempests and whirlwinds have their use; but vicious, ungrateful man is a blot in the fair page of universal beauty. Why was I born of that detested species, whose vices are almost a reproach to the wisdom of the divine Creator! Were men entirely free from vice, all would be uniformity, harmony, and order. A world of moral rectitude should be the result of a perfectly moral agent. Why, why then, O Alla! must I be thus confined in darkness, doubt, and despair!'

Just as he uttered the word despair, he was going to plunge into the lake beneath him, at once to satisfy his doubts, and put a period to his anxiety; when he perceived a most majestic being walking on the surface of the water, and approaching the bank on which he stood. So unexpected an object at once checked his purpose; he stopped, contemplated, and fancied he saw something awful and divine in his aspect.

'Son of Adam,' cried the Genius, 'stop thy rash purpose; the Father of the Faithful has seen thy justice, thy integrity, thy miseries, and hath sent me to afford and administer relief. Give me thine hand, and follow without trembling wherever I shall lead: in me behold the Genius of Conviction, kept by the great Prophet, to turn from their errors those who go astray, not from curiosity, but a rectitude of intention. Follow me, and be wise.'

Asem immediately descended upon the lake, and his guide conducted him along the surface of the water; till, coming near the centre of the lake, they both began to sink; the waters closed over their heads; they descended several hundred fathoms, till Asem, just ready to give up his life as inevitably lost, found himself with his celestial guide in another world, at the bottom of the waters, where human foot had never trod before. His astonishment was beyond description, when he saw a sun like that he had left, a serene sky over his head, and blooming verdure under his feet.

'I plainly perceive your amazement,' said the Genius; 'but suspend it for awhile. This world was formed by Alla, at the request, and under the inspection, of our great Prophet; who once entertained the same doubts which filled your mind when I found you, and from the consequence of which you were so lately rescued. The rational inhabitants of this world are formed agreeable to your own ideas; they are absolutely without vice. In other respects it resembles your earth, but differs from it in being wholly inhabited by men who never do wrong. If you find this world more agreeable than that you so lately left, you have free permission to spend the remainder of your days in it; but permit me for some time to attend you, that I may silence your doubts, and make you better acquainted with your company and your new habitation.'

'A world without vice! Rational beings without immorality!' cried Asem in a rapture; 'I thank thee, O Alla! who hast at length heard my petitions: this, this indeed will produce happiness, ecstasy, and ease. O for an immortality, to spend it among men who are incapable of ingratitude, injustice, fraud, violence, and a thousand other crimes that render society miserable!'

'Cease thine acclamations,' replied the Genius. 'Look around thee; reflect on every object and action before us, and communicate to me the result of thine observations. Lead wherever you think proper, I shall be your attendant and instructor.' Asem and his companion travelled on in silence for some time, the former being entirely lost in astonishment; but at last recovering his former serenity, he could not help observing, that the face of the country bore a near resemblance to that he had left, except that this subterranean world still seemed to retain its primeval wildness.

'Here,' cried Asem, 'I perceive animals of prey and others that seem only designed for their subsistence; it is the very same in the world over our heads. But had I been permitted to instruct our Prophet, I would have removed this defect, and formed no voracious or destructive animals, which only prey on the other parts of the creation.' 'Your tenderness for inferior animals is, I find, remarkable,' said the Genius, smiling. 'But, with regard to meaner creatures, this world exactly resembles the other, and, indeed, for obvious reasons; for the earth can support a more considerable number of animals, by their thus becoming food for each other, than if they had lived entirely on the vegetable productions. So that animals of different natures thus formed, instead of lessening their multitude, subsist in the greatest number possible. But let us hasten on to the inhabited country before us, and see what that offers for instruction.'

They soon gained the utmost verge of the forest, and entered the country inhabited by men without vice; and Asem anticipated in idea the rational delight he hoped to experience in such an innocent society. But they had scarce left the confines of the wood, when they beheld one of the inhabitants flying with hasty steps, and terror in his countenance, from an army of squirrels that closely pursued him. 'Heavens!' cried Asem, 'why does he fly? What can he fear from animals so contemptible?' He had scarce spoke when he perceived two dogs pursuing another of the human species, who with equal terror and haste attempted to avoid them. 'This,' cried Asem to his guide, 'is truly surprising; nor can I conceive the reason for so strange an action.' 'Every species of animals,' replied the Genius, 'has of late grown very powerful in this country; for the inhabitants at first thinking it unjust to use either fraud or force in destroying them, they have insensibly increased, and now frequently ravage their harmless frontiers.' 'But they should have been destroyed,' cried Asem; 'you see the consequence of such neglect.' 'Where is then that tenderness you so lately expressed for subordinate animals?' replied the Genius, smiling; 'you seem to have forgot that branch of justice.' 'I must acknowledge my mistake,' returned Asem; 'I am now convinced that we must be guilty of tyranny and injustice to the brute creation, if we would enjoy the world ourselves. But let us no longer observe the duty of man to these irrational creatures, but survey their connexions with one another.'

As they walked farther up the country, the more he was surprised to see no vestiges of handsome houses, no cities, nor any mark of elegant design. His conductor perceiving his surprise, observed, that the inhabitants of this new world were perfectly content with their ancient simplicity; each had a house, which, though homely, was sufficient to lodge his little family; they were too good to build houses, which could only increase their own pride, and the envy of the spectator; what they built was for convenience, and not for show. 'At least, then,' said Asem, 'they have neither architects, painters, or statuaries, in their society; but these are idle arts, and may be spared. However, before I spend much more time here, you should have my thanks for introducing me into the society of some of their wisest men: there is scarce any pleasure to me equal to a refined conversation; there is nothing of which I am so enamoured as wisdom.' 'Wisdom!' replied his instructor; 'how ridiculous! We have no wisdom here, for we have no occasion for it; true wisdom is only a knowledge of our own duty, and the duty of others to us; but of what use is such wisdom here? each intuitively performs what is right in himself, and expects the same from others. If by wisdom you should mean vain curiosity and empty speculation, as such pleasures have their origin in vanity, luxury, or avarice, we are too good to pursue them.' 'All this may be right,' says Asem; 'but methinks I observe a solitary disposition prevail among the people;

each family keeps separately within their own precincts, without society, or without intercourse.' 'That indeed is true,' replied the other; 'here is no established society; nor should there be any; all societies are made either through fear or friendship; the people we are among are too good to fear each other; and there are no motives to private friendship, where all are equally meritorious.' 'Well then,' said the sceptic, 'as I am to spend my time here, if I am to have neither the polite arts, nor wisdom, nor friendship, in such a world, I should be glad at least of an easy companion, who may tell me his thoughts, and to whom I may communicate mine.' 'And to what purpose should either do this?' says the Genius: 'flattery or curiosity are vicious motives, and never allowed of here; and wisdom is out of the question.' 'Still, however,' said Asem, 'the inhabitants must be happy; each is contented with his own possessions, nor avariciously endeavours to heap up more than is necessary for his own subsistence; each has therefore leisure to pity those that stand in need of his compassion.'

He had scarce spoken, when his ears were assaulted with the lamentations of a wretch who sat by the wayside, and in the most deplorable distress seemed gently to murmur at his own misery. Asem immediately ran to his relief, and found him in the last stage of a consumption. 'Strange,' cried the son of Adam, 'that men who are free from vice should thus suffer so much misery without relief!' 'Be not surprised,' said the wretch who was dying: 'would it not be the utmost injustice for beings who have only just sufficient to support themselves, and are content with a bare subsistence, to take it from their own mouths to put it into mine? They never are possessed of a single meal more than is necessary; and what is barely necessary cannot be dispensed with.' 'They should have been supplied with more than is necessary,' cried Asem; 'and yet I contradict my own opinion but a moment before: all is doubt, perplexity, and confusion. Even the want of ingratitude is no virtue here, since they never received a favour. They have, however, another excellence yet behind; the love of their country is still, I hope, one of their darling virtues.' 'Peace, Asem,' replied the Guardian, with a countenance not less severe than beautiful; 'nor forfeit all thy pretensions to wisdom; the same selfish motives by which we prefer our own interest to that of others, induce us to regard our country preferably to that of another. Nothing less than universal benevolence is free from vice, and that you see is practised here.' —'Strange!' cries the disappointed pilgrim, in an agony of distress; 'what sort of a world am I now introduced to? There is scarce a single virtue, but that of temperance, which they practise; and in that they are no way superior to the very brute creation. There is scarce an amusement which they enjoy; fortitude, liberality, friendship, wisdom, conversation, and love of country, all are virtues entirely unknown here: thus it seems that to be unacquainted with vice is not to know virtue. Take me, O my Genius, back to that very world which I have despised: a world which has Alla for its contriver is much more wisely formed than that which has been projected by Mahomet. Ingratitude, contempt, and hatred, I can now suffer; for perhaps I have deserved them. When I arraigned the wisdom of Providence, I only showed my own ignorance; henceforth let me keep from vice myself, and pity it in others.'

He had scarce ended, when the Genius, assuming an air of terrible complacency, called all his thunders around him, and vanished in a whirlwind. Asem, astonished at the terror of the scene, looked for his imaginary world; when, casting his eyes around, he perceived himself in the very situation, and in the very place, where he first began to repine and despair; his right foot had been just advanced to take the fatal plunge, nor had it been yet withdrawn; so instantly did Providence strike the series of truths just imprinted on his soul. He now departed from the water side in tranquillity, and leaving his horrid mansion, travelled to Segestan, his native city; where he diligently applied himself to commerce, and put in practice that wisdom he had learned in solitude. The frugality of a few years soon produced opulence; the number of his domestics increased; his friends came to him from every part of the city; nor did he receive them with disdain; and a youth of misery was concluded with an old age of elegance, affluence, and ease.

SYDNEY SMITH

1771–1845

EDGEWORTH ON BULLS

Essay on Irish Bulls. By Richard Lovell Edgeworth, and Maria Edgeworth. London, 1802.

We hardly know what to say about this rambling scrambling book; but that we are quite sure the author, when he began any sentence in it, had not the smallest suspicion of what it was about to contain. We say the author, because, in spite of the mixture of sexes in the title-page, we are strongly inclined to suspect that the male contributions exceed the female in a very great degree. The Essay on Bulls is written much with the same mind, and in the same manner, as a schoolboy takes a walk; he moves on for ten yards on the straight road, with surprising perseverance; then sets out after a butterfly, looks for a bird's nest, or jumps backwards and forwards over a ditch. In the same manner, this nimble and digressive gentleman is away after every object which crosses his mind. If you leave him at the end of a comma, in a steady pursuit of his subject, you are sure to find him, before the next full stop, a hundred yards to the right or left, frisking, capering, and grinning in a high paroxysm of merriment and agility. Mr. Edgeworth seems to possess the sentiments of an accomplished gentleman, the information of a scholar, and the vivacity of a first-rate harlequin. He is fuddled with animal spirits, giddy with constitutional joy; in such a state he must have written on, or burst. A discharge of ink was an evacuation absolutely necessary, to avoid fatal and plethoric congestion.

The object of the book is to prove that the practice of making bulls is not more imputable to the Irish than to any other people; and the manner in which he sets about it, is to quote examples of bulls produced in other countries. But this is surely a singular way of reasoning the question: for there are goitres out of the Valais, extortioners who do not worship Moses, oat cakes over the Tweed, and balm beyond the precincts of Gilead. If nothing can be said to exist preeminently and emphatically in one country, which exists at all in another, then Frenchmen are not gay, nor Spaniards grave, nor are gentlemen of the Milesian race remarkable for their disinterested contempt of wealth in their connubial relations. It is probable there is some foundation for a character so generally diffused; though it is also probable that such foundation is extremely enlarged by fame. If there were no foundation for the common opinion, we must suppose national characters formed by chance; and that the Irish might, by accident, have been laughed at as bashful and sheepish; which is impossible. The author puzzles himself a good deal about the nature of bulls, without coming to any decision about the matter. Though the question is not a very easy one, we shall venture to say, that a bull is an apparent congruity and real incongruity of ideas suddenly discovered. And if this account of bulls be just, they are (as might have been supposed) the very reverse of wit; for as wit discovers real relations that are not apparent, bulls admit apparent relations that are not real. The pleasure arising from wit proceeds from our surprise at suddenly discovering two things to be similar in which we suspected no similarity. The pleasure arising from bulls proceeds from our discovering two things to be dissimilar in which a resemblance might have been suspected. The same doctrine will apply to wit and to bulls in action. Practical wit discovers connexion or relation between actions, in which duller understandings discover none; and practical bulls originate from an *apparent* relation between two actions, which more correct understandings immediately perceive to have no relation at all.

Louis XIV, being extremely harassed by the repeated solicitations of a veteran officer for promotion, said one day, loud enough to be heard, 'That gentleman is the most troublesome officer I have in my service.' 'That is precisely the charge (said the old man) which your Majesty's enemies bring against me.'

An English gentleman (says Mr. Edgeworth, in a story cited from Joe Miller,) was writing a letter in a coffee-house; and perceiving that an Irishman stationed behind him was taking that liberty which Parmenio used with his friend Alexander, instead of putting his seal upon the lips of the *curious impertinent*, the English gentleman thought proper to reprove the Hibernian, if not with delicacy, at least with poetical justice. He concluded writing his letter in these words: 'I would say more, but a damned tall Irishman is reading over my shoulder every word I write.'

'You lie, you scoundrel,' said the self-convicted Hibernian (p. 29).

The pleasure derived from the first of these

stories proceeds from the discovery of the relation that subsists between the object he had in view, and the assent of the officer to an observation so unfriendly to that end. In the first rapid glance which the mind throws upon his words, he appears, by his acquiescence, to be pleading against himself. There seems to be no relation between what he says and what he wishes to effect by speaking.

In the second story, the pleasure is directly the reverse. The lie given was *apparently* the readiest means of proving his innocence, and *really* the most effectual way of establishing his guilt. There seems for a moment to be a strong relation between the means and the object; while, in fact, no irrelation can be so complete.

What connexion is there between pelting stones at monkeys and gathering coco-nuts from lofty trees? Apparently none. But monkeys sit upon coco-nut trees; monkeys are imitative animals; and if you pelt a monkey with a stone, he pelts you with a coco-nut in return. This scheme of gathering coco-nuts is very witty, and would be more so, if it did not appear useful: for the idea of utility is always inimical to the idea of wit.[1]

[1] It must be observed, that all the great passions, and many other feelings, extinguish the relish for wit. Thus *lympha pudica Deum vidit et erubuit,* would be witty, were it not bordering on the sublime. The resemblance between the sandal tree imparting (while it falls) its aromatic flavour to the edge of the axe, and the benevolent man rewarding evil with good, would be witty, did it not excite virtuous emotions. There are many mechanical contrivances which excite sensations very similar to wit; but the attention is absorbed by their utility. Some of Merlin's machines, which have no utility at all, are quite similar to wit. A small model of a steam engine, or mere squirt, is wit to a child. A man speculates on the causes of

There appears, on the contrary, to be some relation between the revenge of the Irish rebels against a banker, and the means which they took to gratify it, by burning all his notes wherever they found them; whereas, they could not have rendered him a more essential service. In both these cases of bulls, the one verbal, the other practical, there is an apparent congruity and real incongruity of ideas. In both the cases of wit, there is an apparent incongruity and a real relation.

It is clear that a bull cannot depend upon mere incongruity alone; for if a man were to say that he would ride to London upon a cocked hat, or that he would cut his throat with a pound of pickled salmon, this, though completely incongruous, would not be to make bulls, but to talk nonsense. The stronger the apparent connexion, and the more complete the real disconnexion of the ideas, the greater the surprise and the better the bull. The less apparent, and the more complete the relations established by wit, the higher gratification does it afford. A great deal of the pleasure experienced from bulls proceeds from the sense of superiority in ourselves. Bulls which we invented, or knew to be invented, might please, but in a less degree, for want of this additional zest.

As there must be apparent connexion, and real incongruity, it is seldom that a man of sense and education finds any form of words by which he is

the first, or on its consequences, and so loses the feelings of wit; with the latter, he is too familiar to be surprised. In short, the essence of every species of wit is surprise; which, *vi termini*, must be sudden; and the sensations which wit has a tendency to excite, are impaired or destroyed, as often as they are mingled with much thought or passion.

conscious that he might have been deceived into a bull. To conceive how the person has been deceived, he must suppose a degree of information very different from, and a species of character very heterogeneous to, his own; a process which diminishes surprise, and consequently pleasure. In the above-mentioned story of the Irishman overlooking the man writing, no person of ordinary sagacity can suppose himself betrayed into such a mistake; but he can easily represent to himself a kind of character that might have been so betrayed. There are some bulls so extremely fallacious, that any man may imagine himself to have been betrayed into them; but these are rare: and, in general, it is a poor contemptible species of amusement; a delight in which evinces a very bad taste in wit.

Whether the Irish make more bulls than their neighbours is, as we have before remarked, not a point of much importance; but it is of considerable importance that the character of a nation should not be degraded; and Mr. Edgeworth has great merit in his very benevolent intention of doing justice to the excellent qualities of the Irish. It is not possible to read his book without feeling a strong and a new disposition in their favour. Whether the imitation of the Irish manner be accurate in his little stories we cannot determine; but we feel the same confidence in the accuracy of the imitation, that is often felt in the resemblance of a portrait of which we have never seen the original. It is no very high compliment to Mr. Edgeworth's creative powers, to say, he could not have formed anything, which was not real, so like reality; but such a remark only robs Peter to pay

Paul; and gives everything to his powers of observation, which it takes from those of his imagination. In truth, nothing can be better than his imitation of the Irish manner: It is first-rate painting.

Edgeworth & Co. have another faculty in great perfection. They are eminently masters of the *pathos*. The firm drew tears from us in the stories of little Dominick, and of the Irish beggar who killed his sweetheart: Never was any grief more natural or simple. The first, however, ends in a very foolish way:

> —*formosa superne*
> *Desinit in piscem.*

We are extremely glad that our avocations did not call us from Bath to London, on the day that the Bath coach conversation took place. We except from this wish the story with which the conversation terminates; for as soon as Mr. Edgeworth enters upon a story he excels.

We must confess we have been much more pleased with Mr. Edgeworth in his laughing and in his pathetic, than in his grave and reasoning moods. He meant, perhaps, that we should; and it certainly is not very necessary that a writer should be profound on the subject of bulls. Whatever be the deficiencies of the book, they are, in our estimation, amply atoned for by its merits; by none more, than that lively feeling of compassion which pervades it for the distresses of the wild, kind-hearted, blundering poor of Ireland.

CHARLES LAMB

1775–1834

CHRIST'S HOSPITAL FIVE-AND-THIRTY YEARS AGO

In Mr. Lamb's *Works*, published a year or two since, I find a magnificent eulogy on my old school,[1] such as it was, or now appears to him to have been, between the years 1782 and 1789. It happens, very oddly, that my own standing at Christ's was nearly corresponding with his; and, with all gratitude to him for his enthusiasm for the cloisters, I think he has contrived to bring together whatever can be said in praise of them, dropping all the other side of the argument most ingeniously.

I remember L. at school; and can well recollect that he had some peculiar advantages, which I and others of his schoolfellows had not. His friends lived in town, and were near at hand; and he had the privilege of going to see them, almost as often as he wished, through some invidious distinction, which was denied to us. The present worthy sub-treasurer to the Inner Temple can explain how that happened. He had his tea and hot rolls in a morning, while we were battening upon our quarter of a penny loaf—our *crug*—moistened with attenuated small beer, in wooden piggins, smacking of the pitched leathern jack it was poured from. Our Monday's milk porritch, blue and tasteless, and the pease soup of Saturday, coarse and choking,

[1] 'Recollections of Christ's Hospital.'

were enriched for him with a slice of 'extraordinary bread and butter', from the hot-loaf of the Temple. The Wednesday's mess of millet, somewhat less repugnant (we had three banyan to four meat days in the week)—was endeared to his palate with a lump of double-refined, and a smack of ginger (to make it go down the more glibly) or the fragrant cinnamon. In lieu of our *half-pickled* Sundays, or *quite fresh* boiled beef on Thursdays (strong as *caro equina*), with detestable marigolds floating in the pail to poison the broth—our scanty mutton scrags on Fridays—and rather more savoury, but grudging, portions of the same flesh, rotten-roasted or rare, on the Tuesdays (the only dish which excited our appetites, and disappointed our stomachs, in almost equal proportion)—he had his hot plate of roast veal, or the more tempting griskin (exotics unknown to our palates), cooked in the paternal kitchen (a great thing), and brought him daily by his maid or aunt! I remember the good old relative (in whom love forbade pride) squatting down upon some odd stone in a by-nook of the cloisters, disclosing the viands (of higher regale than those cates which the ravens ministered to the Tishbite); and the contending passions of L. at the unfolding. There was love for the bringer; shame for the thing brought, and the manner of its bringing; sympathy for those who were too many to share in it; and, at top of all, hunger (eldest, strongest of the passions!) predominant, breaking down the stony fences of shame, and awkwardness, and a troubling overconsciousness.

I was a poor friendless boy. My parents, and those who should care for me, were far away.

Those few acquaintances of theirs, which they could reckon upon as being kind to me in the great city, after a little forced notice, which they had the grace to take of me on my first arrival in town, soon grew tired of my holiday visits. They seemed to them to recur too often, though I thought them few enough; and, one after another, they all failed me, and I felt myself alone among six hundred playmates.

O the cruelty of separating a poor lad from his early homestead! The yearnings which I used to have towards it in those unfledged years! How, in my dreams, would my native town (far in the west) come back, with its church, and trees, and faces! How I would wake weeping, and in the anguish of my heart exclaim upon sweet Calne in Wiltshire!

To this late hour of my life, I trace impressions left by the recollection of those friendless holidays. The long warm days of summer never return but they bring with them a gloom from the haunting memory of those *whole-day leaves*, when, by some strange arrangement, we were turned out, for the live-long day, upon our own hands, whether we had friends to go to, or none. I remember those bathing-excursions to the New River, which L. recalls with such relish, better, I think, than he can—for he was a home-seeking lad, and did not much care for such water-pastimes:—How merrily we would sally forth into the fields; and strip under the first warmth of the sun; and wanton like young dace in the streams; getting us appetites for noon, which those of us that were penniless (our scanty morning crust long since exhausted) had not the means of allaying—while the cattle, and the birds, and the fishes, were at feed about us, and we had nothing to satisfy our cravings—the very beauty of the day, and the exercise of the pastime, and the sense of liberty, setting a keener edge upon them!—How faint and languid, finally, we would return, towards nightfall, to our desired morsel, half-rejoicing, half-reluctant, that the hours of our uneasy liberty had expired!

It was worse in the days of winter, to go prowling about the streets objectless—shivering at cold windows of print shops, to extract a little amusement; or haply, as a last resort, in the hopes of a little novelty, to pay a fifty-times repeated visit (where our individual faces should be as well known to the warden as those of his own charges) to the Lions in the Tower—to whose levée, by courtesy immemorial, we had a prescriptive title to admission.

L.'s governor (so we called the patron who presented us to the foundation) lived in a manner under his paternal roof. Any complaint which he had to make was sure of being attended to. This was understood at Christ's, and was an effectual screen to him against the severity of masters, or worse tyranny of the monitors. The oppressions of these young brutes are heart-sickening to call to recollection. I have been called out of my bed, and *waked for the purpose*, in the coldest winter nights—and this not once, but night after night—in my shirt, to receive the discipline of a leathern thong, with eleven other sufferers, because it pleased my callow overseer, when there has been any talking heard after we were gone to bed, to make the six last beds in the dormitory, where the youngest children of us slept, answerable for an offence they neither dared to commit, nor had the power to hinder.—The same execrable tyranny drove the younger part of us from the fires, when our feet were perishing with snow ; and, under the cruellest penalties, forbade the indulgence of a drink of water, when we lay in sleepless summer nights, fevered with the season and the day's sports.

There was one H——, who, I learned in after days, was seen expiating some maturer offence in the hulks. (Do I flatter myself in fancying that this might be the planter of that name, who suffered —at Nevis, I think, or St. Kitts,—some few years since ? My friend Tobin was the benevolent instrument of bringing him to the gallows.) This petty Nero actually branded a boy, who had offended him, with a red-hot iron ; and nearly starved forty of us, with exacting contributions, to the one half of our bread, to pamper a young ass, which, incredible as it may seem, with the connivance of the nurse's daughter (a young flame of his) he had contrived to smuggle in, and keep upon the leads of the *ward*, as they called our dormitories. This game went on for better than a week, till the foolish beast, not able to fare well but he must cry roast meat—happier than Caligula's minion, could he have kept his own counsel—but, foolisher, alas ! than any of his species in the fables—waxing fat, and kicking, in the fullness of bread, one unlucky minute would needs proclaim his good fortune to the world below ; and, laying out his simple throat, blew such a ram's horn blast, as (toppling down the walls of his own Jericho) set concealment any longer at defiance. The client was dismissed, with certain attentions, to Smithfield ; but I never understood that the patron underwent any censure on the occasion. This was in the stewardship of L.'s admired Perry.

Under the same *facile* administration, can L. have forgotten the cool impunity with which the nurses used to carry away openly, in open platters, for their own tables, one out of two of every hot joint, which the careful matron had been seeing scrupulously weighed out for our dinners? These things were daily practised in that magnificent apartment, which L. (grown connoisseur since, we presume) praises so highly for the grand paintings 'by Verrio and others', with which it is 'hung round and adorned'. But the sight of sleek well-fed blue-coat boys in pictures was, at that time, I believe, little consolatory to him, or us, the living ones, who saw the better part of our provisions carried away before our faces by harpies; and ourselves reduced (with the Trojan in the hall of Dido)

> To feed our mind with idle portraiture.

L. has recorded the repugnance of the school to *gags*, or the fat of fresh beef boiled; and sets it down to some superstition. But these unctuous morsels are never grateful to young palates (children are universally fat-haters), and in strong, coarse, boiled meats, *unsalted*, are detestable. A *gag-eater* in our time was equivalent to a *goule*, and held in equal detestation. —— suffered under the imputation:

> . . . 'Twas said
> He ate strange flesh.

He was observed, after dinner, carefully to gather up the remnants left at his table (not many, nor very choice fragments, you may credit me)—

and, in an especial manner, these disreputable morsels, which he would convey away, and secretly stow in the settle that stood at his bedside. None saw when he ate them. It was rumoured that he privately devoured them in the night. He was watched, but no traces of such midnight practices were discoverable. Some reported, that, on leave-days, he had been seen to carry out of the bounds a large blue check handkerchief, full of something. This then must be the accursed thing. Conjecture next was at work to imagine how he could dispose of it. Some said he sold it to the beggars. This belief generally prevailed. He went about moping. None spake to him. No one would play with him. He was excommunicated; put out of the pale of the school. He was too powerful a boy to be beaten, but he underwent every mode of that negative punishment which is more grievous than many stripes. Still he persevered. At length he was observed by two of his schoolfellows, who were determined to get at the secret, and had traced him one leave-day for that purpose, to enter a large worn-out building, such as there exist specimens of in Chancery Lane, which are let out to various scales of pauperism, with open door, and a common staircase. After him they silently slunk in, and followed by stealth up four flights, and saw him tap at a poor wicket, which was opened by an aged woman, meanly clad. Suspicion was now ripened into certainty. The informers had secured their victim. They had him in their toils. Accusation was formally preferred, and retribution most signal was looked for. Mr. Hathaway, the then steward (for this happened a little after my time), with that patient sagacity which tempered all his conduct, determined to investigate the matter, before he proceeded to sentence. The result was, that the supposed mendicants, the receivers or purchasers of the mysterious scraps, turned out to be the parents of ——, an honest couple come to decay—whom this seasonable supply had, in all probability, saved from mendicancy: and that this young stork, at the expense of his own good name, had all this while been only feeding the old birds!—The governors on this occasion, much to their honour, voted a present relief to the family of ——, and presented him with a silver medal. The lesson which the steward read upon RASH JUDGEMENT, on the occasion of publicly delivering the medal to ——, I believe, would not be lost upon his auditory.—I had left school then, but I well remember ——. He was a tall, shambling youth, with a cast in his eye, not at all calculated to conciliate hostile prejudices. I have since seen him carrying a baker's basket. I think I heard he did not do quite so well by himself as he had done by the old folks.

I was a hypochondriac lad; and the sight of a boy in fetters, upon the day of my first putting on the blue clothes, was not exactly fitted to assuage the natural terrors of initiation. I was of tender years, barely turned of seven; and had only read of such things in books, or seen them but in dreams. I was told he had *run away*. This was the punishment for the first offence.—As a novice I was soon after taken to see the dungeons. These were little, square, Bedlam cells, where a boy could just lie at his length upon straw and a blanket—a mattress, I think, was afterwards substituted—with a peep of light, let in askance, from a prison-orifice at top, barely enough to read by. Here the poor boy was locked in by himself all day, without sight of any but the porter who brought him his bread and water—who *might not speak to him*;—or of the beadle, who came twice a week to call him out to receive his periodical chastisement, which was almost welcome, because it separated him for a brief interval from solitude:—and here he was shut up by himself *of nights*, out of the reach of any sound, to suffer whatever horrors the weak nerves, and superstition incident to his time of life, might subject him to.[1] This was the penalty for the second offence. Wouldst thou like, Reader, to see what became of him in the next degree?

The culprit, who had been a third time an offender, and whose expulsion was at this time deemed irreversible, was brought forth, as at some solemn *auto da fé*, arrayed in uncouth and most appalling attire, all trace of his late 'watchet-weeds' carefully effaced, he was exposed in a jacket, resembling those which London lamp-lighters formerly delighted in, with a cap of the same. The effect of this divestiture was such as the ingenious devisers of it could have anticipated. With his pale and frightened features, it was as if some of those disfigurements in Dante had seized upon him. In this disguisement he was brought

[1] One or two instances of lunacy, or attempted suicide, accordingly, at length convinced the governors of the impolicy of this part of the sentence, and the midnight torture to the spirits was dispensed with.—This fancy of dungeons for children was a sprout of Howard's brain; for which (saving the reverence due to Holy Paul) methinks I could willingly spit upon his statue.

into the hall (*L.'s favourite state-room*), where awaited him the whole number of his school-fellows, whose joint lessons and sports he was thenceforth to share no more; the awful presence of the steward, to be seen for the last time; of the executioner beadle, clad in his state robe for the occasion; and of two faces more, of direr import, because never but in these extremities visible. These were governors; two of whom, by choice, or charter, were always accustomed to officiate at these *Ultima Supplicia*; not to mitigate (so at least we understood it), but to enforce the uttermost stripe. Old Bamber Gascoigne, and Peter Aubert, I remember, were colleagues on one occasion, when, the beadle turning rather pale, a glass of brandy was ordered to prepare him for the mysteries. The scourging was, after the old Roman fashion, long and stately. The lictor accompanied the criminal quite round the hall. We were generally too faint with attending to the previous disgusting circumstances to make accurate report with our eyes of the degree of corporal suffering inflicted. Report, of course, gave out the back knotty and livid. After scourging, he was made over, in his *San Benito*, to his friends, if he had any (but commonly such poor runagates were friendless), or to his parish officer, who, to enhance the effect of the scene, had his station allotted to him on the outside of the hall gate.

These solemn pageantries were not played off so often as to spoil the general mirth of the community. We had plenty of exercise and recreation *after* school hours; and, for myself, I must confess, that I was never happier than *in* them. The Upper and the Lower Grammar Schools were held in the same room; and an imaginary line only divided their bounds. Their character was as different as that of the inhabitants on the two sides of the Pyrenees. The Rev. James Boyer was the Upper Master, but the Rev. Matthew Field presided over that portion of the apartment of which I had the good fortune to be a member. We lived a life as careless as birds. We talked and did just what we pleased, and nobody molested us. We carried an accidence, or a grammar, for form; but, for any trouble it gave us, we might take two years in getting through the verbs deponent, and another two in forgetting all that we had learned about them. There was now and then the formality of saying a lesson, but if you had not learned it, a brush across the shoulders (just enough to disturb a fly) was the sole remonstrance. Field never used the rod; and in truth he wielded the cane with no great goodwill—holding it ‘ like a dancer ’. It looked in his hands rather like an emblem than an instrument of authority; and an emblem, too, he was ashamed of. He was a good easy man, that did not care to ruffle his own peace, nor perhaps set any great consideration upon the value of juvenile time. He came among us, now and then, but often stayed away whole days from us; and when he came, it made no difference to us—he had his private room to retire to, the short time he stayed, to be out of the sound of our noise. Our mirth and uproar went on. We had classics of our own, without being beholden to ‘ insolent Greece or haughty Rome ’, that passed current among us—Peter Wilkins—The Adventures of the Hon. Captain Robert Boyle—the Fortunate Blue-coat Boy—and the like. Or we cultivated a turn for mechanic and scientific operations; making little sun-dials of paper; or weaving those ingenious parentheses, called *cat-cradles*; or making dry peas to dance upon the end of a tin pipe; or studying the art military over that laudable game 'French and English', and a hundred other such devices to pass away the time—mixing the useful with the agreeable—as would have made the souls of Rousseau and John Locke chuckle to have seen us.

Matthew Field belonged to that class of modest divines who affect to mix in equal proportion the *gentleman*, the *scholar*, and the *Christian*; but, I know not how, the first ingredient is generally found to be the predominating dose in the composition. He was engaged in gay parties, or with his courtly bow at some episcopal levée, when he should have been attending upon us. He had for many years the classical charge of a hundred children, during the four or five first years of their education; and his very highest form seldom proceeded further than two or three of the introductory fables of Phaedrus. How things were suffered to go on thus, I cannot guess. Boyer, who was the proper person to have remedied these abuses, always affected, perhaps felt, a delicacy in interfering in a province not strictly his own. I have not been without my suspicions, that he was not altogether displeased at the contrast we presented to his end of the school. We were a sort of Helots to his young Spartans. He would sometimes, with ironic deference, send to borrow a rod of the Under Master, and then, with Sardonic grin, observe to one of his upper boys, 'how neat and fresh the twigs looked.' While his pale students were battering their brains over Xenophon and

Plato, with a silence as deep as that enjoined by the Samite, we were enjoying ourselves at our ease in our little Goshen. We saw a little into the secrets of his discipline, and the prospect did but the more reconcile us to our lot. His thunders rolled innocuous for us; his storms came near, but never touched us; contrary to Gideon's miracle, while all around were drenched, our fleece was dry.[1] His boys turned out the better scholars; we, I suspect, have the advantage in temper. His pupils cannot speak of him without something of terror allaying their gratitude; the remembrance of Field comes back with all the soothing images of indolence, and summer slumbers, and work like play, and innocent idleness, and Elysian exemptions, and life itself a 'playing holiday'.

Though sufficiently removed from the jurisdiction of Boyer, we were near enough (as I have said) to understand a little of his system. We occasionally heard sounds of the *Ululantes*, and caught glances of Tartarus. B. was a rabid pedant. His English style was cramped to barbarism. His Easter anthems (for his duty obliged him to those periodical flights) were grating as scrannel pipes.[2]—He would laugh—ay, and heartily—but then it must be at Flaccus's quibble about *Rex*—— or at the

[1] Cowley.

[2] In this and everything B. was the antipodes of his coadjutor. While the former was digging his brains for crude anthems, worth a pig-nut, F. would be recreating his gentlemanly fancy in the more flowery walks of the Muses. A little dramatic effusion of his, under the name of Vertumnus and Pomona, is not yet forgotten by the chroniclers of that sort of literature. It was accepted by Garrick, but the town did not give it their sanction.—B. used to say of it, in a way of half-compliment, half-irony, that it was *too classical for representation*.

tristis severitas in vultu, or *inspicere in patinas*, of Terence—thin jests, which at their first broaching could hardly have had *vis* enough to move a Roman muscle.—He had two wigs, both pedantic, but of different omen. The one serene, smiling, fresh powdered, betokening a mild day. The other, an old discoloured, unkempt, angry caxon, denoting frequent and bloody execution. Woe to the school, when he made his morning appearance in his *passy*, or *passionate wig*. No comet expounded surer.—J. B. had a heavy hand. I have known him double his knotty fist at a poor trembling child (the maternal milk hardly dry upon its lips) with a 'Sirrah, do you presume to set your wits at me?'—Nothing was more common than to see him make a headlong entry into the school-room, from his inner recess, or library, and, with turbulent eye, singling out a lad, roar out, 'Od's my life, sirrah' (his favourite adjuration), 'I have a great mind to whip you,'—then, with as sudden a retracting impulse, fling back into his lair—and, after a cooling lapse of some minutes (during which all but the culprit had totally forgotten the context) drive headlong out again, piecing out his imperfect sense, as if it had been some Devil's Litany, with the expletory yell—'*and I* WILL *too.*'—In his gentler moods, when the *rabidus furor* was assuaged, he had resort to an ingenious method, peculiar, for what I have heard, to himself, of whipping the boy, and reading the Debates, at the same time; a paragraph and a lash between; which in those times, when parliamentary oratory was most at a height and flourishing in these realms, was not calculated to impress the patient with a veneration for the diffuser graces of rhetoric.

Once, and but once, the uplifted rod was known to fall ineffectual from his hand—when droll squinting W—— having been caught putting the inside of the master's desk to a use for which the architect had clearly not designed it, to justify himself, with great simplicity averred, that *he did not know that the thing had been forewarned.* This exquisite irrecognition of any law antecedent to the *oral* or *declaratory*, struck so irresistibly upon the fancy of all who heard it (the pedagogue himself not excepted) that remission was unavoidable.

L. has given credit to B.'s great merits as an instructor. Coleridge, in his literary life, has pronounced a more intelligible and ample encomium on them. The author of the *Country Spectator* doubts not to compare him with the ablest teachers of antiquity. Perhaps we cannot dismiss him better than with the pious ejaculation of C.—when he heard that his old master was on his death-bed: 'Poor J. B.!—may all his faults be forgiven; and may he be wafted to bliss by little cherub boys, all head and wings, with no *bottoms* to reproach his sublunary infirmities.'

Under him were many good and sound scholars bred.—First Grecian of my time was Lancelot Pepys Stevens, kindest of boys and men, since Co-grammar-master (and inseparable companion) with Dr. T——e. What an edifying spectacle did this brace of friends present to those who remembered the anti-socialities of their predecessors!—You never met the one by chance in the street without a wonder, which was quickly dissipated by the almost immediate sub-appearance of the other. Generally arm-in-arm, these kindly coadjutors lightened for each other the toilsome duties of their profession, and when, in advanced age, one found it convenient to retire, the other was not long in discovering that it suited him to lay down the fasces also. Oh, it is pleasant, as it is rare, to find the same arm linked in yours at forty, which at thirteen helped it to turn over the *Cicero De Amicitia*, or some tale of Antique Friendship, which the young heart even then was burning to anticipate!—Co-Grecian with S. was Th——, who has since executed with ability various diplomatic functions at the Northern courts. Th—— was a tall, dark, saturnine youth, sparing of speech, with raven locks.—Thomas Fanshaw Middleton followed him (now Bishop of Calcutta), a scholar and a gentleman in his teens. He has the reputation of an excellent critic; and is author (besides the *Country Spectator*) of a Treatise on the Greek Article, against Sharpe.—M. is said to bear his mitre high in India, where the *regni novitas* (I dare say) sufficiently justifies the bearing. A humility quite as primitive as that of Jewel or Hooker might not be exactly fitted to impress the minds of those Anglo-Asiatic diocesans with a reverence for home institutions, and the church which those fathers watered. The manners of M. at school, though firm, were mild and unassuming.—Next to M. (if not senior to him) was Richards, author of 'The Aboriginal Britons', the most spirited of the Oxford Prize Poems; a pale, studious Grecian.—Then followed poor S——, ill-fated M——! of these the Muse is silent.

> Finding some of Edward's race
> Unhappy, pass their annals by.

Come back into memory, like as thou wert in the dayspring of thy fancies, with hope like a fiery column before thee—the dark pillar not yet turned—Samuel Taylor Coleridge—Logician, Metaphysician, Bard!—How have I seen the casual passer through the Cloisters stand still, entranced with admiration (while he weighed the disproportion between the *speech* and the *garb* of the young Mirandula) to hear thee unfold, in thy deep and sweet intonations, the mysteries of Iamblichus, or Plotinus (for even in those years thou waxedst not pale at such philosophic draughts), or reciting Homer in his Greek, or Pindar—— while the walls of the old Grey Friars re-echoed to the accents of the *inspired charity-boy*!—Many were the 'wit-combats' (to dally awhile with the words of old Fuller), between him and C. V. Le G——, 'which two I behold like a Spanish great galleon, and an English man-of-war: Master Coleridge, like the former, was built far higher in learning, solid, but slow in his performances. C. V. L., with the English man-of-war, lesser in bulk, but lighter in sailing, could turn with all times, tack about, and take advantage of all winds, by the quickness of his wit and invention.'

Nor shalt thou, their compeer, be quickly forgotten, Allen, with the cordial smile, and still more cordial laugh, with which thou wert wont to make the old Cloisters shake, in thy cognition of some poignant jest of theirs; or the anticipation of some more material, and peradventure practical one, of thine own. Extinct are those smiles, with that beautiful countenance, with which (for thou wert the *Nireus formosus* of the school), in the days of thy maturer waggery, thou didst disarm the wrath of infuriated town-damsel, who, incensed by provoking pinch, turning tigress-like round, suddenly converted by thy angel-look, exchanged the half-formed terrible '*bl——*', for a gentler greeting—'*bless thy handsome face!*'

Next follow two, who ought to be now alive, and the friends of Elia—the junior Le G—— and F——; who impelled, the former by a roving temper, the latter by too quick a sense of neglect—ill capable of enduring the slights poor Sizars are sometimes subject to in our seats of learning—exchanged their Alma Mater for the camp; perishing, one by climate, and one on the plains of Salamanca:—Le G——, sanguine, volatile, sweet-natured; F——, dogged, faithful, anticipative of insult, warm-hearted, with something of the old Roman height about him.

Fine, frank-hearted Fr——, the present master of Hertford, with Marmaduke T——, mildest of Missionaries—and both my good friends still—close the catalogue of Grecians in my time.

DETACHED THOUGHTS ON BOOKS AND READING

To mind the inside of a book is to entertain one's self with the forced product of another man's brain. Now I think a man of quality and breeding may be much amused with the natural sprouts of his own.—*Lord Foppington, in 'The Relapse'*.

An ingenious acquaintance of my own was so much struck with this bright sally of his Lordship, that he has left off reading altogether, to the great improvement of his originality. At the hazard of losing some credit on this head, I must confess that I dedicate no inconsiderable portion of my time to other people's thoughts. I dream away my life in others' speculations. I love to lose myself in other men's minds. When I am not walking, I am reading; I cannot sit and think. Books think for me.

I have no repugnances. Shaftesbury is not too genteel for me, nor Jonathan Wild too low. I can read anything which I call *a book*. There are things in that shape which I cannot allow for such.

In this catalogue of *books which are no books—biblia a-biblia*—I reckon Court Calendars, Directories, Pocket Books, Draught Boards, bound and lettered on the back, Scientific Treatises, Almanacs, Statutes at Large: the works of Hume, Gibbon, Robertson, Beattie, Soame Jenyns, and generally, all those volumes which 'no gentleman's library should be without': the *Histories* of Flavius Josephus (that learned Jew), and Paley's *Moral Philosophy*. With these exceptions, I can read almost anything. I bless my stars for a taste so catholic, so unexcluding.

I confess that it moves my spleen to see these *things in books' clothing* perched upon shelves, like false saints, usurpers of true shrines, intruders into the sanctuary, thrusting out the legitimate occupants. To reach down a well-bound semblance of a volume, and hope it some kind-hearted play-book, then, opening what 'seem its leaves', to come bolt upon a withering Population Essay. To expect a Steele or a Farquhar, and find—Adam Smith. To view a well-arranged assortment of block-headed Encyclopaedias (Anglicanas or Metropolitanas) set out in an array of russia, or morocco, when a tithe of that good leather would comfortably re-clothe my shivering folios, would renovate Paracelsus himself, and enable old Raymund Lully to look like himself again in the world. I never see these impostors, but I long to strip them, to warm my ragged veterans in their spoils.

To be strong-backed and neat-bound is the desideratum of a volume. Magnificence comes after. This, when it can be afforded, is not to be lavished upon all kinds of books indiscriminately. I would not dress a set of magazines, for instance, in full suit. The dishabille, or half-binding (with russia backs ever) is *our* costume. A Shakespeare or a Milton (unless the first editions), it were mere foppery to trick out in gay apparel. The possession of them confers no distinction. The exterior of them (the things themselves being so common), strange to say, raises no sweet emotions, no tickling sense of property in the owner. Thomson's *Seasons*, again, looks best (I maintain it) a little torn and dog's-eared. How beautiful to a genuine lover of reading are the sullied leaves, and worn-out appearance, nay, the very odour (beyond russia) if we would not forget kind feelings in fastidiousness, of an old 'Circulating Library' *Tom Jones*, or *Vicar of Wakefield*! How they speak of the thousand thumbs that have turned over their pages with delight!—of the lone sempstress, whom they may have cheered (milliner, or hard-working mantua-maker) after her long day's needle-toil, running far into midnight, when she has snatched an hour, ill spared from sleep, to steep her cares, as in some Lethean cup, in spelling out their enchanting contents! Who would have them a whit less soiled? What better condition could we desire to see them in?

In some respects the better a book is, the less it demands from binding. Fielding, Smollett, Sterne, and all that class of perpetually self-reproductive volumes—Great Nature's Stereotypes—we see them individually perish with less regret, because we know the copies of them to be 'eterne'. But where a book is at once both good and rare—where the individual is almost the species, and when *that* perishes,

> We know not where is that Promethean torch
> That can its light relume,—

such a book, for instance, as the *Life of the Duke of Newcastle*, by his Duchess—no casket is rich enough, no casing sufficiently durable, to honour and keep safe such a jewel.

Not only rare volumes of this description, which seem hopeless ever to be reprinted, but old editions of writers, such as Sir Philip Sidney, Bishop Taylor, Milton in his prose works, Fuller—of whom we *have* reprints, yet the books themselves, though they go about, and are talked of here and there, we know have not endenizened themselves (nor possibly ever will) in the national heart, so as to become stock books—it is good to possess these in durable and costly covers. I do not care for a First Folio of Shakespeare. [You cannot make a *pet* book of an author whom everybody reads.] I rather prefer the common editions of Rowe and Tonson, without notes, and with *plates*, which, being so execrably bad, serve as maps or modest remembrancers, to the text; and, without pretending to any supposable emulation with it, are so much better than the Shakespeare gallery *engravings*, which *did*. I have a community of feeling with my countrymen about his Plays, and I like those editions of him best which have been oftenest tumbled about and handled.—On the contrary,

I cannot read Beaumont and Fletcher but in Folio. The Octavo editions are painful to look at. I have no sympathy with them. If they were as much read as the current editions of the other poet, I should prefer them in that shape to the older one. I do not know a more heartless sight than the reprint of the *Anatomy of Melancholy*. What need was there of unearthing the bones of that fantastic old great man, to expose them in a winding sheet of the newest fashion to modern censure? what hapless stationer could dream of Burton ever becoming popular?—The wretched Malone could not do worse, when he bribed the sexton of Stratford church to let him whitewash the painted effigy of old Shakespeare, which stood there, in rude but lively fashion depicted, to the very colour of the cheek, the eye, the eyebrow, hair, the very dress he used to wear—the only authentic testimony we had, however imperfect, of these curious parts and parcels of him. They covered him over with a coat of white paint. By ——, if I had been a justice of peace for Warwickshire, I would have clapped both commentator and sexton fast in the stocks, for a pair of meddling sacrilegious varlets.

I think I see them at their work—these sapient trouble-tombs.

Shall I be thought fantastical if I confess that the names of some of our poets sound sweeter, and have a finer relish to the ear—to mine, at least—than that of Milton or of Shakespeare? It may be that the latter are more staled and rung upon in common discourse. The sweetest names, and which carry a perfume in the mention, are, Kit Marlowe, Drayton, Drummond of Hawthornden, and Cowley.

Much depends upon *when* and *where* you read a book. In the five or six impatient minutes, before the dinner is quite ready, who would think of taking up the *Fairy Queen* for a stop-gap, or a volume of Bishop Andrewes's sermons?

Milton almost requires a solemn service of music to be played before you enter upon him. But he brings his music, to which, who listens, had need bring docile thoughts, and purged ears.

Winter evenings—the world shut out—with less of ceremony the gentle Shakespeare enters. At such a season the *Tempest*, or his own *Winter's Tale*—

These two poets you cannot avoid reading aloud—to yourself, or (as it chances) to some single person listening. More than one—and it degenerates into an audience.

Books of quick interest, that hurry on for incidents, are for the eye to glide over only. It will not do to read them out. I could never listen to even the better kind of modern novels without extreme irksomeness.

A newspaper, read out, is intolerable. In some of the Bank offices it is the custom (to save so much individual time) for one of the clerks—who is the best scholar—to commence upon the *Times* or the *Chronicle* and recite its entire contents aloud, *pro bono publico*. With every advantage of lungs and elocution, the effect is singularly vapid. In barbers' shops and public-houses a fellow will get up and spell out a paragraph, which he communicates as some discovery. Another follows with *his* selection. So the entire journal transpires at length by piecemeal. Seldom-readers are slow readers, and, without this expedient, no one in the company would probably ever travel through the contents of a whole paper.

Newspapers always excite curiosity. No one ever lays one down without a feeling of disappointment.

What an eternal time that gentleman in black, at Nando's, keeps the paper! I am sick of hearing the waiter bawling out incessantly, 'The *Chronicle* is in hand, Sir.'

Coming into an inn at night—having ordered your supper—what can be more delightful than to find lying in the window-seat, left there time out of mind by the carelessness of some former guest—two or three numbers of the old *Town and Country Magazine*, with its amusing *tête-à-tête* pictures—'The Royal Lover and Lady G——'; 'The Melting Platonic and the old Beau,'—and such-like antiquated scandal? Would you exchange it—at that time, and in that place—for a better book?

Poor Tobin, who latterly fell blind, did not regret it so much for the weightier kinds of reading—the *Paradise Lost*, or *Comus*, he could have *read* to him—but he missed the pleasure of skimming over with his own eye a magazine, or a light pamphlet.

I should not care to be caught in the serious avenues of some cathedral alone, and reading *Candide*.

I do not remember a more whimsical surprise than having been once detected—by a familiar damsel—reclined at my ease upon the grass, on Primrose Hill (her Cythera) reading—*Pamela*. There was nothing in the book to make a man seriously ashamed at the exposure; but as she seated herself down by me, and seemed determined to read in company, I could have wished it had been—any other book. We read on very sociably for a few pages; and, not finding the author much to her taste, she got up, and—went away. Gentle casuist, I leave it to thee to conjecture, whether the blush (for there was one between us) was the property of the nymph or the swain in this dilemma. From me you shall never get the secret.

I am not much a friend to out-of-doors reading. I cannot settle my spirits to it. I knew a Unitarian minister, who was generally to be seen upon Snow Hill (as yet Skinner's Street *was not*), between the hours of ten and eleven in the morning, studying a volume of Lardner. I own this to have been a strain of abstraction beyond my reach. I used to admire how he sidled along, keeping clear of secular contacts. An illiterate encounter with a porter's knot, or a bread basket, would have quickly put to flight all the theology I am master of, and have left me worse than indifferent to the five points.

There is a class of street readers, whom I can never contemplate without affection—the poor gentry, who, not having wherewithal to buy or hire a book, filch a little learning at the open stalls—the owner, with his hard eye, casting envious looks at them all the while, and thinking when they will have done. Venturing tenderly, page after page, expecting every moment when he shall interpose his interdict, and yet unable to deny themselves the gratification, they 'snatch a fearful joy'. Martin B——, in this way, by daily fragments, got through two volumes of *Clarissa*, when the stall-keeper damped his laudable ambition, by asking him (it was in his younger days) whether he meant to purchase the work. M. declares, that under no circumstance in his life did he ever peruse a book with half the satisfaction which he took in those uneasy snatches. A quaint poetess of our day has moralized upon the subject in two very touching but homely stanzas:

I saw a boy with eager eye
Open a book upon a stall,
And read, as he'd devour it all;
Which, when the stall-man did espy,
Soon to the boy I heard him call,
'You Sir, you never buy a book,
Therefore in one you shall not look.'
The boy pass'd slowly on, and with a sigh
He wish'd he never had been taught to read,
Then of the old churl's books he should have had no need.

Of sufferings the poor have many,
Which never can the rich annoy.
I soon perceived another boy,
Who look'd as if he'd not had any
Food, for that day at least, enjoy
The sight of cold meat in a tavern larder.
This boy's case, then thought I, is surely harder,
Thus hungry, longing, thus without a penny,
Beholding choice of dainty-dressèd meat:
No wonder if he wished he ne'er had learn'd to eat.

WILLIAM HAZLITT

1778–1830

ON NICKNAMES

Hae nugae in seria ducunt.

THIS is a more important subject than it seems at first sight. It is as serious in its results as it is contemptible in the means by which these results are brought about. Nicknames, for the most part, govern the world. The history of politics, of religion, of literature, of morals, and of private life, is too often little less than the history of nicknames. What are one-half the convulsions of the civilized world—the frequent overthrow of states and kingdoms—the shock and hostile encounters of mighty continents—the battles by sea and land—the intestine commotions—the feuds of the Vitelli and Orsini, of the Guelphs and Ghibellines—the civil wars in England and the League in France—the jealousies and heart-burnings of cabinets and councils—the uncharitable proscriptions of creeds and sects, Turk, Jew, Pagan, Papist and Puritan, Quaker, and Methodist—the persecutions and massacres—the burnings, tortures, imprisonments, and lingering deaths, inflicted for a different profession of faith—but so many illustrations of the power of this principle? Foxe's *Book of Martyrs*, and Neale's *History of the Puritans*, are comments on the same text. The fires in Smithfield were fanned by nicknames, and a nickname set its seal on the unopened dungeons of the

Holy Inquisition. Nicknames are the talismans and spells that collect and set in motion all the combustible part of men's passions and prejudices, which have hitherto played so much more successful a game, and done their work so much more effectually than reason, in all the grand concerns and petty details of human life, and do not yet seem tired of the task assigned them. Nicknames are the convenient, portable tools by which they simplify the process of mischief, and get through their job with the least time and trouble. These worthless, unmeaning, irritating, envenomed words of reproach are the established signs by which the different compartments of society are ticketed, labelled, and marked out for each other's hatred and contempt. They are to be had, ready cut and dry, of all sorts and sizes, wholesale and retail, for foreign exportation or for home consumption, and for all occasions in life. 'The priest calls the lawyer a cheat, the lawyer beknaves the divine.' The Frenchman hates the Englishman because he is an Englishman; and the Englishman hates the Frenchman for as good a reason. The Whig hates the Tory, and the Tory the Whig. The Dissenter hates the Church of England man, and the Church of England man hates the Dissenter, as if they were of a different species, because they have a different designation. The Mussulman calls the worshipper of the Cross 'Christian dog', spits in his face, and kicks him from the pavement, by virtue of a nickname; and the Christian retorts the indignity upon the Infidel and the Jew by the same infallible rule of right. In France they damn Shakespeare in the lump, by calling him a *barbare*; and we talk of Racine's *verbiage* with inexpressible contempt and self-complacency. Among ourselves, an anti-Jacobin critic denounces a Jacobin poet and his friends, at a venture, 'as infidels and fugitives, who have left their wives destitute, and their children fatherless'—whether they have wives and children or not. The unenlightened savage makes a meal of his enemy's flesh, after reproaching him with the name of his tribe, because he is differently tattooed; and the literary cannibal cuts up the character of his opponent by the help of a nickname. The jest of all this is, that a party nickname is always a relative term, and has its countersign, which has just the same force and meaning, so that both must be perfectly ridiculous and insignificant. A Whig implies a Tory; there must be 'Malcontents' as well as 'Malignants'; Jacobins and anti-Jacobins; English and French. These sorts of *noms-de-guerre* derive all their force from their contraries. Take away the meaning of the one, and you take the sting out of the other. They could not exist but upon the strength of mutual and irreconcilable antipathies; there must be no love lost between them. What is there in the names themselves to give them a preference over each other? 'Sound them, they do become the mouth as well; weigh them, they are as heavy; conjure with them, one will raise a spirit as soon as the other.' If there were not fools and madmen who hated both, there could not be fools and madmen bigoted to either. I have heard an eminent character boast that he had done more to produce the late war by nicknaming Buonaparte 'the Corsican', than all the state papers and documents on the subject put together. And yet Mr. Southey asks triumphantly, 'Is it to be supposed that it is England, *our* England, to whom that war was owing?' As if, in a dispute between two countries, the conclusive argument, which lies in the pronoun *our*, belonged only to one of them. I like Shakespeare's version of the matter better:—

> Hath Britain all the sun that shines? Day, night,
> Are they not but in Britain? I' the world's volume
> *Our* Britain seems as of it, but not in 't;
> In a great pool a swan's nest, prithee, think
> There 's livers out of Britain.

In all national disputes, it is common to appeal to the numbers on your side as decisive on the point. If everybody in England thought the late war right, everybody in France thought it wrong. There were ten millions on one side of the question (or rather of the water), and thirty millions on the other side—that 's all. I remember some one arguing, in justification of our Ministers interfering without occasion, 'That governments would not go to war for nothing'; to which I answered: 'Then they could not go to war at all; for, at that rate, neither of them could be in the wrong, and yet both of them must be in the right, which was absurd.' The only meaning of these vulgar nicknames and party distinctions, where they are urged most violently and confidently, is that others differ from you in some particular or other (whether it be opinion, dress, clime, or complexion), which you highly disapprove of, forgetting that, by the same rule, they have the very same right to be offended at you because you differ from them. Those who have reason on their side do not make the most obstinate and grievous appeals to prejudice and abusive language. I know but of one exception to this general rule, and that is where the things that excite disgust are of such a kind that they cannot well be gone into without offence to decency and good manners; but it is equally certain in this case, that those who are most shocked at the things are not those who are most forward to apply the names. A person will not be fond of repeating a charge, or adverting to a subject, that inflicts a wound on his own feelings, even for the sake of wounding the feelings of another. A man should be very sure that he himself is not what he has always in his mouth. The greatest prudes have been often accounted the greatest hypocrites, and a satirist is at best but a suspicious character. The loudest and most unblushing invectives against vice and debauchery will as often proceed from a desire to inflame and pamper the passions of the writer, by raking into a nauseous subject, as from a wish to excite virtuous indignation against it in the public mind, or to reform the individual. To familiarize the mind to gross ideas is not the way to increase your own or the general repugnance to them. But to return to the subject of nicknames.

The use of this figure of speech is, that it excites a strong idea without requiring any proof. It is a shorthand, compendious mode of getting at a conclusion, and never troubling yourself or anybody else with the formalities of reasoning or the dictates of common sense. It is superior to all evidence, for it does not rest upon any, and operates with the greatest force and certainty in proportion to the utter want of probability. Belief is only a stray impression, and the malignity or extravagance of the accusation passes for a proof of the crime. 'Brevity is the soul of wit'; and of all eloquence a nickname is the most concise, of all arguments the most unanswerable. It gives *carte-blanche* to the imagination, throws the reins on the neck of the passions, and suspends the use of the understanding altogether. It does not stand upon ceremony, on the nice distinctions of right and wrong. It does not wait the slow processes of reason, or stop to unravel the wit of sophistry. It takes everything for granted that serves for nourishment for the spleen. It is instantaneous in its operations. There is nothing to interpose between the effect and it. It is passion without proof, and action without thought —'the unbought grace of life, the cheap defence of nations.' It does not, as Mr. Burke expresses it, 'leave the will puzzled, undecided, and sceptical in the moment of action.' It is a word and a blow. The 'No Popery' cry raised a little while ago let loose all the lurking spite and prejudice which had lain rankling in the proper receptacles for them for above a century, without any knowledge of the past history of the country which had given rise to them, or any reference to their connexion with present circumstances; for the knowledge of the one would have prevented the possibility of their application to the other. Facts present a tangible and definite idea to the mind, a train of causes and consequences, accounting for each other, and leading to a positive conclusion—but no farther. But a nickname is tied down to no such limited service; it is a disposable force, that is almost always perverted to mischief. It clothes itself with all the terrors of uncertain abstraction, and there is no end of the abuse to which it is liable but the cunning of those who employ, or the credulity of those who are gulled by it. It is a reserve of the ignorance, bigotry, and intolerance of weak and vulgar minds, brought up where reason fails, and always ready, at a moment's warning, to be applied to any, the most absurd purposes. If you bring specific charges against a man, you thereby enable him to meet and repel them, if he thinks it worth his while; but a nickname baffles reply, by the very vagueness of the inferences from it, and gives increased activity to the confused, dim, and imperfect notions of dislike connected with it, from their having no settled ground to rest upon. The mind naturally irritates itself against an unknown object of fear or jealousy, and makes up for the blindness of its zeal by an excess of it. We are eager to indulge our hasty feelings to the utmost, lest, by stopping to examine, we should find that there is no excuse for them. The very consciousness of the injustice we may be doing another makes us only the more loud and bitter in our invectives against him. We keep down the admonitions of returning reason, by calling up a double portion of gratuitous and vulgar spite. The will may be said to act with most force *in vacuo*; the passions are the most ungovernable when they are blindfolded. That malignity is always the most implacable which is accompanied with a sense of weakness, because it is never satisfied of its own success or safety. A nickname carries the weight of the pride, the indolence, the cowardice, the ignorance, and the ill nature of mankind on its side. It acts by mechanical sympathy on the nerves of society. Any one who is without character himself may make himself master of the reputation of another by the application of a nickname, as, if you do not mind soiling your fingers, you may always throw dirt on another. No matter how undeserved the imputation, it will stick; for, though it is sport to the bystanders to see you bespattered, they will not stop to see you wipe out the stains. You are not heard in your own defence; it has no effect, it does not tell, excites no sensation, or it is only felt as a disappointment of their triumph over you. Their passions and prejudices are inflamed by the charge, 'As rage with rage doth sympathize'; by vindicating yourself, you merely bring them back to common sense, which is a very sober, mawkish state. *Give a dog an ill name and hang him,* is a proverb. 'A nickname is the heaviest stone that the devil can throw at a man.' It is a bugbear to the imagination, and, though we do not believe in it, it still haunts our apprehensions. Let a nickname be industriously applied to our dearest friend, and let us know that it is ever so false and malicious, yet it will answer its end; it connects the person's name and idea with an ugly association, you think of them with pain together, or it requires an effort of indignation or magnanimity on your part to disconnect them; it becomes an uneasy subject, a sore point, and you will sooner desert your friend, or join in the conspiracy against him, than be constantly forced to repel charges without truth or meaning, and have your penetration or character called in question by a rascal. Nay, such is the unaccountable construction of language and of the human mind, that the affixing the most innocent or praiseworthy appellation to any individual, or set of individuals, *as a nickname,* has all the effect of the most opprobrious epithets.

Thus the cant name, ‘ the Talents,’ was successfully applied as a stigma to the Whigs at one time ; it held them up to ridicule, and made them obnoxious to public feeling, though it was notorious to everybody that the Whig leaders were ‘ the Talents ’, and that their adversaries nicknamed them so from real hatred and pretended derision. Call a man short by his Christian name, as Tom or Dick such-a-one, or by his profession (however respectable), as Canning pelted a noble lord with his left-off title of Doctor, and you undo him for ever, if he has a reputation to lose. Such is the tenaciousness of spite and ill nature, or the jealousy of public opinion, even this will be peg enough to hang doubtful innuendos, weighty dilemmas upon. ‘With so small a web as this will I catch so great a fly as Cassio.’ The public do not like to see their favourites treated with impertinent familiarity; it lowers the tone of admiration very speedily. It implies that some one stands in no great awe of their idol, and he perhaps may know as much about the matter as they do. It seems as if a man whose name, with some contemptuous abbreviation, is always dinned in the public ear, was distinguished for nothing else. By repeating a man's name in this manner you may soon make him sick of it, and of his life too. Children do not like to be *called out of their names*: it is questioning their personal identity. There are political writers who have fairly worried their readers into conviction by abuse and nicknames. People surrender their judgements to escape the persecution of their style, and the disgust and indignation which their incessant violence and vulgarity excite, at last make you hate those who are the objects of it. *Causa causae causa causati.* They make people sick of a subject by making them sick of their arguments.

A parrot may be taught to call names; and if the person who keeps the parrot has a spite to his neighbours, he may give them a great deal of annoyance without much wit, either in the employer or the puppet. The insignificance of the instrument has nothing to do with the efficacy of the means. Hotspur would have had 'a *starling* taught to speak nothing but Mortimer', in the ears of his enemy. Nature, it is said, has given arms to all creatures the most proper to defend themselves, and annoy others: to the lowest she has given the use of nicknames.

There are some droll instances of the effect of proper names combined with circumstances. A young student had come up to London from Cambridge, and went in the evening and planted himself in the pit of the play-house. He had not been seated long, when in one of the front boxes near him he discovered one of his college tutors, with whom he felt an immediate and strong desire to claim acquaintance, and accordingly called out, in a low and respectful voice, 'Dr. Topping!' The appeal was, however, ineffectual. He then repeated in a louder tone, but still in an under key, so as not to excite the attention of any one but his friend, 'Dr. Topping!' The Doctor took no notice. He then grew more impatient, and repeated 'Dr. Topping, Dr. Topping!' two or three times pretty loud, to see whether the Doctor did not or would not hear him. Still the Doctor remained immovable. The joke began at length to get round, and one or two persons, as he continued his invocation of the Doctor's name, joined in with him; these were reinforced by others calling out, 'Dr. Topping, Dr. Topping!' on all sides, so that he could no longer avoid perceiving it, and at length the whole pit rose and roared, 'Dr. Topping!' with loud and repeated cries, and the Doctor was forced to retire precipitately, frightened at the sound of his own name.

The calling people by their Christian or surname is a proof of affection, as well as of hatred. They are generally the best of good fellows with whom their friends take this sort of liberty. *Diminutives* are titles of endearment. Dr. Johnson's calling Goldsmith 'Goldy' did equal honour to both. It showed the regard he had for him. This familiarity may perhaps imply a certain want of formal respect; but formal respect is not necessary to, if it is consistent with, cordial friendship. Titles of honour are the reverse of nicknames; they convey the idea of respect, as the others do of contempt, but they equally mean little or nothing. Junius's motto, *Stat nominis umbra*, is a very significant one; it might be extended farther. A striking instance of the force of names, standing by themselves, is in the respect felt towards Michael Angelo in this country. We know nothing of him but his name. It is an abstraction of fame and greatness. Our admiration of him supports itself, and our idea of his superiority seems self-evident, because it is attached to his name only.

ON ACTORS AND ACTING

Players are 'the abstracts and brief chronicles of the time'; the motley representatives of human nature. They are the only honest hypocrites. Their life is a voluntary dream; a studied madness.

The height of their ambition is to be *beside themselves*. To-day kings, to-morrow beggars, it is only when they are themselves, that they are nothing. Made up of mimic laughter and tears, passing from the extremes of joy or woe at the prompter's call, they wear the livery of other men's fortunes; their very thoughts are not their own. They are, as it were, train-bearers in the pageant of life, and hold a glass up to humanity, frailer than itself. We see ourselves at second-hand in them: they show us all that we are, all that we wish to be, and all that we dread to be. The stage is an epitome, a bettered likeness of the world, with the dull part left out: and indeed, with this omission, it is nearly big enough to hold all the rest. What brings the resemblance nearer is, that, as *they* imitate us, we, in our turn, imitate them. How many fine gentlemen do we owe to the stage? How many romantic lovers are mere Romeos in masquerade? How many soft bosoms have heaved with Juliet's sighs? They teach us when to laugh and when to weep, when to love and when to hate, upon principle and with a good grace! Wherever there is a play-house, the world will go on not amiss. The stage not only refines the manners, but it is the best teacher of morals, for it is the truest and most intelligible picture of life. It stamps the image of virtue on the mind by first softening the rude materials of which it is composed, by a sense of pleasure. It regulates the passions by giving a loose to the imagination. It points out the selfish and depraved to our detestation; the amiable and generous to our admiration; and if it clothes the more seductive vices with the borrowed graces of wit and fancy, even those graces operate as a diversion to the coarser poison of experience and bad example, and often prevent or carry off the infection by inoculating the mind with a certain taste and elegance. To show how little we agree with the common declamations against the immoral tendency of the stage on this score, we will hazard a conjecture, that the acting of the *Beggar's Opera* a certain number of nights every year since it was first brought out, has done more towards putting down the practice of highway robbery, than all the gibbets that ever were erected. A person, after seeing this piece, is too deeply imbued with a sense of humanity, is in too good humour with himself and the rest of the world, to set about cutting throats or rifling pockets. Whatever makes a jest of vice, leaves it too much a matter of indifference for any one in his senses to rush desperately on his ruin for its sake. We suspect that just the contrary effect must be produced by the representation of *George Barnwell*, which is too much in the style of the Ordinary's sermon to meet with any better success. The mind, in such cases, instead of being deterred by the alarming consequences held out to it, revolts against the denunciation of them as an insult offered to its free-will, and, in a spirit of defiance, returns a practical answer to them, by daring the worst that can happen. The most striking lesson ever read to levity and licentiousness, is in the last act of *The Inconstant*, where young Mirabel is preserved by the fidelity of his mistress, Orinda, in the disguise of a page, from the hands of assassins, into whose power he has been allured by the temptations of vice and beauty. There never was a rake who did not become in imagination a reformed man, during the representation of the last trying scenes of this admirable comedy.

If the stage is useful as a school of instruction, it is no less so as a source of amusement. It is the source of the greatest enjoyment at the time, and a never-failing fund of agreeable reflection afterwards. The merits of a new play, or of a new actor, are always among the first topics of polite conversation. One way in which public exhibitions contribute to refine and humanize mankind, is by supplying them with ideas and subjects of conversation and interest in common. The progress of civilization is in proportion to the number of common-places current in society. For instance, if we meet with a stranger at an inn or in a stage-coach, who knows nothing but his own affairs, his shop, his customers, his farm, his pigs, his poultry, we can carry on no conversation with him on these local and personal matters: the only way is to let him have all the talk to himself. But if he has fortunately ever seen Mr. Liston act, this is an immediate topic of mutual conversation, and we agree together the rest of the evening in discussing the merits of that inimitable actor, with the same satisfaction as in talking over the affairs of the most intimate friend.

If the stage thus introduces us familiarly to our contemporaries, it also brings us acquainted with former times. It is an interesting revival of past ages, manners, opinions, dresses, persons, and actions,—whether it carries us back to the wars of York and Lancaster, or half-way back to the heroic times of Greece and Rome, in some translation from the French, or quite back to the age of Charles II in the scenes of Congreve and of Etherege (the gay Sir George!)—happy age, when kings and nobles led purely ornamental lives; when the utmost stretch of a morning's study went no further than the choice of a sword-knot, or the adjustment of a side-curl; when the soul spoke out in all the pleasing eloquence of dress; and beaux and belles, enamoured of themselves in one another's follies, fluttered like gilded butterflies in giddy mazes through the walks of St. James's Park!

A good company of comedians, a Theatre-Royal judiciously managed, is your true Heralds' College; the only Antiquarian Society, that is worth a rush. It is for this reason that there is such an air of romance about players, and that it is pleasanter to see them, even in their own persons, than any of the three learned professions. We feel more respect for John Kemble in a plain coat, than for the Lord Chancellor on the Woolsack. He is surrounded, to our eyes, with a greater number of imposing recollections: he is a more reverend piece of formality; a more complicated tissue of costume. We do not know whether to look upon this accomplished actor as Pierre or King John or Coriolanus or Cato or Leontes or the Stranger. But we see in him a stately hieroglyphic of humanity; a living monument of departed greatness; a sombre comment on the rise and fall of kings. We look after him till he is out of sight, as we listen to a story of one of Ossian's heroes, to 'a tale of other times!'

One of the most affecting things we know is to see a favourite actor take leave of the stage. We were present not long ago when Mr. Bannister quitted it.

We do not wonder that his feelings were overpowered on the occasion: ours were nearly so too. We remembered him in the first heyday of our youthful spirits, in *The Prize*, in which he played so delightfully with that fine old croaker Suett, and Madame Storace,—in the farce of *My Grandmother*, in the *Son-in-Law*, in Autolycus, and in Scrub, in which our satisfaction was at its height. At that time, King, and Parsons, and Dodd, and Quick, and Edwin were in the full vigour of their reputation, who are now all gone. We still feel the vivid delight with which we used to see their names in the play-bills as we went along to the Theatre. Bannister was one of the last of these that remained; and we parted with him as we should with one of our oldest and best friends. The most pleasant feature in the profession of a player, and which, indeed, is peculiar to it, is that we not only admire the talents of those who adorn it, but we contract a personal intimacy with them. There is no class of society whom so many persons regard with affection as actors. We greet them on the stage; we like to meet them in the streets; they almost always recall to us pleasant associations; and we feel our gratitude excited, without the uneasiness of a sense of obligation. The very gaiety and popularity, however, which surround the life of a favourite performer, make the retiring from it a very serious business. It glances a mortifying reflection on the shortness of human life, and the vanity of human pleasures. Something reminds us, that 'all the world 's a stage, and all the men and women merely players'.

WASHINGTON IRVING

1783–1859

JOHN BULL

An old song, made by an aged old pate,
Of an old worshipful gentleman who had a great estate,
That kept a brave old house at a bountiful rate,
And an old porter to relieve the poor at his gate.

With an old study fill'd full of learned old books,
With an old reverend chaplain, you might know him by his looks,
With an old buttery-hatch worn quite off the hooks,
And an old kitchen that maintained half-a-dozen old cooks.

'Like an old courtier,' &c. OLD SONG.

THERE is no species of humour in which the English more excel, than that which consists in caricaturing and giving ludicrous appellations, or nicknames. In this way they have whimsically designated, not merely individuals, but nations; and, in their fondness for pushing a joke, they have not spared even themselves. One would think that, in personifying itself, a nation would be apt to picture something grand, heroic, and imposing; but it is characteristic of the peculiar humour of the English, and of their love for what is blunt, comic, and familiar, that they have embodied their national oddities in the figure of a sturdy, corpulent old fellow, with a three-cornered hat, red waistcoat, leather breeches, and stout oaken cudgel. Thus they have taken a singular delight in exhibiting their most private foibles in a laughable point of view; and have been so successful in their delineations, that there is scarcely a being in actual existence more absolutely present to the public mind than that eccentric personage, John Bull.

Perhaps the continual contemplation of the character thus drawn of them has contributed to fix it upon the nation; and thus to give reality to what at first may have been painted in a great measure from the imagination. Men are apt to acquire peculiarities that are continually ascribed to them. The common orders of English seem wonderfully captivated with the *beau idéal* which they have formed of John Bull, and endeavour to act up to the broad caricature that is perpetually before their eyes. Unluckily, they sometimes make their boasted Bull-ism an apology for their prejudice or grossness; and this I have especially noticed among those truly homebred and genuine sons of the soil who have never migrated beyond the sound of Bow bells. If one of these should be a little uncouth in speech, and apt to utter impertinent truths, he confesses that he is a real John Bull, and always speaks his mind. If he now and then flies into an unreasonable burst of passion about trifles, he observes, that John Bull is a choleric old blade, but then his passion is over in a moment, and he bears no malice. If he betrays a coarseness of taste, and an insensibility to foreign refinements, he thanks Heaven for his ignorance—he is a plain John Bull, and has no relish for frippery and nicknacks. His very proneness to be gulled by strangers, and to pay extravagantly for absurdities, is excused under the plea of munificence—for John is always more generous than wise.

Thus, under the name of John Bull, he will contrive to argue every fault into a merit, and will frankly convict himself of being the honestest fellow in existence.

However little, therefore, the character may have suited in the first instance, it has gradually adapted itself to the nation, or rather they have adapted themselves to each other ; and a stranger who wishes to study English peculiarities, may gather much valuable information from the innumerable portraits of John Bull, as exhibited in the windows of the caricature-shops. Still, however, he is one of those fertile humorists, that are continually throwing out new portraits, and presenting different aspects from different points of view ; and, often as he has been described, I cannot resist the temptation to give a slight sketch of him, such as he has met my eye.

John Bull, to all appearance, is a plain, downright, matter-of-fact fellow, with much less of poetry about him than rich prose. There is little of romance in his nature, but a vast deal of strong natural feeling. He excels in humour more than in wit ; is jolly rather than gay ; melancholy rather than morose ; can easily be moved to a sudden tear, or surprised into a broad laugh ; but he loathes sentiment, and has no turn for light pleasantry. He is a boon companion, if you allow him to have his humour, and to talk about himself ; and he will stand by a friend in a quarrel, with life and purse, however soundly he may be cudgelled.

In this last respect, to tell the truth, he has a propensity to be somewhat too ready. He is a busy-minded personage, who thinks not merely for himself and family, but for all the country round, and is most generously disposed to be everybody's champion. He is continually volunteering his services to settle his neighbour's affairs, and takes it in great dudgeon if they engage in any matter of consequence without asking his advice; though he seldom engages in any friendly office of the kind without finishing by getting into a squabble with all parties, and then railing bitterly at their ingratitude. He unluckily took lessons in his youth in the noble science of defence, and having accomplished himself in the use of his limbs and his weapons, and become a perfect master at boxing and cudgel-play, he has had a troublesome life of it ever since. He cannot hear of a quarrel between the most distant of his neighbours, but he begins incontinently to fumble with the head of his cudgel, and consider whether his interest or honour does not require that he should meddle in the broil. Indeed, he has extended his relations of pride and policy so completely over the whole country, that no event can take place without infringing some of his finely-spun rights and dignities. Couched in his little domain, with these filaments stretching forth in every direction, he is like some choleric, bottle-bellied old spider, who has woven his web over a whole chamber, so that a fly cannot buzz, nor a breeze blow, without startling his repose, and causing him to sally forth wrathfully from his den.

Though really a good-hearted, good-tempered old fellow at bottom, yet he is singularly fond of being in the midst of contention. It is one of his peculiarities, however, that he only relishes the beginning of an affray; he always goes into a fight with alacrity, but comes out of it grumbling even when victorious; and though no one fights with more obstinacy to carry a contested point, yet, when the battle is over, and he comes to the reconciliation, he is so much taken up with the mere shaking of hands, that he is apt to let his antagonist pocket all that they have been quarrelling about. It is not, therefore, fighting that he ought so much to be on his guard against, as making friends. It is difficult to cudgel him out of a farthing; but put him in a good humour, and you may bargain him out of all the money in his pocket. He is like a stout ship, which will weather the roughest storm uninjured, but roll its masts overboard in the succeeding calm.

He is a little fond of playing the magnifico abroad; of pulling out a long purse; flinging his money bravely about at boxing matches, horse races, cock fights, and carrying a high head among 'gentlemen of the fancy'; but immediately after one of these fits of extravagance, he will be taken with violent qualms of economy; stop short at the most trivial expenditure; talk desperately of being ruined and brought upon the parish; and, in such moods, will not pay the smallest tradesman's bill, without violent altercation. He is in fact the most punctual and discontented paymaster in the world; drawing his coin out of his breeches pocket with infinite reluctance; paying to the uttermost farthing, but accompanying every guinea with a growl.

With all his talk of economy, however, he is a bountiful provider, and a hospitable housekeeper. His economy is of a whimsical kind, its chief object being to devise how he may afford to be extravagant; for he will begrudge himself a beefsteak and pint of port one day, that he may roast an ox whole, broach a hogshead of ale, and treat all his neighbours on the next.

His domestic establishment is enormously expensive: not so much from any great outward parade, as from the great consumption of solid beef and pudding; the vast number of followers he feeds and clothes; and his singular disposition to pay hugely for small services. He is a most kind and indulgent master, and, provided his servants humour his peculiarities, flatter his vanity a little now and then, and do not peculate grossly on him before his face, they may manage him to perfection. Everything that lives on him seems to thrive and grow fat. His house-servants are well paid, and pampered, and have little to do. His horses are sleek and lazy, and prance slowly before his state carriage; and his house-dogs sleep quietly about the door, and will hardly bark at a house-breaker.

His family mansion is an old castellated manor-house, grey with age, and of a most venerable, though weather-beaten appearance. It has been built upon no regular plan, but is a vast accumulation of parts, erected in various tastes and ages. The centre bears evident traces of Saxon architecture, and is as solid as ponderous stone and old English oak can make it. Like all the relics of that style, it is full of obscure passages, intricate mazes, and dusky chambers; and though these have been partially lighted up in modern days, yet there are many places where you must still grope in the dark. Additions have been made to the original edifice from time to time, and great alterations have taken place; towers and battlements have been erected during wars and tumults; wings built in time of peace; and outhouses, lodges, and offices, run up according to the whim or convenience of different generations, until it has become one of the most spacious, rambling tenements imaginable. An entire wing is taken up with the family chapel; a reverend pile, that must once have been exceedingly sumptuous, and, indeed, in spite of having been altered and simplified at various periods, has still a look of solemn religious pomp. Its walls within are storied with the monuments of John's ancestors; and it is snugly fitted up with soft cushions and well-lined chairs, where such of his family as are inclined to church services, may doze comfortably in the discharge of their duties.

To keep up this chapel has cost John much money; but he is stanch in his religion, and piqued in his zeal, from the circumstance that many dissenting chapels have been erected in his vicinity, and several of his neighbours, with whom he has had quarrels, are strong papists.

To do the duties of the chapel he maintains, at a large expense, a pious and portly family chaplain. He is a most learned and decorous personage, and a truly well-bred Christian, who always backs the old gentleman in his opinions, winks discreetly at his little peccadilloes, rebukes the children when refractory, and is of great use in exhorting the tenants to read their bibles, say their prayers, and, above all, to pay their rents punctually, and without grumbling.

The family apartments are in a very antiquated taste, somewhat heavy, and often inconvenient, but full of the solemn magnificence of former times; fitted up with rich, though faded tapestry, unwieldy furniture, and loads of massy gorgeous old plate.

The vast fireplaces, ample kitchens, extensive cellars, and sumptuous banqueting-halls,—all speak of the roaring hospitality of days of yore, of which the modern festivity at the manor-house is but a shadow. There are, however, complete suites of rooms apparently deserted and time-worn; and towers and turrets that are tottering to decay; so that in high winds there is danger of their tumbling about the ears of the household.

John has frequently been advised to have the old edifice thoroughly overhauled; and to have some of the useless parts pulled down, and the others strengthened with their materials; but the old gentleman always grows testy on this subject. He swears the house is an excellent house—that it is tight and weather-proof, and not to be shaken by tempests—that it has stood for several hundred years, and, therefore, is not likely to tumble down now—that as to its being inconvenient, his family is accustomed to the inconveniences, and would not be comfortable without them—that as to its unwieldy size and irregular construction, these result from its being the growth of centuries, and being improved by the wisdom of every generation —that an old family, like his, requires a large house to dwell in; new, upstart families may live in modern cottages and snug boxes; but an old English family should inhabit an old English manor-house. If you point out any part of the building as superfluous, he insists that it is material to the strength or decoration of the rest, and the harmony of the whole; and swears that the parts are so built into each other, that if you pull down one, you run the risk of having the whole about your ears.

The secret of the matter is, that John has a great disposition to protect and patronize. He thinks it indispensable to the dignity of an ancient and honourable family, to be bounteous in its appointments, and to be eaten up by dependants; and so, partly from pride and partly from kind-heartedness, he makes it a rule always to give shelter and maintenance to his superannuated servants.

The consequence is, that, like many other venerable family establishments, his manor is encumbered by old retainers whom he cannot turn off, and an old style which he cannot lay down. His mansion is like a great hospital of invalids, and, with all its magnitude, is not a whit too large for its inhabitants. Not a nook or corner but is of use in housing some useless personage. Groups of veteran beef-eaters, gouty pensioners, and retired heroes of the buttery and the larder, are seen lolling about its walls, crawling over its lawns, dozing under its trees, or sunning themselves upon the benches at its doors. Every office and outhouse is garrisoned by these supernumeraries and their families; for they are amazingly prolific, and when they die off, are sure to leave John a legacy of hungry mouths to be provided for. A mattock cannot be struck against the most mouldering tumble-down tower, but out pops, from some cranny or loop-hole, the grey pate of some superannuated hanger-on, who has lived at John's expense all his life, and makes the most grievous outcry at their pulling down the roof from over the head of a worn-out servant of the family. This is an appeal that John's honest heart never can withstand; so that a man, who has faithfully eaten his beef and pudding all his life, is sure to be rewarded with a pipe and tankard in his old days.

A great part of his park, also, is turned into paddocks, where his broken-down chargers are turned loose to graze undisturbed for the remainder of their existence—a worthy example of grateful recollection, which if some of his neighbours were to imitate, would not be to their discredit. Indeed, it is one of his great pleasures to point out these old steeds to his visitors, to dwell on their good qualities, extol their past services, and boast, with some little vainglory, of the perilous adventures and hardy exploits through which they have carried him.

He is given, however, to indulge his veneration for family usages, and family encumbrances, to a whimsical extent. His manor is infested by gangs of gipsies; yet he will not suffer them to be driven off, because they have infested the place time out of mind, and been regular poachers upon every generation of the family. He will scarcely permit a dry branch to be lopped from the great trees that surround the house, lest it should molest the rooks, that have bred there for centuries. Owls have taken possession of the dovecote; but they are hereditary owls, and must not be disturbed. Swallows have nearly choked up every chimney with their nests; martins build in every frieze and cornice; crows flutter about the towers, and perch on every weathercock; and old grey-headed rats may be seen in every quarter of the house, running in and out of their holes undauntedly in broad daylight. In short, John has such a reverence for everything that has been long in the family, that he will not hear even of abuses being reformed, because they are good old family abuses.

All these whims and habits have concurred woefully to drain the old gentleman's purse; and as he prides himself on punctuality in money matters, and wishes to maintain his credit in the neighbourhood, they have caused him great perplexity in meeting his engagements. This, too, has been increased, by the altercations and heart-burnings which are continually taking place in his family. His children have been brought up to different callings, and are of different ways of thinking; and as they have always been allowed to speak their minds freely, they do not fail to exercise the privilege most clamorously in the present posture of his affairs. Some stand up for the honour of the race, and are clear that the old establishment should be kept up in all its state, whatever may be the cost; others, who are more prudent and considerate, entreat the old gentleman to retrench his expenses, and to put his whole system of housekeeping on a more moderate footing. He has, indeed, at times, seemed inclined to listen to their opinions, but their wholesome advice has been completely defeated by the obstreperous conduct of one of his sons. This is a noisy, rattle-pated fellow, of rather low habits, who neglects his business to frequent ale-houses—is the orator of village clubs, and a complete oracle among the poorest of his father's tenants. No sooner does he hear any of his brothers mention reform or retrenchment, than up he jumps, takes the words out of their mouths, and roars out for an overturn. When his tongue is once going nothing can stop it. He rants about the room; hectors the old man about his spendthrift practices; ridicules his tastes and pursuits; insists that he shall turn the old servants out of doors; give the broken-down horses to the hounds; send the fat chaplain packing, and take a field-preacher in his place—nay, that the whole family mansion shall be levelled with the ground, and a plain one of brick and mortar built in its place. He rails at every social entertainment and family festivity, and skulks away growling to the ale-house whenever an equipage drives up to the door. Though constantly complaining of the emptiness of his purse, yet he scruples not to spend all his pocket-money in these tavern convocations, and even runs up scores for the liquor over which he preaches about his father's extravagance.

It may be readily imagined how little such thwarting agrees with the old cavalier's fiery temperament. He has become so irritable, from repeated crossings, that the mere mention of retrenchment or reform is a signal for a brawl between him and the tavern oracle. As the latter is too sturdy and refractory for paternal discipline, having grown out of all fear of the cudgel, they have frequent scenes of wordy warfare, which at times run so high, that John is fain to call in the aid of his son Tom, an officer who has served abroad, but is at present living at home, on half-pay. This last is sure to stand by the old gentleman, right or wrong; likes nothing so much as a racketing, roistering life; and is ready at a wink or nod, to out sabre, and flourish it over the orator's head, if he dares to array himself against paternal authority.

These family dissensions, as usual, have got

abroad, and are rare food for scandal in John's neighbourhood. People begin to look wise, and shake their heads, whenever his affairs are mentioned. They all 'hope that matters are not so bad with him as represented; but when a man's own children begin to rail at his extravagance, things must be badly managed. They understand he is mortgaged over head and ears, and is continually dabbling with money-lenders. He is certainly an open-handed old gentleman, but they fear he has lived too fast; indeed, they never knew any good come of this fondness for hunting, racing, revelling, and prize-fighting. In short, Mr. Bull's estate is a very fine one, and has been in the family a long while; but, for all that, they have known many finer estates come to the hammer.'

What is worst of all, is the effect which these pecuniary embarrassments and domestic feuds have had on the poor man himself. Instead of that jolly round corporation, and smug rosy face, which he used to present, he has of late become as shrivelled and shrunk as a frost-bitten apple. His scarlet gold-laced waistcoat, which bellied out so bravely in those prosperous days when he sailed before the wind, now hangs loosely about him like a mainsail in a calm. His leather breeches are all in folds and wrinkles; and apparently have much ado to hold up the boots that yawn on both sides of his once sturdy legs.

Instead of strutting about, as formerly, with his three-cornered hat on one side; flourishing his cudgel, and bringing it down every moment with a hearty thump upon the ground; looking every one sturdily in the face, and trolling out a stave of a catch or a drinking song; he now goes about whistling thoughtfully to himself, with his head drooping down, his cudgel tucked under his arm, and his hands thrust to the bottom of his breeches pockets, which are evidently empty.

Such is the plight of honest John Bull at present; yet for all this the old fellow's spirit is as tall and as gallant as ever. If you drop the least expression of sympathy or concern, he takes fire in an instant; swears that he is the richest and stoutest fellow in the country; talks of laying out large sums to adorn his house or buy another estate; and with a valiant swagger and grasping of his cudgel, longs exceedingly to have another bout at quarter-staff.

Though there may be something rather whimsical in all this, yet I confess I cannot look upon John's situation, without strong feelings of interest. With all his odd humours and obstinate prejudices, he is a sterling-hearted old blade. He may not be so wonderfully fine a fellow as he thinks himself, but he is at least twice as good as his neighbours represent him. His virtues are all his own; all plain, homebred, and unaffected. His very faults smack of the raciness of his good qualities. His extravagance savours of his generosity; his quarrelsomeness of his courage; his credulity of his open faith; his vanity of his pride; and his bluntness of his sincerity. They are all the redundancies of a rich and liberal character. He is like his own oak; rough without, but sound and solid within; whose bark abounds with excrescences in proportion to the growth and grandeur of the timber; and whose branches make a fearful groaning and murmuring in the least storm, from their very magnitude and luxuriance. There is something, too, in the appearance of his old family mansion that is extremely poetical and picturesque; and, as long as it can be rendered comfortably habitable, I should almost tremble to see it meddled with, during the present conflict of tastes and opinions. Some of his advisers are no doubt good architects, that might be of service; but many, I fear, are mere levellers, who, when they had once got to work with their mattocks on this venerable edifice, would never stop until they had brought it to the ground, and perhaps buried themselves among the ruins. All that I wish is, that John's present troubles may teach him more prudence in future. That he may cease to distress his mind about other people's affairs; that he may give up the fruitless attempt to promote the good of his neighbours, and the peace and happiness of the world, by dint of the cudgel; that he may remain quietly at home; gradually get his house into repair; cultivate his rich estate according to his fancy; husband his income—if he thinks proper; bring his unruly children into order—if he can; renew the jovial scenes of ancient prosperity; and long enjoy, on his paternal lands, a green, an honourable, and a merry old age.

JAMES HENRY LEIGH HUNT

1784–1859

FICTION AND MATTER OF FACT

'There are more things in heaven and earth, Horatio,
Than are dreamt of in your philosophy.'—SHAKESPEARE.

A PASSION for these two things is supposed to be incompatible. It is certainly not; and the supposition is founded on an ignorance of the nature of the human mind, and the very sympathies of the two strangers. Mathematical truth is not the only truth in the world. An unpoetical logician is not the only philosopher. Locke had no taste for fiction: he thought Blackmore as great a genius as Homer; but this was a conclusion he could never have come to, if he had known his premises. Newton considered poetry as on a par with 'ingenious nonsense'; which was an error as great as if he had ranked himself with Tom D'Urfey, or made the apex of a triangle equal to the base of it. Newton has had good for evil returned him by 'a greater than himself'; for the eye of imagination sees farther than the glasses of astronomy. I should say that the poets had praised their scorner too much, illustrious as he is, if it were not delightful to see that there is at least one faculty in the world which knows how to do justice to all the rest. Of all the universal privileges of poetry, this is one of the most peculiar, and marks her for what she is. The mathematician, the schoolman, the wit, the statesman, and the soldier, may all be blind to the merits of poetry, and of one another; but the poet, by the privilege which he possesses of recognizing every species of truth, is aware of the merits of mathematics, of learning, of wit, of politics, and of generalship. He is great in his own art, and he is great in his appreciation of that of others. And this is most remarkable in proportion as he is a *poetical* poet—a high lover of fiction. Milton brought the visible and the invisible together 'on the top of Fiesole', to pay homage to Galileo; and the Tuscan deserved it, for he had an insight into the world of imagination. I cannot but fancy the shade of Newton blushing to reflect that, among the many things which he professed to *know not*, poetry was omitted, of which he knew nothing. Great as he was, he indeed saw nothing in the face of nature but its lines and colours; not the lines and colours of passion and sentiment included, but only squares and their distances, and the anatomy of the rainbow. He thought the earth a glorious planet; he knew it better than any one else, in its connexion with other planets; and yet half the beauty of them all, that which sympathy bestows and imagination colours, was to him a blank. He took space to be the sensorium of the Deity (so noble a fancy could be struck out of the involuntary encounter between his intense sense of a mystery and the imagination he despised!) and yet this very fancy was but an escape from the horror of a vacuum, and a substitution of the mere consciousness of existence for the thoughts and images with which a poet would have accompanied it. He imagined the form of the house, and the presence of the builder; but the life and the variety, the paintings, the imagery, and the music,—the loves and the joys, the whole riches of the place, the whole riches in the distance, the creations heaped upon creation, and the particular as well as aggregate consciousness of all this in the great mind of whose presence he was conscious,—to all this his want of imagination rendered him insensible. The *Fairy Queen* was to him a trifle; the dreams of Shakespeare 'ingenious nonsense'. But courts were something, and so were the fashions there. When the name of the Deity was mentioned, he took off his hat![1]

There are two worlds; the world that we can measure with line and rule, and the world that we feel with our hearts and imaginations. To be sensible of the truth of only one of these, is to know truth but by halves. Milton said, that he 'dared be known to think Spenser a better teacher than Scotus or Aquinas'. He did not say than Plato or Pythagoras, who understood the two spheres within our reach. Both of these, and Milton himself, were as great lovers of physical and political truth as any men; but they knew that it was not all; they felt much beyond, and they

[1] Sir Isaac Newton rejected the doctrine of the Trinity, because he could not reconcile it to his arithmetic. The 'French Prophets', not being cognizable by the mathematics, were very near having him for a proselyte. His strength and his weakness were hardly equal in this distinction: but one of them, at least, serves to show how more than conventional his understanding was inclined to be, when taken out of its only faculty; and I do not presume to think that any criticism of mine can be thought even invidious against it. I do not deny the sun, because I deny that the sun has a right to deny the universe. I am writing upon Matter of Fact now myself, and Matter of Fact will have me say what I do.

made experiments upon more. It is doubted by the critics, whether Chaucer's delight in the handling of fictions, or in the detection and scrutiny of a piece of truth, was the greater. Chaucer was a conscientious Reformer, which is a man who has a passion for truth; and so was Milton. So, in his way, was Ariosto himself, and indeed most great poets; part of the very perfection of their art, which is verisimilitude, being closely connected with their sense of truth in all things. But it is not necessary to be great, in order to possess a reasonable variety of perception. That nobody may despair of being able to indulge the two passions together, I can answer for them by my own experience. I can pass, with as much pleasure as ever, from the reading of one of Hume's Essays to that of the *Arabian Nights*, and vice versa; and I think, the longer I live, the closer, if possible, will the union grow.[1] The roads are found to approach nearer, in proportion as we advance upon either; and they both terminate in the same prospect.

I am far from meaning that there is nothing real in either road. The path of matter of fact is as solid as ever; but they who do not see the reality of the other, keep but a blind and prone beating upon their own surface. To drop the metaphor, matter of fact is our perception of the grosser and

[1] It has done so. This Essay was written in the year 1824; and within the last few years I have had the pleasure of reading (besides poets) three different histories of Philosophy, histories of Rome and England, some of the philosophy of Hume himself, much of Abraham Tucker's, all the novels of Fielding and Smollett (including *Gil Blas*), Mr. Lane's *Arabian Nights, Don Quixote*, a heap of English Memoirs. and the whole of the romances of Mrs. Radcliffe.

more external shapes of truth; fiction represents the residuum and the mystery. To love matter of fact is to have a lively sense of the visible and immediate; to love fiction is to have as lively a sense of the possible and the remote. Now these two senses, if they exist at all, are of necessity as real, the one as the other. The only proof of either is in our perception. To a blind man, the most visible colours no more exist, than the hues of a fairy tale to a man destitute of fancy. To a man of fancy, who sheds tears over a tale, the chair in which he sits has no truer existence in its way, than the story that moves him. His being touched is his proof in both instances.

But, says the mechanical understanding, modern discoveries have acquainted us with the cause of lightning and thunder, the nature of optical delusions, and fifty other apparent wonders; and therefore there is no more to be feigned about them. Fancy has done with them, at least with their causes; and witches and will-o'-the-wisps being abolished, poetry is at a stand. The strong glass of science has put an end to the assumptions of fiction.

This is a favourite remark with a pretty numerous set of writers; and it is a very desperate one. It looks like reasoning; and by a singular exercise of the very faculty which it asserts the death of, many persons take the look of an argument for the proof of it. Certainly, no observation can militate more strongly against existing matter of fact; and this is the reason why it is made. The mechanical writers of verse find that it is no longer so easy to be taken for poets, because fancy and imagination are more than usually in request: so they would have their revenge, by asserting, that poetry is no longer to be written.

When an understanding of this description is told, that thunder is caused by a collision of clouds, and that lightning is a well-known result of electricity, there may be an end, if he pleases, of his poetry with him. He may, if he thinks fit, or if he cannot help it, no longer see anything in the lightning but the escape of a subtle fluid, or hear anything more noble in the thunder than the crack of a bladder of water. Much good may his ignorance do him. But it is not so with understandings of a loftier or a more popular kind. The wonder of children, and the lofty speculations of the wise, meet alike on a point, higher than he can attain to, and look over the threshold of the world. Mechanical knowledge is a great and a glorious tool in the hands of man, and will change the globe. But it will still leave untouched the invisible sphere above and about us; still leave us all the great and all the gentle objects of poetry,—the heavens and the human heart, the regions of genii and fairies, the fanciful or passionate images that come to us from the seas, and from the flowers, and all that we behold.

It is, in fact, remarkable, that the growth of science, and the re-appearance of a more poetical kind of poetry, have accompanied one another. Whatever may be the difference of opinion as to the extent to which our modern poets have carried their success, their inclinations cannot be doubted. How is it that poetical impulse has taken this turn in a generation pronounced to be so mechanical? Whence has arisen among us this exceeding fondness for the fictions of the East, for solitary and fanciful reveries, for the wild taste of the Germans (themselves more scientific and wild than ever), and even for a new and more primitive use of the old Pagan mythology, so long and so mechanically abused by the Chloes and Venuses of the French? Politics may be thought a very unlikely cause for poetry, and it is so with mere politicians; yet politics, pushed further than common, have been the cause of the new and greater impetus given to the sympathies of imagination; for the more we know of any one ground of knowledge, the further we see into the general domains of intellect, if we are not mere slaves of the soil. A little philosophy, says Bacon, takes men away from religion; a greater brings them round to it. This is the case with the reasoning faculty and poetry. We reason to a certain point, and are content with the discoveries of second causes. We reason further, and find ourselves in the same airy depths as of old. The imagination recognizes its ancient field, and begins ranging about at will, doubly bent upon liberty, because of the trammels with which it has been threatened.

Take the following Apologue.—During a wonderful period of the world, the kings of the earth leagued themselves together to destroy all opposition; to root out, if they could, the very thoughts of mankind. Inquisition was made for blood. The ears of the grovelling lay in wait for every murmur. On a sudden, during this great hour of danger, there arose in a hundred parts of the world, a cry, to which the cry of the Blatant Beast was a whisper. It proceeded from the wonderful multiplication of an extraordinary creature, which had already turned the cheeks of the tyrants pallid. It groaned and it grew loud: it spoke with a hundred tongues; it grew fervidly on the ear, like the noise of millions of wheels. And the sound of millions of wheels was in it, together with other marvellous and awful noises. There was the sharpening of swords, the braying of trumpets, the neighing of war-horses, the laughter of solemn voices, the rushing by of lights, the movement of impatient feet, a tread as if the world were coming. And ever and anon there were pauses with 'a still small voice', which made a trembling in the night time. But still the glowing sound of the wheels renewed itself; gathering early towards the morning. And when you came up to one of these creatures, you saw with fear and reverence, its mighty conformation, being like wheels indeed, and a great vapour. And ever and anon the vapour boiled, and the wheels went rolling, and the creature threw out of its mouth visible words, that fell into the air by millions, and spoke to the uttermost parts of the earth. And the nations (for it was a loving though a fearful creature) fed upon its words like the air they breathed: and the monarchs paused, for they knew their masters.

This is Printing by Steam.—It will be said that it is an allegory, and that all allegories are but fictions, and flat ones. I am far from producing it as a specimen of the poetical power now in existence. Allegory itself is out of fashion, though it was a favourite exercise of our old poets when the public were familiar with shows and spectacles. But allegory is the readiest shape into which imagination can turn a thing mechanical; and in the one before us is contained the mechanical truth and the spiritual truth of that very matter of fact thing called a Printing Press: each of them as true as the other, or neither could take place. A business of screws and iron wheels is, or appears to be, a very commonplace matter; but not so the will of the hand that sets them in motion; not so the operations of the mind that directs them what to utter. We are satisfied respecting the one by science; but what is it that renders us sensible of the wonders of the other, and their connexion with the great mysteries of nature? Thought—Fancy—*Imagination.* What signifies to her the talk about electricity, and suction, and gravitation, and alembics, and fifty other mechanical operations of the marvellous? This is but the bone and muscle of wonder. Soul, and not body, is her pursuit; the first cause, not the second; the whole effect, not a part of it; the will, the invention, the marvel itself. As long as this lies hidden, she still fancies what agents for it she pleases. The science of atmospherical phenomena hinders not her angels from 'playing in the plighted clouds'. The analysis of a bottle of salt water does not prevent her from 'taking the wings of the morning, and remaining in the uttermost parts of the sea'. You must prove to her first, that you understand the simple elements, when decomposed; the reason that brings them together; the power that puts them in action; the relations which they have to a thousand things besides ourselves and our wants; the necessity of all this perpetual motion; the understanding that looks out of the eye; love, joy, sorrow, death and life, the future, the universe, the whole invisible abyss. Till you know all this, and can plant the dry sticks of your reasons, as trophies of possession, in every quarter of space, how shall you oust her from her dominion?

SHAKESPEARE'S BIRTHDAY

NEXT Friday, making the proper allowance of twelve days from the 23rd of April, according to the change of the Style, is the birthday of Shakespeare. Pleasant thoughts must be associated with him in everything. If he is not to be born in April, he must be born in May. Nature will have him with her on her blithest holidays, like her favourite lover.

O thou divine human creature,—greater name than even divine poet or divine philosopher,—and yet thou wast all three,—a very spring and vernal abundance of all fair and noble things is to be found in thy productions! They are truly a second nature. We walk in them, with whatever society we please; either with men, or fair women, or circling spirits, or with none but the whispering airs and leaves. Thou makest worlds of green trees and gentle natures for us, in thy forests of Arden, and thy courtly retirements of Navarre. Thou bringest us among the holiday lasses on the green sward; layest us to sleep among fairies in the bowers of midsummer; wakest us with the song of the lark and the silver-sweet voices of lovers; bringest more music to our ears, both from earth and from the planets; anon settest us upon enchanted islands, where it welcomes us again, from the touching of invisible instruments; and after all, restorest us to our still desired haven, the arms of humanity. Whether grieving us or making us glad, thou makest us kinder and happier. The tears which thou fetchest down are like the rains of April, softening the times that come after them. Thy smiles are those of the month of love, the more blessed and universal for the tears.

The birthdays of such men as Shakespeare ought to be kept, in common gratitude and affection, like those of relations whom we love. He has said, in a line full of him, that

> One touch of nature makes the whole world kin.

How near does he become to us with his thousand touches! The lustre and utility of intellectual power is so increasing in the eyes of the world, that we do not despair of seeing the time when his birthday will be a subject of public rejoicing; when the regular feast will be served up in tavern and dwelling-house, the bust crowned with laurel, and the theatres sparkle with illuminations. The town is lucky enough once more to have a manager who is an enthusiast. If Mr. Elliston would light up the front of his theatre next Friday with the name of Shakespeare, we would warrant him a call from the pit, and whole shouts of acknowledgement.

In the meantime it is in the power of every admirer of Shakespeare to honour the day privately. Rich or poor, busy or at leisure, all may do it. The busiest finds time to eat his dinner, and may pitch one considerate glass of wine down his throat. The poorest may call him to mind, and drink his memory in honest water. We had mechanically written health, as if he were alive. So he is in spirit;—and the spirit of such a writer is so constantly with us, that it would be a good thing, a judicious extravagance, a contemplative piece of jollity, to drink his health instead of his memory. But this, we fear, should be an impulse. We must content ourselves with having felt it here, and drinking it in imagination. To act upon it, as a proposal of the day before yesterday, might be too much like getting up an extempore gesture, or practising an unspeakable satisfaction.

An outline, however, may be drawn of the manner in which such a birthday might be spent. The tone and colouring would be filled up, of course, according to the taste of the parties. If any of our readers, then, have leisure as well as inclination to devote a day to the memory of Shakespeare, we would advise them, in the first place, to walk out, whether alone or in company, and enjoy during the morning as much as possible of those beauties of nature of which he has left us such exquisite pictures. They would take a volume of him in their hands, the most suitable to the occasion; not to hold themselves bound to sit down and read it, nor even to refer to it, if the original work of nature should occupy them too much; but to read it, if they read anything; and to feel that Shakespeare was with them substantially as well as spiritually; —that they had him with them under their arm. There is another thought connected with his presence, which may render the Londoner's walk the more interesting. Shakespeare had neither the vanity which induces a man to be disgusted with what everybody can enjoy; nor on the other hand the involuntary self-degradation which renders us incapable of enjoying what is abased by our own familiarity of acquaintanceship. About the metropolis, therefore, there is perhaps not a single rural spot, any more than about Stratford-upon-Avon, which he has not himself enjoyed. The south side of London was the one nearest his theatre. Hyde Park was then, as it is now, one of the fashionable promenades. Richmond also was in high pride of estimation. At Greenwich

Elizabeth held her court, and walked abroad amid the gallant service of the Sidneys and Raleighs. And Hampstead and Highgate, with the country about them, were as they have been ever since, the favourite resort of the lovers of natural productions. Nay, without repeating what we said in a former number about the Mermaid in Cornhill, the Devil Tavern in Fleet Street, the Boar's Head in East-cheap, and other town associations with Shake-speare, the reader who cannot get out of London on his birthday, and who has the luck to be hard at work in Chancery Lane or the Borough, may be pretty certain that Shakespeare has admired the fields and the May flowers there; for the fields were close to the latter, perhaps came up to the very walls of the theatre; and the suburban mansion and gardens of his friend Lord Southamp-ton occupied the spot now called Southampton Buildings. It was really a country neighbourhood. The Old Bourne (Holborn) ran by, with a bridge over it; and Gray's Inn was an academic bower in the fields.

The dinner does not much signify. The sparest or the most abundant will equally suit the various fortunes of the great poet; only it will be as well for those who can afford wine to pledge Falstaff in a cup of 'sherris sack', which seems to have been a sort of sherry negus. After dinner Shakespeare's volumes will come well on the table; lying among the dessert like laurels, where there is one, and supplying it where there is not. Instead of songs, the persons present may be called upon for scenes. But no stress need be laid on this proposition, if they do not like to read out loud. The pleasure of the day should be as much at liberty as possible; and if the company prefer conversation, it will not be very easy for them to touch upon any subjects which Shakespeare shall not have touched upon also. If the enthusiasm is in high taste, the ladies should be crowned with violets, which (next to the roses of their lips) seem to have been his favourite flower. After tea should come singing and music, especially the songs which Arne set from his plays, and the ballad of 'Thou soft-flowing Avon'. If an engraving or bust of him could occupy the principal place in the room, it would look like the 'present deity' of the occasion; and we have known a very pleasant effect produced by everybody's bringing some quotation applicable to him from his works, and laying it before his image, to be read in the course of the evening.

The Editor would have dilated on these matters, not so much to recommend what the enthusiasm of the moment will suggest, as to enjoy them with the reader, and have his company, as it were, at an imaginary meeting. But he is too unwell now to write much, and should have taken the liberty of compiling almost the whole of his present number, could he have denied himself the pleasure of saying a few words on so happy an occasion.

THOMAS DE QUINCEY

1785–1859

ON THE KNOCKING AT THE GATE IN *MACBETH*

FROM my boyish days I had always felt a great perplexity on one point in *Macbeth*. It was this: the knocking at the gate, which succeeds to the murder of Duncan, produced to my feelings an effect for which I never could account. The effect was, that it reflected back upon the murderer a peculiar awfulness and a depth of solemnity; yet, however obstinately I endeavoured with my understanding to comprehend this, for many years I never could see *why* it should produce such an effect.

Here I pause for one moment, to exhort the reader never to pay any attention to his understanding, when it stands in opposition to any other faculty of his mind. The mere understanding, however useful and indispensable, is the meanest faculty in the human mind, and the most to be distrusted; and yet the great majority of people trust to nothing else, which may do for ordinary life, but not for philosophical purposes. Of this out of ten thousand instances that I might produce, I will cite one. Ask of any person whatsoever, who is not previously prepared for the demand by a knowledge of the perspective, to draw in the rudest way the commonest appearance which depends upon the laws of that science; as, for instance, to represent the effect of two walls standing at right angles to each other, or the appearance of the houses on each side of a street, as seen by a person looking down the street from one extremity. Now in all cases, unless the person has happened to observe in pictures how it is that artists produce these effects, he will be utterly unable to make the smallest approximation to it. Yet why? For he has actually seen the effect every day of his life. The reason is—that he allows his understanding to overrule his eyes. His understanding, which includes no intuitive knowledge of the laws of vision, can furnish him with no reason why a line which is known and can be proved to be a horizontal line, should not *appear* a horizontal line; a line that made any angle with the perpendicular, less than a right angle, would seem to him to indicate that his houses were all tumbling down together. Accordingly, he makes the line of his houses a horizontal line, and fails, of course, to produce the effect demanded. Here, then, is one instance out of many, in which not only the understanding is allowed to overrule the eyes, but where the understanding is positively allowed to obliterate the eyes, as it were; for not only does the man believe the evidence of his understanding in opposition to that of his eyes, but (what is monstrous!) the idiot is not aware that his eyes ever gave such evidence. He does not know that he has seen (and therefore *quoad* his consciousness has *not* seen) that which he *has* seen every day of his life.

But to return from this digression, my understanding could furnish no reason why the knocking at the gate in *Macbeth* should produce any effect, direct or reflected. In fact, my understanding said positively that it could *not* produce any effect. But I knew better; I felt that it did; and I waited and clung to the problem until further knowledge should enable me to solve it. At length, in 1812, Mr. Williams made his début on the stage of Ratcliffe Highway, and executed those unparalleled murders which have procured for him such a brilliant and undying reputation. On which murders, by the way, I must observe, that in one respect they have had an ill effect, by making the connoisseur in murder very fastidious in his taste, and dissatisfied by anything that has been since done in that line. All other murders look pale by the deep crimson of his; and, as an amateur once said to me in a querulous tone, 'There has been absolutely nothing *doing* since his time, or nothing that 's worth speaking of.' But this is wrong; for it is unreasonable to expect all men to be great artists, and born with the genius of Mr. Williams. Now it will be remembered, that in the first of these murders (that of the Marrs), the same incident (of a knocking at the door, soon after the work of extermination was complete) did actually occur, which the genius of Shakespeare has invented; and all good judges, and the most eminent dilettanti, acknowledged the felicity of Shakespeare's suggestion, as soon as it was actually realized. Here, then, was a fresh proof that I was right in relying on my own feeling, in opposition to my understanding; and I again set myself to study the problem; at length I solved it to my own satisfaction, and my solution is this. Murder, in ordinary cases, where the sympathy is wholly directed to the case of the murdered person, is an incident of coarse and vulgar horror; and for this reason, that it flings the interest exclusively upon the natural but ignoble instinct by which we cleave to life; an instinct which, as being indispensable to the primal law of self-preservation, is the same in kind (though different in degree) amongst all living creatures: this instinct, therefore, because it annihilates all distinctions, and degrades the greatest of men to the level of 'the poor beetle that we tread on', exhibits human nature in its most abject and humiliating attitude. Such an attitude would little suit the purposes of the poet. What then must he do? He must throw the interest on the murderer. Our sympathy must be with *him* (of course I mean a sympathy of comprehension, a sympathy by which we enter into his feelings, and are made to understand them,—not a sympathy of pity or approbation[1]). In the murdered person, all strife of thought, all flux and reflux of passion and of purpose, are crushed by one overwhelming panic; the fear of instant death smites him 'with its petrific mace'. But in the murderer, such a murderer as a poet will condescend to, there must be raging some great storm of passion—jealousy, ambition, vengeance, hatred—which will create a hell within him; and into this hell we are to look.

[1] It seems almost ludicrous to guard and explain my use of a word, in a situation where it would naturally explain itself. But it has become necessary to do so, in consequence of the unscholarlike use of the word sympathy, at present so general, by which, instead of taking it in its proper sense, as the act of reproducing in our minds the feelings of another, whether for hatred, indignation, love, pity, or approbation, it is made a mere synonym of the word *pity*; and hence, instead of saying 'sympathy *with* another', many writers adopt the monstrous barbarism of 'sympathy *for* another'.

In *Macbeth*, for the sake of gratifying his own enormous and teeming faculty of creation, Shakespeare has introduced two murderers: and, as usual in his hands, they are remarkably discriminated: but, though in Macbeth the strife of mind is greater than in his wife, the tiger spirit not so awake, and his feelings caught chiefly by contagion from her,—yet, as both were finally involved in the guilt of murder, the murderous mind of necessity is finally to be presumed in both. This was to be expressed; and on its own account, as well as to make it a more proportionable antagonist to the unoffending nature of their victim, 'the gracious Duncan,' and adequately to expound 'the deep damnation of his taking off', this was to be expressed with peculiar energy. We were to be made to feel that the human nature, i.e. the divine nature of love and mercy, spread through the hearts of all creatures, and seldom utterly withdrawn from man—was gone, vanished, extinct; and that the fiendish nature had taken its place. And, as this effect is marvellously accomplished in the *dialogues* and *soliloquies* themselves, so it is finally consummated by the expedient under consideration; and it is to this that I now solicit the reader's attention. If the reader has ever witnessed a wife, daughter, or sister in a fainting-fit, he may chance to have observed that the most affecting moment in such a spectacle is *that* in which a sigh and a stirring announce the recommencement of suspended life. Or, if the reader has ever been present in a vast metropolis, on the day when some great national idol was carried in funeral pomp to his grave, and chancing to walk near the course through which it passed, has felt powerfully in the silence and desertion of the streets, and in the stagnation of ordinary business, the deep interest which at that moment was possessing the heart of man—if all at once he should hear the death-like stillness broken up by the sound of wheels rattling away from the scene, and making known that the transitory vision was dissolved, he will be aware that at no moment was his sense of the complete suspension and pause in ordinary human concerns so full and affecting, as at that moment when the suspension ceases, and the goings-on of human life are suddenly resumed. All action in any direction is best expounded, measured, and made apprehensible, by reaction. Now apply this to the case in *Macbeth*. Here, as I have said, the retiring of the human heart, and the entrance of the fiendish heart was to be expressed and made sensible. Another world has stepped in; and the murderers are taken out of the region of human things, human purposes, human desires. They are transfigured: Lady Macbeth is 'unsexed'; Macbeth has forgot that he was born of woman; both are conformed to the image of devils; and the world of devils is suddenly revealed. But how shall this be conveyed and made palpable? In order that a new world may step in, this world must for a time disappear. The murderers, and the murder must be insulated—cut off by an immeasurable gulf from the ordinary tide and succession of human affairs—locked up and sequestered in some deep recess; we must be made sensible that the world of ordinary life is suddenly arrested—laid asleep—tranced—racked into a dread armistice; time must be annihilated; relation to things without abolished; and all must pass self-withdrawn into a deep syncope and suspension of earthly passion. Hence it is, that when the deed is done, when the work of darkness is perfect, then the world of darkness passes away like a pageantry in the clouds: the knocking at the gate is heard; and it makes known audibly that the reaction has commenced; the human has made its reflux upon the fiendish; the pulses of life are beginning to beat again; and the re-establishment of the goings-on of the world in which we live, first makes us profoundly sensible of the awful parenthesis that had suspended them.

O mighty poet! Thy works are not as those of other men, simply and merely great works of art; but are also like the phenomena of nature, like the sun and the sea, the stars and the flowers; like frost and snow, rain and dew, hail-storm and thunder, which are to be studied with entire submission of our own faculties, and in the perfect faith that in them there can be no too much or too little, nothing useless or inert—but that, the further we press in our discoveries, the more we shall see proofs of design and self-supporting arrangement where the careless eye had seen nothing but accident!

LEVANA AND OUR LADIES OF SORROW

Oftentimes at Oxford I saw Levana in my dreams. I knew her by her Roman symbols. Who is Levana? Reader, that do not pretend to have leisure for very much scholarship, you will not be angry with me for telling you. Levana was the Roman goddess that performed for the new-born infant the earliest office of ennobling kindness

—typical, by its mode, of that grandeur which belongs to man everywhere, and of that benignity in powers invisible, which even in Pagan worlds sometimes descends to sustain it. At the very moment of birth, just as the infant tasted for the first time the atmosphere of our troubled planet, it was laid on the ground. *That* might bear different interpretations. But immediately, lest so grand a creature should grovel there for more than one instant, either the paternal hand, as proxy for the goddess Levana, or some near kinsman, as proxy for the father, raised it upright, bade it look erect as the king of all this world, and presented its forehead to the stars, saying, perhaps, in his heart—'Behold what is greater than yourselves!' This symbolic act represented the function of Levana. And that mysterious lady, who never revealed her face (except to me in dreams), but always acted by delegation, had her name from the Latin verb (as still it is the Italian verb) *levare*, to raise aloft.

This is the explanation of Levana. And hence it has arisen that some people have understood by Levana the tutelary power that controls the education of the nursery. She, that would not suffer at his birth even a prefigurative or mimic degradation for her awful ward, far less could be supposed to suffer the real degradation attaching to the non-development of his powers. She therefore watches over human education. Now, the word *edŭco*, with the penultimate short, was derived (by a process often exemplified in the crystallization of languages) from the word *edūco*, with the penultimate long. Whatsoever *educes* or develops—*educates*. By the education of Levana, therefore, is meant—not the poor machinery that moves by spelling-books and grammars, but that mighty system of central forces hidden in the deep bosom of human life, which by passion, by strife, by temptation, by the energies of resistance, works for ever upon children—resting not day or night, any more than the mighty wheel of day and night themselves, whose moments, like restless spokes, are glimmering for ever as they revolve.

If, then, these are the ministries by which Levana works, how profoundly must she reverence the agencies of grief! But you, reader, think—that children generally are not liable to grief such as mine. There are two senses in the word *generally*—the sense of Euclid where it means *universally* (or in the whole extent of the *genus*), and a foolish sense of this world where it means *usually*. Now I am far from saying that children universally are capable of grief like mine. But there are more than you ever heard of, who die of grief in this island of ours. I will tell you a common case. The rules of Eton require that a boy on the *Foundation* should be there twelve years: he is superannuated at eighteen, consequently he must come at six. Children torn away from mothers and sisters at that age not unfrequently die. I speak of what I know. The complaint is not entered by the registrar as grief; but *that* it is. Grief of that sort, and at that age, has killed more than ever have been counted amongst its martyrs.

Therefore it is that Levana often communes with the powers that shake man's heart: therefore it is that she dotes upon grief. 'These ladies,' said I softly to myself, on seeing the ministers with whom Levana was conversing, 'these are the Sorrows; and they are three in number, as the *Graces* are three, who dress man's life with beauty; the *Parcae* are three, who weave the dark arras of man's life in their mysterious loom always with colours sad in part, sometimes angry with tragic crimson and black; the *Furies* are three, who visit with retributions called from the other side of the grave offences that walk upon this; and once even the *Muses* were but three, who fit the harp, the trumpet, or the lute, to the great burdens of man's impassioned creations. These are the Sorrows, all three of whom I know.' The last words I say *now*; but in Oxford I said—'one of whom I know, and the others too surely I *shall* know.' For already, in my fervent youth, I saw (dimly relieved upon the dark background of my dreams) the imperfect lineaments of the awful sisters. These sisters—by what name shall we call them?

If I say simply—'The Sorrows,' there will be a chance of mistaking the term; it might be understood of individual sorrow—separate cases of sorrow,—whereas I want a term expressing the mighty abstractions that incarnate themselves in all individual sufferings of man's heart; and I wish to have these abstractions presented as impersonations, that is, as clothed with human attributes of life, and with functions pointing to flesh. Let us call them, therefore, *Our Ladies of Sorrow*. I know them thoroughly, and have walked in all their kingdoms. Three sisters they are, of one mysterious household; and their paths are wide apart; but of their dominion there is no end. Them I saw often conversing with Levana, and sometimes about myself. Do they talk, then? Oh, no! Mighty phantoms like these disdain the infirmities of language. They may utter voices through the organs of man when they dwell in human hearts, but amongst themselves is no voice nor sound—eternal silence reigns in *their* kingdoms. *They* spoke not as they talked with Levana. *They* whispered not. *They* sang not. Though oftentimes methought they *might* have sung ; for I upon earth had heard their mysteries oftentimes deciphered by harp and timbrel, by dulcimer and organ. Like God, whose servants they are, they utter their pleasure, not by sounds that perish, or by words that go astray, but by signs in heaven—by changes on earth—by pulses in secret rivers—heraldries painted on darkness—and hieroglyphics written on the tablets of the brain. *They* wheeled in mazes ; *I* spelled the steps. *They* telegraphed from afar ; *I* read the signals. *They* conspired together ; and on the mirrors of darkness *my* eye traced the plots. *Theirs* were the symbols,—*mine* are the words.

What is it the sisters are ? What is it that they do ? Let me describe their form, and their presence ; if form it were that still fluctuated in its outline ; or presence it were that for ever advanced to the front, or for ever receded amongst shades.

The eldest of the three is named *Mater Lachrymarum*, Our Lady of Tears. She it is that night and day raves and moans, calling for vanished faces. She stood in Rama, when a voice was heard of lamentation—Rachel weeping for her children, and refusing to be comforted. She it was that stood in Bethlehem on the night when Herod's sword swept its nurseries of Innocents and the little feet were stiffened for ever, which, heard at times as they tottered along floors overhead, woke pulses of love in household hearts that were not unmarked in heaven.

Her eyes are sweet and subtle, wild and sleepy by turns; oftentimes rising to the clouds; oftentimes challenging the heavens. She wears a diadem round her head. And I knew by childish memories that she could go abroad upon the winds, when she heard the sobbing of litanies or the thundering of organs, and when she beheld the mustering of summer clouds. This sister, the elder, it is that carries keys more than papal at her girdle, which open every cottage and every palace. She, to my knowledge, sate all last summer by the bedside of the blind beggar, him that so often and so gladly I talked with, whose pious daughter, eight years old, with the sunny countenance, resisted the temptations of play and village mirth to travel all day long on dusty roads with her afflicted father. For this did God send her a great reward. In the spring-time of the year, and whilst yet her own spring was budding, He recalled her to Himself. But her blind father mourns for ever over *her*; still he dreams at midnight that the little guiding hand is locked within his own; and still he wakens to a darkness that is *now* within a second and a deeper darkness. This *Mater Lachrymarum* also has been sitting all this winter of 1844–5 within the bedchamber of the Czar, bringing before his eyes a daughter (not less pious) that vanished to God not less suddenly, and left behind her a darkness not less profound. By the power of her keys it is that Our Lady of Tears glides a ghostly intruder into the chambers of sleepless men, sleepless women, sleepless children, from Ganges to the Nile, from Nile to Mississippi.

And her, because she is the first-born of her house, and has the widest empire, let us honour with the title of 'Madonna'.

The second sister is called *Mater Suspiriorum*, Our Lady of Sighs. She never scales the clouds, nor walks abroad upon the winds. She wears no diadem. And her eyes, if they were ever seen, would be neither sweet nor subtle; no man could read their story; they would be found filled with perishing dreams, and with wrecks of forgotten delirium. But she raises not her eyes; her head, on which sits a dilapidated turban, droops for ever; for ever fastens on the dust. She weeps not. She groans not. But she sighs inaudibly at intervals. Her sister, Madonna, is oftentimes stormy and frantic; raging in the highest against heaven; and demanding back her darlings. But Our Lady of Sighs never clamours, never defies, dreams not of rebellious aspirations. She is humble to abjectness. Hers is the meekness that belongs to the hopeless. Murmur she may, but it is in her sleep. Whisper she may, but it is to herself in the twilight. Mutter she does at times, but it is in solitary places that are desolate as she is desolate, in ruined cities, and when the sun has gone down to his rest. This sister is the visitor of the Pariah, of the Jew, of the bondsman to the oar in Mediterranean galleys, of the English criminal in Norfolk Island, blotted out from the books of remembrance in sweet far-off England, of the baffled penitent reverting his eye for ever upon a solitary grave, which to him seems the altar overthrown of some past and bloody sacrifice, on which altar no oblations can now be availing, whether towards pardon that he might implore, or towards reparation that he might attempt. Every slave that at noonday looks up to the tropical sun with timid reproach, as he points with one hand to the earth, our general mother, but for *him* a stepmother, as he points with the other hand to the Bible, our general teacher, but against *him* sealed and sequestered;—every woman sitting in darkness, without love to shelter her head, or hope to illumine her solitude, because the heaven-born instincts kindling in her nature germs of holy affections, which God implanted in her womanly bosom, having been stifled by social necessities, now burn sullenly to waste, like sepulchral lamps amongst the ancients;—every nun defrauded of her unreturning May-time by wicked kinsmen, whom God will judge;—every captive in every dungeon;—all that are betrayed, and all that are rejected; outcasts by traditionary law, and children of *hereditary* disgrace—all these walk with Our Lady of Sighs. She also carries a key; but she needs it little. For her kingdom is chiefly amongst the tents of Shem, and the houseless vagrant of every clime. Yet in the very highest ranks of man she finds chapels of her own; and even in glorious England there are some that, to the world, carry their heads as proudly as the reindeer, who yet secretly have received her mark upon their foreheads.

But the third sister, who is also the youngest—— Hush! whisper, whilst we talk of *her*! Her kingdom is not large, or else no flesh should live; but within that kingdom all power is hers. Her head, turreted like that of Cybele, rises almost beyond the reach of sight. She droops not; and her eyes rising so high, *might* be hidden by distance.

But, being what they are, they cannot be hidden; through the treble veil of crape which she wears, the fierce light of a blazing misery, that rests not for matins or for vespers—for noon of day or noon of night—for ebbing or for flowing tide—may be read from the very ground. She is the defier of God. She also is the mother of lunacies, and the suggestress of suicides. Deep lie the roots of her power; but narrow is the nation that she rules. For she can approach only those in whom a profound nature has been upheaved by central convulsions; in whom the heart trembles and the brain rocks under conspiracies of tempest from without and tempest from within. Madonna moves with uncertain steps, fast or slow, but still with tragic grace. Our Lady of Sighs creeps timidly and stealthily. But this youngest sister moves with incalculable motions, bounding, and with a tiger's leaps. She carries no key; for, though coming rarely amongst men, she storms all doors at which she is permitted to enter at all. And *her* name is *Mater Tenebrarum*—Our Lady of Darkness.

These were the *Semnai Theai*, or Sublime Goddesses—these were the *Eumenides*, or Gracious Ladies (so called by antiquity in shuddering propitiation)—of my Oxford dreams. Madonna spoke. She spoke by her mysterious hand. Touching my head, she beckoned to Our Lady of Sighs; and *what* she spoke, translated out of the signs which (except in dreams) no man reads, was this:—

'Lo! here is he, whom in childhood I dedicated to my altars. This is he that once I made my darling. Him I led astray, him I beguiled, and from heaven I stole away his young heart to mine.

Through me did he become idolatrous; and through me it was, by languishing desires, that he worshipped the worm, and prayed to the wormy grave. Holy was the grave to him; lovely was its darkness; saintly its corruption. Him, this young idolater, I have seasoned for thee, dear gentle Sister of Sighs! Do thou take him now to *thy* heart, and season him for our dreadful sister. And thou'—turning to the *Mater Tenebrarum*, she said—'wicked sister, that temptest and hatest, do thou take him from *her*. See that thy sceptre lie heavy on his head. Suffer not woman and her tenderness to sit near him in his darkness. Banish the frailties of hope—wither the relentings of love—scorch the fountains of tears: curse him as only thou canst curse. So shall he be accomplished in the furnace—so shall he see the things that ought *not* to be seen—sights that are abominable, and secrets that are unutterable. So shall he read elder truths, sad truths, grand truths, fearful truths. So shall he rise again *before* he dies. And so shall our commission be accomplished which from God we had—to plague his heart until we had unfolded the capacities of his spirit.'

THOMAS CARLYLE

1795–1881

THE OPERA [1]

(Dear P.,—Not having anything of my own which I could contribute (as is my wish and duty) to this pious Adventure of yours, and not being able in these busy days to get anything ready, I decide to offer you a bit of an Excerpt from that singular *Conspectus of England*, lately written, not yet printed, by Professor Ezechiel Peasemeal, a distinguished American friend of mine. Dr. Peasemeal will excuse my printing it here. His *Conspectus*, a work of some extent, has already been crowned by the Phi Beta Kappa Society of Buncombe, which includes, as you know, the chief thinkers of the New World; and it will probably be printed entire in their 'Transactions' one day. Meanwhile let your readers have the first taste of it; and much good may it do them and you!'—T.C.)

MUSIC is well said to be the speech of angels; in fact, nothing among the utterances allowed to man is felt to be so divine. It brings us near to the Infinite; we look for moments, across the cloudy elements, into the eternal Sea of Light, when song leads and inspires us. Serious nations, all nations that can still listen to the mandate of Nature, have prized song and music as the highest; as a vehicle for worship, for prophecy, and for whatsoever in them was divine. Their singer was a *vates*, admitted to the council of the universe, friend of the gods, and choicest benefactor to man.

[1] *Keepsake* for 1852. The 'dear P.' there, I recollect, was my old friend Procter (Barry Cornwall); and his 'pious Adventure' had reference to that same publication, under touching human circumstances which had lately arisen.

Reader, it was actually so in Greek, in Roman, in Moslem, Christian, most of all in Old-Hebrew times: and if you look how it now is, you will find a change that should astonish you. Good Heavens, from a Psalm of Asaph to a seat at the London Opera in the Haymarket, what a road have men travelled! The waste that is made in music is probably among the saddest of all our squanderings of God's gifts. Music has, for a long time past, been avowedly mad, divorced from sense and the reality of things; and runs about now as an open Bedlamite, for a good many generations back, bragging that she has nothing to do with sense and reality, but with fiction and delirium only; and stares with unaffected amazement, not able to suppress an elegant burst of witty laughter, at my suggesting the old fact to her.

Fact nevertheless it is, forgotten, and fallen ridiculous as it may be. Tyrtaeus, who had a little music, did not sing Barbers of Seville, but the need of beating back one's country's enemies; a most *true* song, to which the hearts of men did burst responsive into fiery melody, followed by fiery strokes before long. Sophocles also sang, and showed in grand dramatic rhythm and melody, not a fable but a fact, the best he could interpret it; the judgements of Eternal Destiny upon the erring sons of men. Aeschylus, Sophocles, all noble poets were priests as well; and sang the *truest* (which was also the divinest) they had been privileged to discover here below. To 'sing the praise of God', that, you will find, if you can interpret old words, and see what new things they mean, was always, and will always be, the business of the singer. He who forsakes that business, and, wasting our divinest gifts, sings the praise of Chaos, what shall we say of him!

David, King of Judah, a soul inspired by divine music and much other heroism, was wont to pour himself in song; he, with seer's eye and heart, discerned the Godlike amid the Human; struck tones that were an echo of the sphere-harmonies, and are still felt to be such. Reader, art thou one of a thousand, able still to *read* a Psalm of David, and catch some echo of it through the old dim centuries; feeling far off, in thy own heart, what it once was to other hearts made as thine? To sing it attempt not, for it is impossible in this late time; only know that it once was sung. Then go to the Opera, and hear, with unspeakable reflections, what things men now sing!

. . . .

Of the Haymarket Opera, my account, in fine, is this. Lustres, candelabras, painting, gilding at discretion; a hall as of the Caliph Alraschid, or him that commanded the slaves of the Lamp; a hall as if fitted-up by the genii, regardless of expense. Upholstery, and the outlay of human capital, could do no more. Artists, too, as they are called, have been got together from the ends of the world, regardless likewise of expense, to do dancing and singing, some of them even geniuses in their craft. One singer in particular, called Coletti or some such name, seemed to me, by the cast of his face, by the tones of his voice, by his general bearing, so far as I could read it, to be a man of deep and ardent sensibilities, of delicate intuitions, just sympathies; originally an almost poetic soul, or man of *genius*, as we term it; stamped by Nature as capable of far other work than squalling here, like a blind Samson, to make the Philistines sport!

Nay, all of them had aptitudes, perhaps of a distinguished kind; and must, by their own and other people's labour, have got a training equal or superior in toilsomeness, earnest assiduity, and patient travail, to what breeds men to the most arduous trades. I speak not of kings, grandees, or the like show-figures; but few soldiers, judges, men of letters, can have had such pains taken with them. The very ballet-girls, with their muslin saucers round them, were perhaps little short of miraculous; whirling and spinning there in strange mad vortexes, and then suddenly fixing themselves motionless, each upon her left or right great toe, with the other leg stretched out at an angle of ninety degrees—as if you had suddenly pricked into the floor, by one of their points, a pair, or rather a multitudinous cohort, of mad, restlessly jumping and clipping scissors, and so bidden them rest, with opened blades, and stand still, in the Devil's name! A truly notable motion; marvellous, almost miraculous, were not the people there so used to it. Motion peculiar to the Opera; perhaps the ugliest, and surely one of the most difficult, ever taught a female creature in this world. Nature abhors it; but art does at least admit it to border on the impossible. One little Cerito, or Taglioni the Second, that night when I was there, went bounding from the floor as if she had been made of Indian-rubber, or filled with hydrogen gas, and inclined by positive levity to bolt through the ceiling; perhaps neither Semiramis nor Catherine the Second had bred herself so carefully.

Such talent, and such martyrdom of training,

gathered from the four winds, was now here, to do its feat and be paid for it. Regardless of expense, indeed! The purse of Fortunatus seemed to have opened itself, and the divine art of Musical Sound and Rhythmic Motion was welcomed with an explosion of all the magnificences which the other arts, fine and coarse, could achieve. For you are to think of some Rossini or Bellini in the rear of it, too; to say nothing of the Stanfields, and hosts of scene-painters, machinists, engineers, enterprisers;—fit to have taken Gibraltar, written the History of England, or reduced Ireland into Industrial Regiments, had they so set their minds to it!

Alas, and of all these notable or noticeable human talents, and excellent perseverances and energies, backed by mountains of wealth, and led by the divine art of Music and Rhythm vouchsafed by Heaven to them and us, what was to be the issue here this evening? An hour's amusement, not amusing either, but wearisome and dreary, to a high-dizened select populace of male and female persons, who seemed to me not much worth amusing! Could any one have pealed into their hearts once, one true thought, and glimpse of Self-vision: 'High-dizened, most expensive persons, Aristocracy so-called, or *Best* of the World, beware, beware what proofs you are giving here of betterness and bestness!' And then the salutary pang of conscience in reply: 'A select populace, with money in its purse, and drilled a little by the posture-master: good Heavens! if that were what, here and everywhere in God's Creation, I *am*? And a world all dying because I am, and show myself to be, and to have long been, even that? John, the carriage, the carriage; swift! Let me go home in silence, to reflection, perhaps to sackcloth and ashes!' This, and not amusement, would have profited those high-dizened persons.

Amusement, at any rate, they did not get from Euterpe and Melpomene. These two Muses, sent for regardless of expense, I could see, were but the vehicle of a kind of service which I judged to be Paphian rather. Young beauties of both sexes used their opera glasses, you could notice, not entirely for looking at the stage. And, it must be owned, the light, in this explosion of all the upholsteries, and the human fine arts and coarse, was magical; and made your fair one an Armida,—if you liked her better so. Nay, certain old Improper-Females (of quality), in their rouge and jewels, even these looked some *reminiscence* of enchantment; and I saw this and the other lean domestic Dandy, with icy smile on his old worn face; this and the other Marquis Chatabagues, Prince Mahogany, or the like foreign Dignitary, tripping into the boxes of said females, grinning there awhile, with dyed moustachios and macassar oil graciosity, and then tripping out again;—and, in fact, I perceived that Coletti and Cerito and the Rhythmic Arts were a mere accompaniment here.

Wonderful to see; and sad, if you had eyes! Do but think of it. Cleopatra threw pearls into her drink, in mere waste; which was reckoned foolish of her. But here had the Modern Aristocracy of men brought the divinest of its Arts, heavenly Music itself; and, piling all the upholsteries and ingenuities that other human art could do, had lighted them into a bonfire to illuminate an hour's flirtation of Chatabagues, Mahogany, and these improper persons! Never in Nature had I seen such waste before. O Coletti, you whose inborn melody, once of kindred, as I judged, to 'the Melodies Eternal', might have valiantly weeded-out this and the other false thing from the ways of men, and made a bit of God's Creation more melodious—they have purchased you away from that; chained you to the wheel of Prince Mahogany's chariot, and here you make sport for a macassar Chatabagues and his improper-females past the prime of life! Wretched spiritual Nigger, oh, if you *had* some genius, and were not a born Nigger with mere appetite for pumpkin, should you have endured such a lot? I lament for you beyond all other expenses. Other expenses are light; you are the Cleopatra's pearl that should not have been flung into Mahogany's claret-cup. And Rossini, too, and Mozart and Bellini—Oh, Heavens! when I think that Music too is condemned to be mad, and to burn herself, to this end, on such a funeral pile—your celestial Opera-house grows dark and infernal to me! Behind its glitter stalks the shadow of Eternal Death; through it too, I look not 'up into the divine eye', as Richter has it, 'but down into the bottomless eye-socket—not up towards God, Heaven, and the Throne of Truth, but too truly down towards Falsity, Vacuity, and the dwelling-place of Everlasting Despair. . . .'

Good sirs, surely I by no means expect the Opera will abolish itself this year or the next. But if you ask me, Why heroes are not born now, why heroisms are not done now? I will answer you: It is a world all calculated for strangling of heroisms. At every ingress into life, the genius of the world lies in wait for heroisms, and by seduction or compulsion unweariedly does its utmost to pervert them or extinguish them. Yes; to its Hells of sweating tailors, distressed needlewomen and the like, this Opera of yours is the appropriate Heaven! Of a truth, if you will read a Psalm of Asaph till you understand it, and then come hither and hear the Rossini-and-Coletti Psalm, you will find the ages have altered a good deal. . . .

Nor do I wish all men to become Psalmist Asaphs and fanatic Hebrews. Far other is my wish; far other, and wider, is now my notion of this Universe. Populations of stern faces, stern as any Hebrew, but capable withal of bursting into inextinguishable laughter on occasion:—do you understand that new and better form of character? Laughter also, if it come from the heart, is a heavenly thing. But, at least and lowest, I would have you a Population abhorring phantasms;—abhorring *unveracity* in all things; and in your 'amusements', which are voluntary and not compulsory things, abhorring it most impatiently of all.

THOMAS BABINGTON MACAULAY

1800–1859

JOHN BUNYAN[1]

THIS is an eminently beautiful and splendid edition of a book which well deserves all that the printer and the engraver can do for it. The Life of Bunyan is, of course, not a performance which can add much to the literary reputation of such a writer as Mr. Southey. But it is written in excellent English, and, for the most part, in an excellent spirit. Mr. Southey propounds, we need not say, many opinions from which we altogether dissent; and his attempts to excuse the odious persecution to which Bunyan was subjected have sometimes moved our indignation. But we will avoid this topic. We are at present much more inclined to join in paying homage to the genius of a great man than to engage in a controversy concerning Church-government and toleration.

We must not pass without notice the engravings with which this volume is decorated. Some of Mr. Heath's woodcuts are admirably designed and executed. Mr. Martin's illustrations do not please us quite so well. His Valley of the Shadow of Death is not that Valley of the Shadow of Death which Bunyan imagined. At all events, it is not that dark and horrible glen which has from childhood been in our mind's eye. The valley is a

[1] *The Pilgrim's Progress, with a Life of John Bunyan.* By ROBERT SOUTHEY, Esq., LL.D., Poet-Laureate. 8vo. London: 1830.

cavern: the quagmire is a lake: the straight path runs zigzag: and Christian appears like a speck in the darkness of the immense vault. We miss, too, those hideous forms which make so striking a part of the description of Bunyan, and which Salvator Rosa would have loved to draw. It is with unfeigned diffidence that we pronounce judgement on any question relating to the art of painting. But it appears to us that Mr. Martin has not of late been fortunate in his choice of subjects. He should never have attempted to illustrate the *Paradise Lost*. There can be no two manners more directly opposed to each other than the manner of his painting and the manner of Milton's poetry. Those things which are mere accessories in the descriptions become the principal objects in the pictures; and those figures which are most prominent in the descriptions can be detected in the pictures only by a very close scrutiny. Mr. Martin has succeeded perfectly in representing the pillars and candelabras of Pandaemonium. But he has forgotten that Milton's Pandaemonium is merely the background to Satan. In the picture, the Archangel is scarcely visible amidst the endless colonnades of his infernal palace. Milton's Paradise, again, is merely the background to his Adam and Eve. But in Mr. Martin's picture the landscape is everything. Adam, Eve, and Raphael, attract much less notice than the lake and the mountains, the gigantic flowers, and the giraffes which feed upon them. We read that James II sat to Verelst, the great flower-painter. When the performance was finished, his majesty appeared in the midst of a bower of sun-flowers and tulips, which completely drew away all attention from the central figure. All who looked at the portrait took it for a flower-piece. Mr. Martin, we think, introduces his immeasurable spaces, his innumerable multitudes, his gorgeous prodigies of architecture and landscape, almost as unseasonably as Verelst introduced his flower-pots and nosegays. If Mr. Martin were to paint Lear in the storm, we suspect that the blazing sky, the sheets of rain, the swollen torrents, and the tossing forest would draw away all attention from the agonies of the insulted king and father. If he were to paint the death of Lear, the old man asking the by-standers to undo his button, would be thrown into the shade by a vast blaze of pavilions, standards, armour, and heralds' coats. Mr. Martin would illustrate the *Orlando Furioso* well, the *Orlando Innamorato* still better, the *Arabian Nights* best of all. Fairy palaces and gardens, porticoes of agate, and groves flowering with emeralds and rubies, inhabited by people for whom nobody cares, these are his proper domain. He would succeed admirably in the enchanted ground of Alcina, or the mansion of Aladdin. But he should avoid Milton and Bunyan.

The characteristic peculiarity of *The Pilgrim's Progress* is that it is the only work of its kind which possesses a strong human interest. Other allegories only amuse the fancy. The allegory of Bunyan has been read by many thousands with tears. There are some good allegories in Johnson's works, and some of still higher merit by Addison. In these performances there is, perhaps, as much wit and ingenuity as in *The Pilgrim's Progress*. But the pleasure which is produced by the Vision of Mirza, the Vision of Theodore, the genealogy of Wit, or the contest between Rest and Labour, is exactly similar to the pleasure which we derive from one of Cowley's odes or from a canto of *Hudibras*. It is a pleasure which belongs wholly to the understanding, and in which the feelings have no part whatever. Nay, even Spenser himself, though assuredly one of the greatest poets that ever lived, could not succeed in the attempt to make allegory interesting. It was in vain that he lavished the riches of his mind on the House of Pride and the House of Temperance. One unpardonable fault, the fault of tediousness, pervades the whole of the *Fairy Queen*. We become sick of Cardinal Virtues and Deadly Sins, and long for the society of plain men and women. Of the persons who read the first canto, not one in ten reaches the end of the first book, and not one in a hundred perseveres to the end of the poem. Very few and very weary are those who are in at the death of the Blatant Beast. If the last six books, which are said to have been destroyed in Ireland, had been preserved, we doubt whether any heart less stout than that of a commentator would have held out to the end.

It is not so with *The Pilgrim's Progress*. That wonderful book, while it obtains admiration from the most fastidious critics, is loved by those who are too simple to admire it. Dr. Johnson, all whose studies were desultory, and who hated, as he said, to read books through, made an exception in favour of *The Pilgrim's Progress*. That work was one of the two or three works which he wished longer. It was by no common merit that the illiterate sectary extracted praise like this from the most pedantic of critics and the most bigoted of Tories. In the wildest parts of Scotland *The Pilgrim's Progress* is the delight of the peasantry.

In every nursery *The Pilgrim's Progress* is a greater favourite than *Jack the Giant-killer*. Every reader knows the straight and narrow path as well as he knows a road in which he has gone backward and forward a hundred times. This is the highest miracle of genius, that things which are not should be as though they were, that the imaginations of one mind should become the personal recollections of another. And this miracle the tinker has wrought. There is no ascent, no declivity, no resting-place, no turn-stile, with which we are not perfectly acquainted. The wicket gate, and the desolate swamp which separates it from the City of Destruction, the long line of road, as straight as a rule can make it, the Interpreter's house, and all its fair shows, the prisoner in the iron cage, the palace, at the doors of which armed men kept guard, and on the battlements of which walked persons clothed all in gold, the cross and the sepulchre, the steep hill and the pleasant arbour, the stately front of the House Beautiful by the wayside, the chained lions crouching in the porch, the low, green valley of Humiliation, rich with grass and covered with flocks, all are as well known to us as the sights of our own street. Then we come to the narrow place where Apollyon strode right across the whole breadth of the way, to stop the journey of Christian, and where afterwards the pillar was set up to testify how bravely the pilgrim had fought the good fight. As we advance, the valley becomes deeper and deeper. The shade of the precipices on both sides falls blacker and blacker. The clouds gather overhead. Doleful voices, the clanking of chains, and the rushing of many feet to and fro, are heard through the darkness. The way, hardly discernible in gloom, runs close by the mouth of the burning pit, which sends forth its flames, its noisome smoke, and its hideous shapes, to terrify the adventurer. Thence he goes on, amidst the snares and pitfalls, with the mangled bodies of those who have perished lying in the ditch by his side. At the end of the long dark valley he passes the dens in which the old giants dwelt, amidst the bones of those whom they had slain.

Then the road passes straight on through a waste moor, till at length the towers of a distant city appear before the traveller; and soon he is in the midst of the innumerable multitudes of Vanity Fair. There are the jugglers and the apes, the shops and the puppet-shows. There are Italian Row, and French Row, and Spanish Row, and Britain Row, with their crowds of buyers, sellers, and loungers, jabbering all the languages of the earth.

Thence we go on by the little hill of the silver mine, and through the meadow of lilies, along the bank of that pleasant river which is bordered on both sides by fruit-trees. On the left side branches off the path leading to the horrible castle, the court-yard of which is paved with the skulls of pilgrims; and right onward are the sheepfolds and orchards of the Delectable Mountains.

From the Delectable Mountains, the way lies through the fogs and briers of the Enchanted Ground, with here and there a bed of soft cushions spread under a green arbour. And beyond is the land of Beulah, where the flowers, the grapes, and the songs of birds never cease, and where the sun shines night and day. Thence are plainly seen the golden pavements and streets of pearl, on the other side of that black and cold river over which there is no bridge.

All the stages of the journey, all the forms which cross or overtake the pilgrims, giants, and hobgoblins, ill-favoured ones and shining ones, the tall, comely, swarthy Madam Bubble, with her great purse by her side, and her fingers playing with the money, the black man in the bright vesture, Mr. Worldly Wiseman and my Lord Hategood, Mr. Talkative and Mrs. Timorous, all are actually existing beings to us. We follow the travellers through their allegorical progress with interest not inferior to that with which we follow Elizabeth from Siberia to Moscow, or Jeanie Deans from Edinburgh to London. Bunyan is almost the only writer who ever gave to the abstract the interest of the concrete. In the works of many celebrated authors, men are mere personifications. We have not a jealous man, but jealousy, not a traitor, but perfidy, not a patriot, but patriotism. The mind of Bunyan, on the contrary, was so imaginative that personifications, when he dealt with them, became men. A dialogue between two qualities, in his dream, has more dramatic effect than a dialogue between two human beings in most plays. In this respect the genius of Bunyan bore a great resemblance to that of a man who had very little else in common with him, Percy Bysshe Shelley. The strong imagination of Shelley made him an idolater in his own despite. Out of the most indefinite terms of a hard, cold, dark, metaphysical system, he made a gorgeous Pantheon, full of beautiful, majestic, and life-like forms. He turned atheism itself into a mythology, rich with visions as glorious as the gods that live in the marble of Phidias, or the virgin saints that smile on us from the canvas of Murillo. The Spirit of Beauty, the Principle of Good, the Principle of Evil, when he treated of them, ceased to be abstractions. They took shape and colour. They were no longer mere words; but 'intelligible forms'; 'fair humanities'; objects of love, of adoration, or of fear. As there can be no stronger sign of a mind destitute of the poetical faculty than that tendency which was so common among the writers of the French school to turn images into abstractions, Venus, for example, into Love, Minerva into Wisdom, Mars into War, and Bacchus into Festivity, so there can be no stronger sign of a mind truly poetical than a disposition to reverse this abstracting process, and to make individuals out of generalities. Some of the metaphysical and ethical theories of Shelley were certainly most absurd and pernicious. But we doubt whether any modern poet has possessed in an equal degree some of the highest qualities of the great ancient masters. The words bard and inspiration, which seem so cold and affected when applied to other modern writers, have a perfect propriety when applied to him. He was not an author, but a bard. His poetry seems not to have been an art, but an inspiration. Had he lived to the full age of man, he might not improbably have given to the world some great work of the very highest rank in design and execution. But, alas!

> ὁ Δάφνις ἔβα ῥόον· ἔκλυσε δίνα
> τὸν Μώσαις φίλον ἄνδρα, τὸν οὐ Νύμφαισιν ἀπεχθῆ.

But we must return to Bunyan. *The Pilgrim's Progress* undoubtedly is not a perfect allegory.

The types are often inconsistent with each other; and sometimes the allegorical disguise is altogether thrown off. The river, for example, is emblematic of death; and we are told that every human being must pass through the river. But Faithful does not pass through it. He is martyred, not in shadow, but in reality, at Vanity Fair. Hopeful talks to Christian about Esau's birthright and about his own convictions of sin as Bunyan might have talked with one of his own congregation. The damsels at the House Beautiful catechize Christiana's boys, as any good ladies might catechize any boys at a Sunday School. But we do not believe that any man, whatever might be his genius, and whatever his good luck, could long continue a figurative history without falling into many inconsistencies. We are sure that inconsistencies, scarcely less gross than the worst into which Bunyan has fallen, may be found in the shortest and most elaborate allegories of the *Spectator* and the *Rambler*. The *Tale of a Tub* and the *History of John Bull* swarm with similar errors, if the name of error can be properly applied to that which is unavoidable. It is not easy to make a simile go on all-fours. But we believe that no human ingenuity could produce such a centipede as a long allegory in which the correspondence between the outward sign and the thing signified should be exactly preserved. Certainly no writer, ancient or modern, has yet achieved the adventure. The best thing, on the whole, that an allegorist can do, is to present to his readers a succession of analogies, each of which may separately be striking and happy, without looking very nicely to see whether they harmonize with each other.

This Bunyan has done; and, though a minute scrutiny may detect inconsistencies in every page of his Tale, the general effect which the Tale produces on all persons, learned and unlearned, proves that he has done well. The passages which it is most difficult to defend are those in which he altogether drops the allegory, and puts in the mouth of his pilgrims religious ejaculations and disquisitions, better suited to his own pulpit at Bedford or Reading than to the Enchanted Ground or to the Interpreter's Garden. Yet even these passages, though we will not undertake to defend them against the objections of critics, we feel that we could ill spare. We feel that the story owes much of its charm to these occasional glimpses of solemn and affecting subjects, which will not be hidden, which force themselves through the veil, and appear before us in their native aspect. The effect is not unlike that which is said to have been produced on the ancient stage, when the eyes of the actor were seen flaming through his mask, and giving life and expression to what would else have been an inanimate and uninteresting disguise.

It is very amusing and very instructive to compare *The Pilgrim's Progress* with the *Grace Abounding*. The latter work is indeed one of the most remarkable pieces of autobiography in the world. It is a full and open confession of the fancies which passed through the mind of an illiterate man, whose affections were warm, whose nerves were irritable, whose imagination was ungovernable, and who was under the influence of the strongest religious excitement. In whatever age Bunyan had lived, the history of his feelings would, in all probability, have been very curious. But the time in which his lot was cast was the time of a great stirring of the human mind. A tremendous burst of public feeling, produced by the tyranny of the hierarchy, menaced the old ecclesiastical institutions with destruction. To the gloomy regularity of one intolerant Church had succeeded the licence of innumerable sects, drunk with the sweet and heady must of their new liberty. Fanaticism, engendered by persecution, and destined to engender persecution in turn, spread rapidly through society. Even the strongest and most commanding minds were not proof against this strange taint. Any time might have produced George Fox and James Naylor. But to one time alone belong the frantic delusions of such a statesman as Vane, and the hysterical tears of such a soldier as Cromwell.

The history of Bunyan is the history of a most excitable mind in an age of excitement. By most of his biographers he has been treated with gross injustice. They have understood in a popular sense all those strong terms of self-condemnation which he employed in a theological sense. They have, therefore, represented him as an abandoned wretch, reclaimed by means almost miraculous, or, to use their favourite metaphor, 'as a brand plucked from the burning.' Mr. Ivimey calls him the depraved Bunyan and the wicked Tinker of Elstow. Surely Mr. Ivimey ought to have been too familiar with the bitter accusations which the most pious people are in the habit of bringing against themselves, to understand literally all the strong expressions which are to be found in the *Grace Abounding*. It is quite clear, as Mr. Southey most justly remarks, that Bunyan never was a vicious man. He married very early; and he solemnly declares that he was strictly faithful to his wife. He does not appear to have been a drunkard. He owns, indeed, that, when a boy, he never spoke without an oath. But a single admonition cured him of this bad habit for life; and the cure must have been wrought early; for at eighteen he was in the army of the Parliament; and, if he had carried the vice of profaneness into that service, he would doubtless have received something more than an admonition from Sergeant Bind-their-kings-in-chains, or Captain Hew-Agag-in-pieces-before-the-Lord. Bell-ringing and playing at hockey on Sundays seem to have been the worst vices of this depraved tinker. They would have passed for virtues with Archbishop Laud. It is quite clear that, from a very early age, Bunyan was a man of strict life and of a tender conscience. 'He had been,' says Mr. Southey, 'a blackguard.' Even this we think too hard a censure. Bunyan was not, we admit, so fine a gentleman as Lord Digby; but he was a blackguard no otherwise than as every labouring man that ever lived has been a blackguard. Indeed, Mr. Southey acknowledges this. 'Such he might have been expected to be by his birth, breeding, and vocation. Scarcely, indeed, by possibility, could he have been otherwise.' A man whose manners and sentiments are decidedly below those of his class deserves to be called a blackguard. But it is surely unfair to apply so strong a word of reproach to one who is only what the great mass of every community must inevitably be.

Those horrible internal conflicts which Bunyan has described with so much power of language prove, not that he was a worse man than his neighbours, but that his mind was constantly occupied by religious considerations, that his fervour exceeded his knowledge, and that his imagination exercised despotic power over his body and mind. He heard voices from heaven. He saw strange visions of distant hills, pleasant and sunny as his own Delectable Mountains. From those abodes he was shut out, and placed in a dark and horrible wilderness, where he wandered through ice and snow, striving to make his way into the happy region of light. At one time he was seized with an inclination to work miracles. At another time he thought himself actually possessed by the devil. He could distinguish the blasphemous whispers. He felt his infernal enemy pulling at his clothes behind him. He spurned with his feet and struck with his hands at the destroyer. Sometimes he was tempted to sell his part in the salvation of mankind. Sometimes a violent impulse urged him to start up from his food, to fall on his knees, and to break forth into prayer. At length he fancied that he had committed the unpardonable sin. His agony convulsed his robust frame. He was, he says, as if his breast-bone would split; and this he took for a sign that he was destined to burst asunder like Judas. The agitation of his nerves made all his movements tremulous; and this trembling, he supposed, was a visible mark of his reprobation, like that which had been set on Cain. At one time, indeed, an encouraging voice seemed to rush in at the window, like the noise of wind, but very pleasant, and commanded, as he says, a great calm in his soul. At another time, a word of comfort 'was spoke loud unto him; it showed a great word; it seemed to be writ in great letters'.

But these intervals of ease were short. His state, during two years and a half, was generally the most horrible that the human mind can imagine. 'I walked,' says he, with his own peculiar eloquence, 'to a neighbouring town; and sat down upon a settle in the street, and fell into a very deep pause about the most fearful state my sin had brought me to; and, after long musing, I lifted up my head; but methought I saw as if the sun that shineth in the heavens did grudge to give me light; and as if the very stones in the street, and tiles upon the houses, did band themselves against me. Methought that they all combined together to banish me out of the world. I was abhorred of them, and unfit to dwell among them, because I had sinned against the Saviour. Oh, how happy now was every creature over I! for they stood fast, and kept their station. But I was gone and lost.' Scarcely any madhouse could produce an instance of delusion so strong, or of misery so acute.

It was through this Valley of the Shadow of Death, overhung by darkness, peopled with devils, resounding with blasphemy and lamentation, and passing amidst quagmires, snares, and pitfalls, close by the very mouth of hell, that Bunyan journeyed to that bright and fruitful land of Beulah, in which he sojourned during the latter period of his pilgrimage. The only trace which his cruel sufferings and temptations seem to have left behind them was an affectionate compassion for those who were still in the state in which he had once been. Religion has scarcely ever worn a form so calm and soothing as in his allegory. The feeling which predominates through the whole book is a feeling of tenderness for weak, timid, and harassed minds. The character of Mr. Fearing, of Mr. Feeblemind, of Mr. Despondency and his daughter Miss Muchafraid, the account of poor Littlefaith who was robbed by the three thieves of his spending money, the description of Christian's terror in the dungeons of Giant Despair and in his passage through the river, all clearly show how strong a sympathy Bunyan felt, after his own mind had become clear and cheerful, for persons afflicted with religious melancholy.

Mr. Southey, who has no love for the Calvinists, admits that, if Calvinism had never worn a blacker appearance than in Bunyan's works, it would never have become a term of reproach. In fact, those works of Bunyan with which we are acquainted are by no means more Calvinistic than the articles and homilies of the Church of England. The moderation of his opinions on the subject of predestination gave offence to some zealous persons. We have seen an absurd allegory, the heroine of which is named Hephzibah, written by some raving supralapsarian preacher who was dissatisfied with the mild theology of *The Pilgrim's Progress.* In this foolish book, if we recollect rightly, the Interpreter is called the Enlightener, and the House Beautiful is Castle Strength. Mr. Southey tells us that the Catholics had also their *Pilgrim's Progress*, without a Giant Pope, in which the Interpreter is the Director, and the House Beautiful Grace's Hall. It is surely a remarkable proof of the power of Bunyan's genius, that two religious parties, both of which regarded his opinions as heterodox, should have had recourse to him for assistance.

There are, we think, some characters and scenes in *The Pilgrim's Progress*, which can be fully comprehended and enjoyed only by persons familiar with the history of the times through which Bunyan lived. The character of Mr. Greatheart, the guide, is an example. His fighting is, of course, allegorical; but the allegory is not strictly preserved. He delivers a sermon on imputed righteousness to his companions; and, soon after, he gives battle to Giant Grim, who had taken upon him to back the lions. He expounds the fifty-third chapter of *Isaiah* to the household and guests of Gaius; and then he sallies out to attack Slaygood, who was of the nature of flesh-eaters, in his den. These are inconsistencies; but they are inconsistencies which add, we think, to the interest of the narrative. We have not the least doubt that Bunyan had in view some stout old Greatheart of Naseby and Worcester, who prayed with his men before he drilled them, who knew the spiritual state of every dragoon in his troop, and who, with the praises of God in his mouth, and a two-edged sword in his hand, had turned to flight, on many fields of battle, the swearing, drunken bravoes of Rupert and Lunsford.

Every age produces such men as By-ends. But the middle of the seventeenth century was eminently prolific of such men. Mr. Southey thinks that the satire was aimed at some particular individual; and this seems by no means improbable. At all events, Bunyan must have known many of those hypocrites who followed religion only when religion walked in silver slippers, when the sun shone, and when the people applauded. Indeed, he might have easily found all the kindred of By-ends among the public men of his time. He might have found among the peers my Lord Turn-about, my Lord Time-server, and my Lord Fair-speech; in the House of Commons, Mr. Smoothman, Mr. Anything, and Mr. Facing-both-ways; nor would 'the parson of the parish, Mr. Two-tongues', have been wanting. The town of Bedford probably contained more than one politician who, after contriving to raise an estate by seeking the Lord during the reign of the saints, contrived to keep what he had got by persecuting the saints during the reign of the strumpets—and more than one priest who, during repeated changes in the discipline and doctrines of the Church, had remained constant to nothing but his benefice.

One of the most remarkable passages in *The Pilgrim's Progress* is that in which the proceedings against Faithful are described. It is impossible to doubt that Bunyan intended to satirize the mode in which state trials were conducted under Charles II. The licence given to the witnesses for the prosecution, the shameless partiality and ferocious insolence of the judge, the precipitancy and the blind rancour of the jury, remind us of those odious mummeries which, from the Restoration to the Revolution, were merely forms preliminary to hanging, drawing, and quartering. Lord Hategood performs the office of counsel for the prisoners as well as Scroggs himself could have performed it.

Judge. Thou runagate, heretic, and traitor, hast thou heard what these honest gentlemen have witnessed against thee?

Faithful. May I speak a few words in my own defence?

Judge. Sirrah, sirrah! thou deservest to live no longer, but to be slain immediately upon the place; yet, that all

men may see our gentleness to thee, let us hear what thou, vile runagate, hast to say.

No person who knows the state trials can be at a loss for parallel cases. Indeed, write what Bunyan would, the baseness and cruelty of the lawyers of those times 'sinned up to it still', and even went beyond it. The imaginary trial of Faithful, before a jury composed of personified vices, was just and merciful, when compared with the real trial of Alice Lisle before that tribunal where all the vices sat in the person of Jeffreys.

The style of Bunyan is delightful to every reader, and invaluable as a study to every person who wishes to obtain a wide command over the English language. The vocabulary is the vocabulary of the common people. There is not an expression, if we except a few technical terms of theology, which would puzzle the rudest peasant. We have observed several pages which do not contain a single word of more than two syllables. Yet no writer has said more exactly what he meant to say. For magnificence, for pathos, for vehement exhortation, for subtle disquisition, for every purpose of the poet, the orator, and the divine, this homely dialect, the dialect of plain working men, was perfectly sufficient. There is no book in our literature on which we would so readily stake the fame of the old unpolluted English language, no book which shows so well how rich that language is in its own proper wealth, and how little it has been improved by all that it has borrowed.

Cowper said, forty or fifty years ago, that he dared not name John Bunyan in his verse, for fear of moving a sneer. To our refined forefathers, we suppose, Lord Roscommon's *Essay on Translated*

Verse, and the Duke of Buckinghamshire's *Essay on Poetry*, appeared to be compositions infinitely superior to the allegory of the preaching tinker. We live in better times; and we are not afraid to say, that, though there were many clever men in England during the latter half of the seventeenth century, there were only two minds which possessed the imaginative faculty in a very eminent degree. One of those minds produced *Paradise Lost*, the other *The Pilgrim's Progress*.

RALPH WALDO EMERSON

1803–1882

GIFTS

Gifts of one who loved me,—
'Twas high time they came;
When he ceased to love me,
Time they stopped for shame.

It is said that the world is in a state of bankruptcy, that the world owes the world more than the world can pay, and ought to go into chancery, and be sold. I do not think this general insolvency, which involves in some sort all the population, to be the reason of the difficulty experienced at Christmas and New Year, and other times, in bestowing gifts; since it is always so pleasant to be generous, though very vexatious to pay debts. But the impediment lies in the choosing. If, at any time, it comes into my head that a present is due from me to somebody, I am puzzled what to give, until the opportunity is gone. Flowers and fruits are always fit presents;—flowers, because they are a proud assertion that a ray of beauty outvalues all the utilities of the world. These gay natures contrast with the somewhat stern countenance of ordinary nature; they are like music heard out of a workhouse. Nature does not cocker us: we are children, not pets: she is not fond: everything is dealt to us without fear or favour, after severe universal laws. Yet these delicate flowers look like the frolic and interference of love and beauty. Men used to tell us that we love flattery, even though we are not deceived by it, because it shows that we are of importance enough to be courted. Something like that pleasure, the flowers give us: what am I to whom these sweet hints are addressed? Fruits are acceptable gifts, because they are the flower of commodities, and admit of fantastic values being attached to them. If a man should send to me to come a hundred miles to visit him, and should set before me a basket of fine summer-fruit, I should think there was some proportion between the labour and the reward.

For common gifts, necessity makes pertinences and beauty every day, and one is glad when an imperative leaves him no option, since if the man at the door has no shoes you have not to consider whether you could procure him a paint-box. And as it is always pleasing to see a man eat bread, or drink water, in the house or out of doors, so it is always a great satisfaction to supply these first wants. Necessity does everything well. In our condition of universal dependence, it seems heroic to let the petitioner be the judge of his necessity, and to give all that is asked, though at great inconvenience. If it be a fantastic desire, it is better to leave to others the office of punishing him. I can think of many parts I should prefer playing to that of the Furies. Next to things of necessity, the rule for a gift, which one of my friends prescribed, is, that we might convey to some person that which properly belonged to his character, and was easily associated with him in thought. But our tokens of compliment and love are for the most part barbarous. Rings and other jewels are not gifts, but apologies for gifts. The only gift is a portion of thyself. Thou must bleed for me. Therefore the poet brings his poem; the shepherd, his lamb; the farmer, corn; the miner, a gem; the sailor, coral and shells; the painter, his picture; the girl, a handkerchief of her own sewing. This is right and pleasing, for it restores society in so far to its primary basis, when a man's biography is conveyed in his gift, and every man's wealth is an index of his merit. But it is a cold, lifeless business when you go to the shops to buy me something, which does not represent your life and talent, but a goldsmith's. This is fit for kings, and rich men who represent kings, and a false state of property, to make presents of gold and silver stuffs, as a kind of symbolical sin-offering, or payment of blackmail.

The law of benefits is a difficult channel, which requires careful sailing, or rude boats. It is not the office of a man to receive gifts. How dare you give them? We wish to be self-sustained. We do not quite forgive a giver. The hand that feeds us is in some danger of being bitten. We can receive anything from love, for that is a way of receiving it from ourselves; but not from any one who assumes to bestow. We sometimes hate the meat which we eat, because there seems something of degrading dependence in living by it.

Brother, if Jove to thee a present make
Take heed that from his hands thou nothing take.

We ask the whole. Nothing less will content us. We arraign society, if it do not give us, besides earth, and fire, and water, opportunity, love, reverence, and objects of veneration.

He is a good man who can receive a gift well. We are either glad or sorry at a gift, and both emotions are unbecoming. Some violence, I think, is done, some degradation borne, when I rejoice or grieve at a gift. I am sorry when my independence is invaded, or when a gift comes from such as do not know my spirit, and so the act is not supported; and if the gift pleases me overmuch, then I should be ashamed that the donor should read my heart, and see that I love his commodity and not him. The gift, to be true, must be the flowing of the giver unto me, correspondent to my flowing unto him. When the waters are at a level, then my goods pass to him, and his to me. All his are mine, all mine his. I say to him, 'How can you give me this pot of oil, or this flagon of wine, when all your oil and wine is mine?' which belief of mine this gift seems to deny. Hence the fitness of beautiful, not useful things for gifts. This giving is flat usurpation, and therefore when the beneficiary is ungrateful, as all beneficiaries hate all Timons, not at all considering the value of the gift, but looking back to the greater store it was taken from, I rather sympathize with the beneficiary than with the anger of my lord Timon. For, the expectation of gratitude is mean, and is continually punished by the total insensibility of the obliged person. It is a great happiness to get off without injury and heart-burning from one who has had the ill luck to be served by you. It is a very onerous business, this of being served, and the debtor naturally wishes to give you a slap. A golden text for these gentlemen is that which I so admire in the Buddhist, who never thanks, and who says, 'Do not flatter your benefactors.'

The reason of these discords I conceive to be, that there is no commensurability between a man and any gift. You cannot give anything to a magnanimous person. After you have served him, he at once puts you in debt by his magnanimity. The service a man renders his friend is trivial and selfish, compared with the service he knows his friend stood in readiness to yield him, alike before he had begun to serve his friend, and now also. Compared with that goodwill I bear my friend, the benefit it is in my power to render him seems small. Besides, our action on each other, good as well as evil, is so incidental and at random, that we can seldom hear the acknowledgements of any person who would thank us for a benefit without some shame and humiliation. We can rarely strike a direct stroke, but must be content with an oblique one; we seldom have the satisfaction of yielding a direct benefit, which is directly received. But rectitude scatters favours on every side without knowing it, and receives with wonder the thanks of all people.

I fear to breathe any treason against the majesty of love, which is the genius and god of gifts, and to whom we must not affect to prescribe. Let him give kingdoms or flower-leaves indifferently. There are persons from whom we always expect fairy tokens; let us not cease to expect them. This is prerogative, and not to be limited by our municipal rules. For the rest, I like to see that we cannot be bought and sold. The best of hospitality and of generosity is also not in the will, but in fate. I find that I am not much to you; you do not need me; you do not feel me; then am I thrust out of doors, though you proffer me house and lands. No services are of any value, but only likeness. When I have attempted to join myself to others by services, it proved an intellectual trick,—no more. They eat your service like apples, and leave you out. But love them, and they feel you, and delight in you all the time.

EDGAR ALLAN POE

1809–1849

PHILOSOPHY OF FURNITURE

IN the internal decoration, if not in the external architecture of their residences, the English are supreme. The Italians have but little sentiment beyond marbles and colours. In France, *meliora probant, deteriora sequuntur*—the people are too much a race of gad-abouts to maintain those household proprieties of which, indeed, they have a delicate appreciation, or at least the elements of a proper sense. The Chinese and most of the eastern races have a warm but inappropriate fancy. The Scotch are *poor* decorists. The Dutch have, perhaps, an indeterminate idea that a curtain is not a cabbage. In Spain they are *all* curtains—a nation of hangmen. The Russians do not furnish. The Hottentots and Kickapoos are very well in their way. The Yankees alone are preposterous.

How this happens, it is not difficult to see. We have no aristocracy of blood, and having therefore as a natural, and indeed as an inevitable thing, fashioned for ourselves an aristocracy of dollars, the *display of wealth* has here to take the place and perform the office of the heraldic display in monarchical countries. By a transition readily understood, and which might have been as readily foreseen, we have been brought to merge in simple *show* our notions of taste itself.

To speak less abstractly. In England, for

example, no mere parade of costly appurtenances would be so likely as with us, to create an impression of the beautiful in respect to the appurtenances themselves—or of taste as regards the proprietor: —this for the reason, first, that wealth is not, in England, the loftiest object of ambition as constituting a nobility; and secondly, that there, the true nobility of blood, confining itself within the strict limits of legitimate taste, rather avoids than affects that mere costliness in which a *parvenu* rivalry may at any time be successfully attempted. The people *will* imitate the nobles, and the result is a thorough diffusion of the proper feeling. But in America, the coins current being the sole arms of the aristocracy, their display may be said, in general, to be the sole means of aristocratic distinction; and the populace, looking always upward for models, are insensibly led to confound the two entirely separate ideas of magnificence and beauty. In short, the cost of an article of furniture has at length come to be, with us, nearly the sole test of its merit in a decorative point of view—and this test, once established, has led the way to many analogous errors, readily traceable to the one primitive folly.

There could be nothing more directly offensive to the eye of an artist than the interior of what is termed in the United States—that is to say, in Appallachia—a well-furnished apartment. Its most usual defect is a want of keeping. We speak of the keeping of a room as we would of the keeping of a picture—for both the picture and the room are amenable to those undeviating principles which regulate all varieties of art; and very nearly the same laws by which we decide on the higher merits of a painting, suffice for decision on the adjustment of a chamber.

A want of keeping is observable sometimes in the character of the several pieces of furniture, but generally in their colours or modes of adaptation to use. *Very* often the eye is offended by their inartistical arrangement. Straight lines are too prevalent—too uninterruptedly continued—or clumsily interrupted at right angles. If curved lines occur, they are repeated into unpleasant uniformity. By undue precision, the appearance of many a fine apartment is utterly spoiled.

Curtains are rarely well disposed, or well chosen in respect to other decorations. With formal furniture, curtains are out of place; and an extensive volume of drapery of any kind is, under any circumstances, irreconcilable with good taste—the proper quantum, as well as the proper adjustment, depending upon the character of the general effect.

Carpets are better understood of late than of ancient days, but we still very frequently err in their patterns and colours. The soul of the apartment is the carpet. From it are deduced not only the hues but the forms of all objects incumbent. A judge at common law may be an ordinary man; a good judge of a carpet *must be* a genius. Yet we have heard discoursing of carpets, with the air '*d'un mouton qui rêve*', fellows who should not and who could not be entrusted with the management of their own *moustaches*. Every one knows that a large floor *may* have a covering of large figures, and that a small one *must* have a covering of small—yet this is not all the knowledge in the world. As regards texture, the Saxony is alone admissible. Brussels is the preterpluperfect tense of fashion, and Turkey is taste in its dying agonies. Touching pattern—a carpet should *not* be bedizened out like a Riccaree Indian—all red chalk, yellow ochre, and cock's feathers. In brief—distinct grounds, and vivid circular or cycloid figures, *of no meaning*, are here Median laws. The abomination of flowers, or representations of well-known objects of any kind, should not be endured within the limits of Christendom. Indeed, whether on carpets, or curtains, or tapestry, or ottoman coverings, all upholstery of this nature should be rigidly Arabesque. As for those antique floor-cloths still occasionally seen in the dwellings of the rabble—cloths of huge, sprawling, and radiating devices, stripe-interspersed, and glorious with all hues, among which no ground is intelligible—these are but the wicked invention of a race of time-servers and money-lovers—children of Baal and worshippers of Mammon—Benthams, who, to spare thought and economize fancy, first cruelly invented the Kaleidoscope, and then established joint-stock companies to twirl it by steam.

Glare is a leading error in the philosophy of American household decoration—an error easily recognized as deduced from the perversion of taste just specified. We are violently enamoured of gas and of glass. The former is totally inadmissible within doors. Its harsh and unsteady light offends. No one having both brains and eyes will use it. A mild, or what artists term a cool light, with its consequent warm shadows, will do wonders for even an ill-furnished apartment. Never was a more lovely thought than that of the astral lamp. We mean, of course, the astral lamp proper—the lamp of Argand, with its original plain ground-glass shade, and its tempered and uniform moonlight rays. The cut-glass shade is a weak invention of the enemy. The eagerness with which we have adopted it, partly on account of its *flashiness*, but principally on account of its *greater cost*, is a good commentary on the proposition with which we began. It is not too much to say, that the deliberate employer of a cut-glass shade is either radically deficient in taste, or blindly subservient to the caprices of fashion. The light proceeding from one of these gaudy abominations is unequal, broken, and painful. It alone is sufficient to mar a world of good effect in the furniture subjected to its influence. Female loveliness, in especial, is more than one-half disenchanted beneath its evil eye.

In the matter of glass, generally, we proceed upon false principles. Its leading feature is *glitter*—and in that one word how much of all that is detestable do we express! Flickering, unquiet lights, are *sometimes* pleasing—to children and idiots always so—but in the embellishment of a room they should be scrupulously avoided. In truth, even strong *steady* lights are inadmissible. The huge and unmeaning glass chandeliers, prism-cut, gas-lighted, and without shade, which dangle in our most fashionable drawing-rooms, may be cited as the quintessence of all that is false in taste or preposterous in folly.

The rage for *glitter*—because its idea has become, as we before observed, confounded with that of magnificence in the abstract—has led us, also, to the exaggerated employment of mirrors. We line our dwellings with great British plates, and then imagine we have done a fine thing. Now the slightest thought will be sufficient to convince any one who has an eye at all of the ill effect of numerous looking-glasses, and especially of large ones. Regarded apart from its reflection, the mirror presents a continuous, flat, colourless, unrelieved surface,—a thing always and obviously unpleasant. Considered as a reflector, it is potent in producing a monstrous and odious uniformity: and the evil is here aggravated, not in merely direct proportion with the augmentation of its sources, but in a ratio constantly increasing. In fact, a room with four or five mirrors arranged at random, is, for all purposes of artistic show, a room of no shape at all. If we add to this evil, the attendant glitter upon glitter, we have a perfect farrago of discordant and displeasing effects. The veriest bumpkin, on entering an apartment so bedizened, would be instantly aware of something wrong, although he might be altogether unable to assign a cause for his dissatisfaction. But let the same person be led into a room tastefully furnished, and he would be startled into an exclamation of pleasure and surprise.

It is an evil growing out of our republican institutions that here a man of large purse has usually a very little soul which he keeps in it. The corruption of taste is a portion or a pendant of the dollar-manufacture. As we grow rich our ideas grow rusty. It is, therefore, not among *our* aristocracy that we must look (if at all, in Appallachia,) for the spirituality of a British *boudoir*. But we have seen apartments in the tenure of Americans of moderate means, which, in negative merit at least, might vie with any of the *ormolu'd* cabinets of our friends across the water. Even *now*, there is present to our mind's eye a small and not ostentatious chamber with whose decorations no fault can be found. The proprietor lies asleep on a sofa—the weather is cool—the time is near midnight: we will make a sketch of the room during his slumber.

It is oblong—some thirty feet in length and twenty-five in breadth—a shape affording the best (ordinary) opportunities for the adjustment of furniture. It has but one door—by no means a wide one—which is at one end of the parallelogram, and but two windows, which are at the other. These latter are large, reaching down to the floor—have deep recesses—and open on an Italian *veranda*. Their panes are of a crimson-tinted glass, set in rosewood framings, more massive than usual. They are curtained within the recess, by a thick silver tissue adapted to the shape of the window, and hanging loosely in small volumes. Without the recess are curtains of an exceedingly rich crimson silk, fringed with a deep network of gold, and lined with the silver tissue, which is the material of the exterior blind. There are no cornices; but the folds of the whole fabric (which are sharp rather than massive, and have an airy appearance,) issue from beneath a broad entablature of rich giltwork, which encircles the room at the junction of the ceiling and walls. The drapery is thrown open also, or closed, by means of a thick rope of gold loosely enveloping it, and resolving itself readily into a knot; no pins or other such devices are apparent. The colours of the curtains and their fringe—the tints of crimson and gold—appear everywhere in profusion, and determine the *character* of the room. The carpet—of Saxony material—is quite half an inch thick, and is of the same crimson ground, relieved simply by the appearance of a gold cord (like that festooning the curtains) slightly relieved above the surface of the *ground*, and thrown upon it in such a manner as to form a succession of short irregular curves—one occasionally overlaying the other. The walls are prepared with a glossy paper of a silver grey tint, spotted with small Arabesque devices of a fainter hue of the prevalent crimson. Many paintings relieve the expanse of the paper. These are chiefly landscapes of an imaginative cast—such as the fairy grottoes of Stanfield, or the lake of the Dismal Swamp of Chapman. There are, nevertheless, three or four female heads, of an ethereal beauty—portraits in the manner of Sully. The tone of each picture is warm, but dark. There are no 'brilliant effects'. *Repose* speaks in all. Not one is of small size. Diminutive paintings give that *spotty* look to a room, which is the blemish of so many a fine work of Art overtouched. The frames are broad but not deep, and richly carved, without being *dulled* or filigreed. They have the whole lustre of burnished gold. They lie flat on the walls, and do not hang off with cords. The designs themselves are often seen to better advantage in this latter position, but the general appearance of the chamber is injured. But one mirror—and this not a very large one—is visible. In shape it is nearly circular—and it is hung so that a reflection of the person can be obtained from it in none of the ordinary sitting-places of the room. Two large low sofas of rosewood and crimson silk, gold-flowered, form the only seats, with the exception of two light conversation chairs, also of rosewood.

There is a pianoforte (rosewood, also,) without cover, and thrown open. An octagonal table, formed altogether of the richest gold-threaded marble, is placed near one of the sofas. This is also without cover—the drapery of the curtains has been thought sufficient. Four large and gorgeous Sèvres vases, in which bloom a profusion of sweet and vivid flowers, occupy the slightly rounded angles of the room. A tall candelabrum, bearing a small antique lamp with highly perfumed oil, is standing near the head of my sleeping friend. Some light and graceful hanging shelves, with golden edges and crimson silk cords with gold tassels, sustain two or three hundred magnificently bound books. Beyond these things, there is no furniture, if we except an Argand lamp, with a plain crimson-tinted ground-glass shade, which depends from the lofty vaulted ceiling by a single slender gold chain, and throws a tranquil but magical radiance over all.

WILLIAM MAKEPEACE THACKERAY

1811–1863

DE FINIBUS

WHEN Swift was in love with Stella, and dispatching her a letter from London thrice a month by the Irish packet, you may remember how he would begin letter No. XXIII, we will say, on the very day when XXII had been sent away, stealing out of the coffee-house or the assembly so as to be able to prattle with his dear; 'never letting go her kind hand, as it were,' as some commentator or other has said in speaking of the Dean and his amour. When Mr. Johnson, walking to Dodsley's, and touching the posts in Pall Mall as he walked, forgot to pat the head of one of them, he went back and imposed his hands on it,—impelled I know not by what superstition. I have this I hope not dangerous mania too. As soon as a piece of work is out of hand, and before going to sleep, I like to begin another: it may be to write only half a dozèn lines: but that is something towards Number the Next. The printer's boy has not yet reached Green Arbour Court with the copy. Those people who were alive half an hour since, Pendennis, Clive Newcome, and (what do you call him? what was the name of the last hero? I remember now!) Philip Firmin have hardly drunk their glass of wine, and the mammas have only this minute got the children's cloaks on, and have been bowed out of my premises—and here I come back to the study again: *tamen usque recurro.* How lonely it looks now all these people are gone! My dear good friends, some folks are utterly tired of you, and say, 'What a poverty of friends the man has! He is always asking us to meet those Pendennises, Newcomes, and so forth. Why does he not introduce us to some new characters? Why is he not thrilling like Twostars, learned and profound like Threestars, exquisitely humorous and human like Fourstars? Why, finally, is he not somebody else?' My good people, it is not only impossible to please you all, but it is absurd to try. The dish which one man devours, another dislikes. Is the dinner of to-day not to your taste? Let us hope to-morrow's entertainment will be more agreeable. . . . I resume my original subject. What an odd, pleasant, humorous, melancholy feeling it is to sit in the study, alone and quiet, now all these people are gone who have been boarding and lodging with me for twenty months! They have interrupted my rest: they have plagued me at all sorts of minutes: they have thrust themselves upon me when I was ill, or wished to be idle, and I have growled out a 'Be hanged to you, can't you leave me alone now?' Once or twice they have prevented my going out to dinner. Many and many a time they have prevented my coming home, because I knew they were there waiting in the study, and a plague take them! and I have left home and family, and gone to dine at the Club, and told nobody where I went. They have bored me, those people. They have plagued me at all sorts of uncomfortable hours. They have made such a disturbance in my mind and house, that sometimes I have hardly known what was going on in my family, and scarcely have heard what my neighbour said to me. They are gone at last; and you would expect me to be at ease? Far from it. I should almost be glad if Woolcomb would walk in and talk to me; or Twysden reappear, take his place in that chair opposite me, and begin one of his tremendous stories.

Madmen, you know, see visions, hold conversations with, even draw the likeness of, people invisible to you and me. Is this making of people out of fancy madness? and are novel-writers at all entitled to strait-waistcoats? I often forget people's names in life; and in my own stories contritely own that I make dreadful blunders regarding them; but I declare, my dear sir, with respect to the personages introduced into your humble servant's fables, I know the people utterly —I know the sound of their voices. A gentleman came in to see me the other day, who was so like the picture of Philip Firmin in Mr. Walker's charming drawings in the *Cornhill Magazine*, that he was quite a curiosity to me. The same eyes, beard, shoulders, just as you have seen them from month to month. Well, he is not like the Philip Firmin in my mind. Asleep, asleep in the grave, lies the bold, the generous, the reckless, the tender-hearted creature whom I have made to pass through those adventures which have just been brought to an end. It is years since I heard the laughter ringing, or saw the bright blue eyes. When I knew him both were young. I become young as I think of him. And this morning he was alive again in this room, ready to laugh, to fight, to weep. As I write, do you know, it is the grey of evening; the house is quiet; everybody is out; the room is getting a little dark, and I look rather wistfully up from the paper with perhaps ever so little fancy that HE MAY COME IN.—— No? No movement. No grey shade, growing more palpable, out of which at last look the well-known eyes. No, the printer came and took him away with the last page of the proofs. And with the printer's boy did the whole *cortège* of ghosts flit away, invisible? Ha! stay! what is this? Angels and ministers of grace! The door opens, and a dark form—enters, bearing a black—a black suit of clothes. It is John. He says it is time to dress for dinner.

. . . .

Every man who has had his German tutor, and has been coached through the famous *Faust* of Goethe (thou wert my instructor, good old Weissenborn, and these eyes beheld the great master himself in dear little Weimar town!) has read those charming verses which are prefixed to the drama, in which the poet reverts to the time when his work was first composed, and recalls the friends now departed, who once listened to his song. The dear shadows rise up around him, he says; he lives in the past again. It is to-day which appears vague and visionary. We humbler writers cannot create Fausts, or raise up monumental works that shall endure for all ages; but our books are diaries, in which our own feelings must of necessity be set down. As we look to the page written last month, or ten years ago, we remember the day and its events; the child ill, mayhap, in the adjoining room, and the doubts and fears which racked the brain as it still pursued its work; the dear old friend who read the commencement of the tale, and whose gentle hand shall be laid in ours no more. I own for my part that, in reading pages which this hand penned formerly, I often lose sight of the text under my eyes. It is not the words I see; but that past day; that bygone page of life's history; that tragedy, comedy it may be, which our little home company was enacting; that merrymaking which we shared; that funeral which we followed; that bitter, bitter grief which we buried.

And, such being the state of my mind, I pray gentle readers to deal kindly with their humble servant's manifold shortcomings, blunders, and slips of memory. As sure as I read a page of my own composition, I find a fault or two, half a dozen. Jones is called Brown. Brown, who is dead, is brought to life. Aghast, and months after the number was printed, I saw that I had called Philip Firmin, Clive Newcome. Now Clive Newcome is the hero of another story by the reader's most obedient writer. The two men are as different, in my mind's eye, as—as Lord Palmerston and Mr. Disraeli let us say. But there is that blunder at page 990, line 76, volume 84 of the *Cornhill Magazine*, and it is past mending; and I wish in my life I had made no worse blunders or errors than that which is hereby acknowledged.

Another Finis written. Another mile-stone passed on this journey from birth to the next world! Sure it is a subject for solemn cogitation. Shall we continue this story-telling business and be voluble to the end of our age? Will it not be presently time, O prattler, to hold your tongue, and let younger people speak? I have a friend, a painter, who, like other persons who shall be nameless, is growing old. He has never painted with such laborious finish as his works now show. This master is still the most humble and diligent of scholars. Of Art, his mistress, he is always an eager, reverent pupil. In his calling, in yours, in mine, industry and humility will help and comfort us. A word with you. In a pretty large experience I have not found the men who write books superior in wit or learning to those who don't write at all. In regard of mere information, non-writers must often be superior to writers. You don't expect a lawyer in full practice to be conversant with all kinds of literature; he is too busy with his law; and so a writer is commonly too busy with his own books to be able to bestow attention on the works of other people. After a day's work (in which I have been depicting, let us say, the agonies of Louisa on parting with the Captain, or the atrocious behaviour of the wicked Marquess to Lady Emily) I march to the club, proposing to improve my mind and keep myself 'posted up', as the Americans phrase it, with the literature of the day. And what happens? Given, a walk after luncheon, a pleasing book, and a most comfortable arm-chair by the fire, and you know the rest. A doze ensues. Pleasing book drops suddenly, is picked up once with an air of some confusion, is laid presently softly in lap: head falls on comfortable arm-chair cushion: eyes close: soft nasal music is heard. Am I telling club secrets? Of afternoons, after lunch, I say, scores of sensible fogies have a doze. Perhaps I have fallen asleep over that very book to which 'Finis' has just been written. And if the writer sleeps, what happens to the readers? says Jones, coming down upon me with his lightning wit. What? You *did* sleep over it? And a very good thing too. These eyes have more than once seen a friend dozing over pages which this hand has written. There is a vignette somewhere in one of my books of a friend so caught napping with *Pendennis*, or the *Newcomes*, in his lap; and if a writer can give you a sweet, soothing, harmless sleep, has he not done you a kindness? So is the author who excites and interests you worthy of your thanks and benedictions. I am troubled with fever and ague, that seizes me at odd intervals and prostrates me for a day. There is cold fit, for which, I am thankful to say, hot brandy-and-water is prescribed, and this induces hot fit, and so on. In one or two of these fits I have read novels with the most fearful contentment of mind. Once, on the Mississippi, it was my dearly beloved *Jacob Faithful*: once at Frankfort O. M., the delightful *Vingt ans après* of Monsieur Dumas: once at Tunbridge Wells, the thrilling *Woman in White*: and these books gave me amusement from morning till sunset. I remember those ague fits with a great deal of pleasure and gratitude. Think of a whole day in bed, and a good novel for a companion! No cares: no remorse about idleness: no visitors: and the Woman in White or the Chevalier d'Artagnan to tell me stories from dawn to night! 'Please, ma'am, my master's compliments, and can he have the third volume?' (This message was sent to an astonished friend and neighbour who lent me, volume by volume, the *W. in W.*) How do you like your novels? I like mine strong, 'hot with,' and no mistake: no love-making: no observations about society: little dialogue, except where the characters are bullying each other:

plenty of fighting: and a villain in the cupboard, who is to suffer tortures just before Finis. I don't like your melancholy Finis. I never read the history of a consumptive heroine twice. If I might give a short hint to an impartial writer (as the *Examiner* used to say in old days), it would be to act, *not* à la mode le pays de Pole (I think that was the phraseology), but *always* to give quarter. In the story of *Philip*, just come to an end, I have the permission of the author to state that he was going to drown the two villains of the piece—a certain Doctor F—— and a certain Mr. T. H—— on board the *President*, or some other tragic ship —but you see I relented. I pictured to myself Firmin's ghastly face amid the crowd of shuddering people on that reeling deck in the lonely ocean, and thought, 'Thou ghastly lying wretch, thou shalt not be drowned: thou shalt have a fever only; a knowledge of thy danger; and a chance— ever so small a chance—of repentance.' I wonder whether he *did* repent when he found himself in the yellow-fever, in Virginia? The probability is, he fancied that his son had injured him very much, and forgave him on his deathbed. Do you imagine there is a great deal of genuine right-down remorse in the world? Don't people rather find excuses which make their minds easy; endeavour to prove to themselves that they have been lamentably belied and misunderstood; and try and forgive the persecutors who *will* present that bill when it is due; and not bear malice against the cruel ruffian who takes them to the police-office for stealing the spoons? Years ago I had a quarrel with a certain well-known person (I believed a statement regarding him which his friends imparted to me, and which turned out to be quite incorrect). To his dying day that quarrel was never quite made up. I said to his brother, 'Why is your brother's soul still dark against me? It is I who ought to be angry and unforgiving: for I was in the wrong.' In the region which they now inhabit (for Finis has been set to the volumes of the lives of both here below), if they take any cognizance of our squabbles, and tittle-tattles, and gossips on earth here, I hope they admit that my little error was not of a nature unpardonable. If you have never committed a worse, my good sir, surely the score against you will not be heavy. Ha, *dilectissimi fratres!* It is in regard of sins *not* found out that we may say or sing (in an undertone, in a most penitent and lugubrious minor key), *Miserere nobis miseris peccatoribus.*

Among the sins of commission which novel-writers not seldom perpetrate, is the sin of grandiloquence, or tall-talking, against which, for my part, I will offer up a special *libera me.* This is the sin of schoolmasters, governesses, critics, sermoners, and instructors of young or old people. Nay (for I am making a clean breast, and liberating my soul), perhaps of all the novel-spinners now extant, the present speaker is the most addicted to preaching. Does he not stop perpetually in his story and begin to preach to you? When he ought to be engaged with business, is he not for ever taking the Muse by the sleeve, and plaguing her with some of his cynical sermons? I cry *peccavi* loudly and heartily. I tell you I would like to be able to write a story which should show no egotism whatever—in which there should be no reflections, no cynicism, no vulgarity (and so forth), but an incident in every other page, a villain, a battle, a mystery in every chapter. I should like to be able to feed a reader so spicily as to leave him hungering and thirsting for more at the end of every monthly meal.

Alexandre Dumas describes himself, when inventing the plan of a work, as lying silent on his back for two whole days on the deck of a yacht in a Mediterranean port. At the end of the two days he arose, and called for dinner. In those two days he had built his plot. He had moulded a mighty clay, to be cast presently in perennial brass. The chapters, the characters, the incidents, the combinations were all arranged in the artist's brain ere he set a pen to paper. My Pegasus won't fly, so as to let me survey the field below me. He has no wings, he is blind of one eye certainly, he is restive, stubborn, slow; crops a hedge when he ought to be galloping, or gallops when he ought to be quiet. He never will show off when I want him. Sometimes he goes at a pace which surprises me. Sometimes, when I most wish him to make the running, the brute turns restive, and I am obliged to let him take his own time. I wonder do other novel-writers experience this fatalism? They *must* go a certain way, in spite of themselves. I have been surprised at the observations made by some of my characters. It seems as if an occult Power was moving the pen. The personage does or says something, and I ask, how the Dickens did he come to think of that? Every man has remarked in dreams, the vast dramatic power which is sometimes evinced; I won't say the surprising power, for nothing does surprise you in dreams. But those strange characters you meet make instant observations of which you never can have thought previously. In like manner, the imagination foretells things. We spake anon of the inflated style of some writers. What also if there is an *afflated* style,—when a writer is like a Pythoness on her oracle tripod, and mighty words, words which he cannot help, come blowing, and bellowing, and whistling, and moaning through the speaking pipes of his bodily organ? I have told you it was a very queer shock to me the other day when, with a letter of introduction in his hand, the artist's (not my) Philip Firmin walked into this room, and sat down in the chair opposite. In the novel of *Pendennis*, written ten years ago, there is an account of a certain Costigan, whom I had invented (as I suppose authors invent their personages out of scraps, heel-taps, odds and ends of characters). I was smoking in a tavern parlour one night—and this Costigan came into the room alive—the very man:—the most remarkable resemblance of the printed sketches of the man, of the rude drawings in which I had depicted him. He had the same little coat, the same battered hat, cocked on one eye, the same twinkle in that eye. 'Sir,' said I, knowing him to be an old friend whom I had met in unknown regions, 'sir,' I said, 'may I offer you a glass of brandy-and-water?' '*Bedad, ye may*,' says he, '*and I'll sing ye a song tu*.' Of course he spoke with an Irish brogue. Of course he had been in the army. In ten minutes he pulled out an army agent's account, whereon his name was written. A few months after we read of him in a police-court. How had I come to know him, to divine him? Nothing shall convince me that I have not seen that man in the world of spirits. In the world of spirits and water I know I did: but that is a mere quibble of words. I was not surprised when he spoke in an Irish brogue. I had had cognizance of him before somehow. Who has not felt that little shock which arises when a person, a place, some words in a book (there is always a collocation) present themselves to you, and you know that you have before met the same person, words, scene, and so forth?

They used to call the good Sir Walter the 'Wizard of the North'. What if some writer should appear who can write so *enchantingly* that he shall be able to call into actual life the people whom he invents? What if Mignon, and Margaret, and Goetz von Berlichingen are alive now (though I don't say they are visible), and Dugald Dalgetty and Ivanhoe were to step in at that open window by the little garden yonder? Suppose Uncas and our noble old Leather-stocking were to glide silent in? Suppose Athos, Porthos, and Aramis should enter with a noiseless swagger, curling their mustachios? And dearest Amelia Booth, on Uncle Toby's arm; and Tittlebat Titmouse, with his hair dyed green; and all the Crummles company of comedians, with the Gil Blas troop; and Sir Roger de Coverley; and the greatest of all crazy gentlemen, the Knight of La Mancha, with his blessed squire? I say to you, I look rather wistfully towards the window, musing upon these people. Were any of them to enter, I think I should not be very much frightened. Dear old friends, what pleasant hours I have had with them! We do not see each other very often, but when we do, we are ever happy to meet. I had a capital half-hour with Jacob Faithful last night; when the last sheet was corrected, when 'Finis' had been written, and the printer's boy, with the copy, was safe in Green Arbour Court.

So you are gone, little printer's boy, with the last scratches and corrections on the proof, and a fine flourish by way of Finis at the story's end. The last corrections? I say those last corrections seem never to be finished. A plague upon the weeds! Every day, when I walk in my own little literary garden-plot, I spy some, and should like to have a spud, and root them out. Those idle words, neighbour, are past remedy. That turning back to the old pages produces anything but elation of mind. Would you not pay a pretty fine to be able to cancel some of them? Oh, the sad old pages, the dull old pages! Oh, the cares, the *ennui*, the squabbles, the repetitions, the old conversations over and over again! But now and again a kind thought is recalled, and now and again a dear memory. Yet a few chapters more, and then the last: after which, behold Finis itself come to an end, and the Infinite begun.

CHARLES DICKENS

1812–1870

BROKERS' AND MARINE-STORE SHOPS

When we affirm that brokers' shops are strange places, and that if an authentic history of their contents could be procured, it would furnish many a page of amusement, and many a melancholy tale, it is necessary to explain the class of shops to which we allude. Perhaps when we make use of the term 'Brokers' Shop', the minds of our readers will at once picture large, handsome warehouses, exhibiting a long perspective of French-polished dining-tables, rosewood chiffoniers, and mahogany wash-hand-stands, with an occasional vista of a four-post bedstead and hangings, and an appropriate foreground of dining-room chairs. Perhaps they will imagine that we mean a humble class of second-hand furniture repositories. Their imagination will then naturally lead them to that street at the back of Long Acre, which is composed almost entirely of brokers' shops; where you walk through groves of deceitful, showy-looking furniture, and where the prospect is occasionally enlivened by a bright red, blue, and yellow hearth-rug, embellished with the pleasing device of a mail-coach at full speed, or a strange animal, supposed to have been originally intended for a dog, with a mass of worsted-work in his mouth, which conjecture has likened to a basket of flowers.

This, by the by, is a tempting article to young

wives in the humbler ranks of life, who have a first-floor front to furnish—they are lost in admiration, and hardly know which to admire most. The dog is very beautiful, but they have a dog already on the best tea-tray, and two more on the mantel-piece. Then, there is something so genteel about that mail-coach ; and the passengers outside (who are all hat) give it such an air of reality !

The goods here are adapted to the taste, or rather to the means, of cheap purchasers. There are some of the most beautiful *looking* Pembroke tables that were ever beheld : the wood as green as the trees in the Park, and the leaves almost as certain to fall off in the course of a year. There is also a most extensive assortment of tent and turn-up bedsteads, made of stained wood, and innumerable specimens of that base imposition on society—a sofa bedstead.

A turn-up bedstead is a blunt, honest piece of furniture ; it may be slightly disguised with a sham drawer ; and sometimes a mad attempt is even made to pass it off for a bookcase ; ornament it as you will, however, the turn-up bedstead seems to defy disguise, and to insist on having it distinctly understood that he is a turn-up bedstead, and nothing else—that he is indispensably necessary, and that being so useful, he disdains to be ornamental.

How different is the demeanour of a sofa bedstead ! Ashamed of its real use, it strives to appear an article of luxury and gentility—an attempt in which it miserably fails. It has neither the respectability of a sofa, nor the virtues of a bed ; every man who keeps a sofa bedstead in his house, becomes a party to a wilful and designing fraud—we question whether you could insult him more, than by insinuating that you entertain the least suspicion of its real use.

To return from this digression, we beg to say, that neither of these classes of brokers' shops forms the subject of this sketch. The shops to which we advert, are immeasurably inferior to those on whose outward appearance we have slightly touched. Our readers must often have observed in some by-street, in a poor neighbourhood, a small dirty shop, exposing for sale the most extraordinary and confused jumble of old, worn-out, wretched articles, that can well be imagined. Our wonder at their ever having been bought, is only to be equalled by our astonishment at the idea of their ever being sold again. On a board, at the side of the door, are placed about twenty books—all odd volumes; and as many wine-glasses—all different patterns; several locks, an old earthenware pan, full of rusty keys; two or three gaudy chimney-ornaments—cracked, of course; the remains of a lustre, without any drops; a round frame like a capital O, which has once held a mirror; a flute, complete with the exception of the middle joint; a pair of curling-irons; and a tinder-box. In front of the shop window are ranged some half-dozen high-backed chairs, with spinal complaints and wasted legs; a corner cupboard; two or three very dark mahogany tables with flaps like mathematical problems; some pickle-jars, some surgeons' ditto, with gilt labels and without stoppers; an unframed portrait of some lady who flourished about the beginning of the thirteenth century, by an artist who never flourished at all; an incalculable host of miscellanies of every description, including bottles and cabinets, rags and bones, fenders and street-door knockers, fire-irons, wearing apparel and bedding, a hall-lamp, and a room-door. Imagine, in addition to this incongruous mass, a black doll in a white frock, with two faces—one looking up the street, and the other looking down, swinging over the door; a board with the squeezed-up inscription 'Dealer in marine stores', in lanky white letters, whose height is strangely out of proportion to their width; and you have before you precisely the kind of shop to which we wish to direct your attention.

Although the same heterogeneous mixture of things will be found at all these places, it is curious to observe how truly and accurately some of the minor articles which are exposed for sale—articles of wearing apparel, for instance—mark the character of the neighbourhood. Take Drury Lane and Covent Garden for example.

This is essentially a theatrical neighbourhood. There is not a potboy in the vicinity who is not, to a greater or less extent, a dramatic character. The errand-boys and chandler's-shop-keepers' sons are all stage-struck: they 'gets up' plays in back kitchens hired for the purpose, and will stand before a shop-window for hours, contemplating a great staring portrait of Mr. Somebody or other, of the Royal Coburg Theatre, 'as he appeared in the character of Tongo the Denounced.' The consequence is, that there is not a marine-store shop in the neighbourhood, which does not exhibit for sale some faded articles of dramatic finery, such as three or four pairs of soiled buff boots with turn-over red tops, heretofore worn by a 'fourth robber', or 'fifth mob'; a pair of rusty broadswords, a few gauntlets, and certain resplendent ornaments, which, if they were yellow instead of white, might be taken for insurance plates of the Sun Fire Office. There are several of these shops in the narrow streets and dirty courts, of which there are so many near the national theatres, and they all have tempting goods of this description, with the addition, perhaps, of a lady's pink dress covered with spangles ; white wreaths, stage shoes, and a tiara like a tin lamp reflector. They have been purchased of some wretched supernumeraries, or sixth-rate actors, and are now offered for the benefit of the rising generation, who, on condition of making certain weekly payments, amounting in the whole to about ten times their value, may avail themselves of such desirable bargains.

Let us take a very different quarter, and apply it to the same test. Look at a marine-store dealer's, in that reservoir of dirt, drunkenness, and drabs : thieves, oysters, baked potatoes, and pickled salmon—Ratcliff Highway. Here, the wearing apparel is all nautical. Rough blue jackets, with mother-of-pearl buttons, oil-skin hats, coarse checked shirts, and large canvas trousers that look as if they were made for a pair of bodies instead of a pair of legs, are the staple commodities. Then, there are large bunches of cotton pocket-handkerchiefs, in colour and pattern unlike any one ever saw before, with the exception of those on the backs of the three young ladies without bonnets who passed just now. The furniture is much the same as elsewhere, with the addition of one or two models of ships, and some old prints of naval engagements in still older frames. In the window are a few compasses, a small tray containing silver watches in clumsy thick cases; and tobacco-boxes, the lid of each ornamented with a ship, or an anchor, or some such trophy. A sailor generally pawns or sells all he has before he has been long ashore, and if he does not, some favoured companion kindly saves him the trouble. In either case, it is an even chance that he afterwards unconsciously repurchases the same things at a higher price than he gave for them at first.

Again: pay a visit with a similar object, to a part of London, as unlike both of these as they are to each other. Cross over to the Surrey side, and look at such shops of this description as are to be found near the King's Bench prison, and in 'the Rules'. How different, and how strikingly illustrative of the decay of some of the unfortunate residents in this part of the metropolis! Imprisonment and neglect have done their work. There is contamination in the profligate denizens of a debtor's prison; old friends have fallen off; the recollection of former prosperity has passed away; and with it all thoughts for the past, all care for the future. First, watches and rings, then cloaks, coats, and all the more expensive articles of dress, have found their way to the pawnbroker's. That miserable resource has failed at last, and the sale of some trifling article at one of these shops has been the only mode left of raising a shilling or two, to meet the urgent demands of the moment. Dressing-cases and writing-desks, too old to pawn but too good to keep; guns, fishing-rods, musical instruments, all in the same condition; have first been sold, and the sacrifice has been but slightly felt. But hunger must be allayed, and what has already become a habit is easily resorted to, when an emergency arises. Light articles of clothing, first of the ruined man, then of his wife, at last of their children, even of the youngest, have been parted with, piecemeal. There they are, thrown carelessly together until a purchaser presents himself, old, and patched and repaired, it is true ; but the make and materials tell of better days ; and the older they are, the greater the misery and destitution of those whom they once adorned.

JAMES ANTHONY FROUDE

1818–1894

ETHICAL DOUBTS CONCERNING REINEKE FUCHS

In a recent dissatisfied perusal of Mr. Macaulay's collected articles, we were especially offended by his curious and undesirable Essay on Machiavelli. Declining the various solutions which have been offered to explain how a man supposed to be so great could have lent his genius to the doctrine of 'the Prince', he has advanced an hypothesis of his own, which may or may not be true, as an interpretation of Machiavelli's character, but which, as an exposition of a universal ethical theory, is as detestable as what it is brought forward to explain. ... We will not show Mr. Macaulay the disrespect of supposing that he has unsuccessfully attempted an elaborate piece of irony. It is possible that he may have been exercising his genius with a paradox, but the subject is not of the sort in which we can patiently permit such exercises. It is hard work with all of us to keep ourselves straight, even when we see the road with all plainness as it lies out before us; and clever men must be good enough to find something else to amuse themselves with, instead of dusting our eyes with sophistry.

In Mr. Macaulay's conception of human nature, the basenesses and the excellences of mankind are no more than accidents of circumstance, the results of national feeling and national capabilities; and cunning and treachery, and lying, and such other 'natural defences of the weak against the strong', are in themselves neither good nor bad, except as thinking makes them so. They are the virtues of a weak people, and they will be as much admired, and are as justly admirable; they are to the full as compatible with the highest graces and most lofty features of the heart and intellect as any of those opposite so-called heroisms which we are generally so unthinking as to allow to monopolize the name. . . . Cunning is the only resource of the feeble; and why may we not feel for victorious cunning as strong a sympathy as for the bold, downright, open bearing of the strong? . . . That there may be no mistake in the essayist's meaning, that he may drive the nail home into the English understanding, he takes an illustration which shall be familiar to all of us in the characters of Iago and Othello. To our northern thought, the free and noble nature of the Moor is wrecked through a single infirmity, by a fiend in the human form. To one of Machiavelli's Italians, Iago's keen-edged intellect would have appeared as admirable as Othello's daring appears to us, and Othello himself little better than a fool and a savage. . . . It is but a change of scene, of climate, of the animal qualities of the frame, and evil has become a good, and good has become evil. . . . Now, our displeasure with Mr. Macaulay is, not that he has advanced a novel and mischievous theory: it was elaborated long ago in the finely-tempered dialectics of the Schools of Rhetoric, at Athens; and so long as such a phenomenon as a cultivated rogue remains possible among mankind, it will reappear in all languages and under any number of philosophical disguises.

. . . Seldom or never, however, has it appeared with so little attempt at disguise. It has been left for questionable poets and novelists to idealize the rascal genus; philosophers have escaped into the ambiguities of general propositions, and we do not remember elsewhere to have met with a serious ethical thinker deliberately laying two whole organic characters, with their vices and virtues in full life and bloom, side by side, asking himself which is best, and answering gravely that it is a matter of taste.

Mr. Macaulay has been bolder than his predecessors; he has shrunk from no conclusion, and looked directly into the very heart of the matter; he has struck, as we believe, the very lowest stone of our ethical convictions, and declared that the foundation quakes under it.

For, ultimately, how do we know that right is right, and wrong is wrong? People in general accept it on authority; but authority itself must repose on some ulterior basis; and what is that? . . . Are we to say that in morals there is a system of primary axioms, out of which we develop our conclusions, and apply them, as they are needed, to life? It does not appear so. The analogy of morals is rather with art than with geometry. The grace of heaven gives us good men, and gives us beautiful creations; and we, perceiving by the instincts within ourselves that celestial presence in the objects on which we gaze, find out for ourselves the laws which make them what they are, not by comparing them with any antecedent theory, but by careful analysis of our own impressions, by asking ourselves what it is which we admire in them, and calling that good, and calling that beautiful.

So, then, if admiration be the first fact, if the sense of it be the ultimate ground on which the after temple of morality, as a system, upraises itself, if we can be challenged here on our own ground, and fail to make it good, what we call the life of the soul becomes a dream of a feeble enthusiast, and we moralists a mark for the sceptic's finger to point at with scorn.

Bold and ably urged arguments against our own convictions, if they do not confuse us, will usually send us back over our ground to re-examine the strength of our positions: and if we are honest with ourselves, we shall very often find points of some uncertainty left unguarded, of which the show of the strength of our enemy will oblige us to see better to the defence. . . . It was not without some shame, and much uneasiness, that, while we were ourselves engaged in this process, full of indignation with Mr. Macaulay, we heard a clear voice ringing in our ear, 'Who art thou that judgest another?' and warning us of the presence in our own heart of a sympathy, which we could not deny, with the sadly questionable hero of the German epic, *Reynard the Fox*. With our vulpine friend, we were on the edge of the very same abyss, if, indeed, we were not rolling in the depth of it. By what sophistry could we justify ourselves, if not by the very same which we had just been so eagerly condemning? And our conscience whispered to us that we had been swift to detect a fault in another, because it was the very fault to which, in our own heart of hearts, we had a latent leaning.

Was it so indeed, then? Was Reineke no better than Iago? Was the sole difference between them, that the *vates sacer* who had sung the exploits of

Reineke loved the wicked rascal, and entangled us in loving him? It was a question to be asked.... And yet we had faith enough in the straightforwardness of our own sympathies to feel sure that it must admit of some sort of answer. And, indeed, we rapidly found an answer satisfactory enough to give us time to breathe, in remembering that Reineke, with all his roguery, has no malice in him.... It is not in his nature to hate; he could not do it if he tried. The characteristic of Iago is that deep motiveless malignity which rejoices in evil as its proper element, which loves evil as good men love virtue. In his calculations on the character of the Moor, he despises his unsuspicious trustingness as imbecility, while he hates him as a man because his nature is the perpetual opposite and perpetual reproach of his own.... Now Reineke would not have hurt a creature, not even Scharfenebbe, the crow's wife, when she came to peck his eyes out, if he had not been hungry; and that γαστρὸς ἀνάγκη, that craving of the stomach, makes a difference quite infinite. It is true that, like Iago, he rejoices in the exercise of his intellect; the sense of his power, and the scientific employment of his time are a real delight to him; but then, as we said, he does not love evil for its own sake; he is only somewhat indifferent to it. If the other animals venture to take liberties with him, he will repay them in their own coin, and get his quiet laugh at them at the same time; but the object generally for which he lives is the natural one of getting his bread for himself and his family; and, as the great moralist says, 'It is better to be bad for something than for nothing.' Badness generally is undesirable; but badness in its essence, which may be called heroic badness, is gratuitous.

But this first thought served merely to give us a momentary relief from our alarm, and we determined we would sift the matter to the bottom, and no more expose ourselves to be taken at such disadvantage. We went again to the poem, with our eyes open, and our moral sense as keenly awake as a genuine wish to understand our feelings could make it. We determined that we would really know what we did feel and what we did not. We would not be lightly scared away from our friend, but neither would we any more allow our judgement to be talked down by that fluent tongue of his; he should have justice from us, he and his biographer, as far as it lay with us to discern justice and to render it.

And really on this deliberate perusal it did seem little less than impossible that we could find any conceivable attribute illustrated in Reineke's proceedings which we could dare to enter in our catalogue of virtue, and not blush to read it there. What sin is there in the Decalogue in which he has not steeped himself to the lips? To the lips, shall we say? nay, over head and ears—rolling and rollicking in sin. Murder, and theft, and adultery, sacrilege, perjury, lying—his very life is made of them. On he goes to the end, heaping crime on crime, and lie on lie, and at last, when it seems that justice, which has been so long vainly halting after him, has him really in her iron grasp, there is a solemn appeal to heaven, a challenge, a battle ordeal, in which, by means we may not venture even to whisper, the villain prospers, and comes out glorious, victorious, amidst the applause of a gazing world; and, to crown it all, the poet tells us that under the disguise of the animal name and form the world of man is represented, and the true course of it; and the idea of the book is, that we who read it may learn therein to discern between good and evil, and choose the first and avoid the last. It seemed beyond the power of sophistry to whitewash Reineke, and the interest which still continued to cling to him in us seemed too nearly to resemble the unwisdom of the multitude, with whom success is the one virtue and failure the only crime.

It appeared, too, that although the animal disguises were too transparent to endure a moment's reflection, yet that they were so gracefully worn that such moment's reflection was not to be come at without an effort. Our imagination following the costume did imperceptibly betray our judgement; we admired the human intellect, the ever ready prompt sagacity and presence of mind. We delighted in the satire on the foolishnesses and greedinesses of our own fellow mankind; but in our regard for the hero we forgot his humanity wherever it was his interest that we should forget it, and while we admired him as a man we judged him only as a fox. We doubt whether it would have been possible if he had been described as an open acknowledged biped in coat and trousers, to have retained our regard for him. Something or other in us, either real rightmindedness, or humbug, or hypocrisy, would have obliged us to mix more censure with our liking than most of us do in the case as it stands. It may be that the dress of the fox throws us off our guard, and lets out a secret or two which we commonly conceal even from ourselves. When we have to pass an opinion upon bad people, who at the same time are clever and attractive, we say rather what we think we ought to feel than our real sensations; while with Reineke, being but an animal, we forget to make ourselves up, and for once our genuine tastes show themselves freely. . . . Some degree of truth there undoubtedly is in this. . . . But making all allowance for it—making all and over allowance for the trick which is passed upon our senses, there still remained a feeling unresolved. The poem was not solely the apotheosis of a rascal in whom we were betrayed into taking an interest. And it was not a satire merely on the world, and on the men whom the world delight to honour; there was still something which really deserved to be liked in Reineke, and what it was we had as yet failed to discover.

'Two are better than one,' and we resolved in our difficulty to try what our friends might have to say about it; the appearance of the Wurtemburg animals at the Exhibition came fortunately à propos to our assistance: a few years ago it was rare to find a person who had read the Fox Epic; and still more, of course, to find one whose judgement would be worth taking about it; but now the charming figures of Reineke himself, and the Lion King, and Isegrim, and Bruin, and Bellyn, and Hintze, and Grimbart, had set all the world asking who and what they were, and the story began to get itself known. The old editions, which had long slept unbound in reams upon the shelves, began to descend and clothe themselves in green and crimson. . . . Mr. Dickens sent a summary of it round the households of England. Everybody began to talk of Reineke; and now, at any rate, we said to ourselves, we shall see whether we are alone in our liking—whether others share in this strange sympathy, or whether it be some unique and monstrous moral obliquity in ourselves.

We set to work, therefore, with all earnestness, feeling our way first with fear and delicacy, as conscious of our own delinquency, to gather judgements which should be wiser than our own, and correct ourselves, if it proved that we required correction, with whatever severity might be necessary. The result of which labour of ours was not a little surprising; we found that women invariably, with that clear moral instinct of theirs, at once utterly reprobated and detested our poor Reynard; detested the hero and detested the bard who sang of him with so much sympathy; while men we found almost invariably feeling just as we felt ourselves, only with this difference, that we saw no trace of uneasiness in them about the matter. It was no little comfort to us, moreover, to find that the exceptions were rather among the half-men, the would-be extremely good, but whose goodness was of that dead and passive kind which spoke to but a small elevation of thought or activity; while just in proportion as a man was strong, and real, and energetic, was his ability to see good in Reineke. It was really most strange, one near friend of ours, a man who, as far as we knew (and we knew him well) had never done a wrong thing, when we ventured to hint something about roguery, replied, 'You see, he was such a clever rogue, that he had a right.' Another, whom we pressed more closely with that treacherous cannibal feast at Malepartus, on the body of poor Lampe, said, off-hand and with much impatience of such questioning, 'Such fellows were made to be eaten.' What could we do? It had come to this,—as in the exuberance of our pleasure with some dear child, no ordinary epithet will sometimes reach to express the vehemence of our affection, and borrowing language out of the opposites, we call him little rogue or little villain, so here, reversing the terms of the analogy, we bestow the fullness of our regard on Reineke because of that transcendently successful roguery.

When we asked our friends how they came to feel as they did, they had little to say. They were not persons who could be suspected of any latent disposition towards evil doing, and yet though it appeared as if they were falling under the description of those unhappy ones who, if they did not such things themselves, yet 'had pleasure in those who did them', they did not care to justify themselves. The fact was so: ἀρχὴ τὸ ὅτι: it was a fact—what could we want more? Some few attempted feebly to maintain that the book was a satire. But this only moved the difficulty a single step; for the fact of the sympathy remained unimpaired, and if it was a satire we were ourselves the objects of it. Others urged what we said above, that the story was only of poor animals that, according to Descartes, not only had no souls, but scarcely even life in any original and sufficient sense, and therefore we need not trouble ourselves. But one of two alternatives it seemed we were bound to choose, either of which was fatal to the proposed escape. Either there was a man hiding under the fox's skin, or else, if real foxes have such brains as Reineke was furnished withal, no honest doubt could be entertained that some sort of conscience was not forgotten in the compounding of him, and he must be held answerable according to his knowledge.

What would Mr. Carlyle say of it, we thought, with his might and right? 'The just thing in the long run is the strong thing.' But Reineke had a long run out and came in winner. Does he only 'seem to succeed'? Who does succeed, then, if he no more than seems? The vulpine intellect knows where the geese live, it is elsewhere said; but among Reineke's victims we do not remember one goose, in the literal sense of goose; and as to geese metaphorical, at least the whole visible world lies down complacently at his feet. Nor does Mr. Carlyle's expressed language on this very poem serve any better to help us—nay, it seems as if he feels uneasy in the neighbourhood of so strong a rascal, so briefly he dismisses him. 'Worldly prudence is the only virtue which is certain of its reward.' Nay, but there is more in it than that: no worldly prudence would command the voices which have been given in to us for Reineke.

Three only possibilities lay now before us: either we should, on searching, find something solid in this Fox's doings to justify success; or else the just thing was not always the strong thing; or it might be, that such very semblance of success was itself the most miserable failure; that the wicked man who was struck down and foiled, and foiled again, till he unlearnt his wickedness, or till he was disabled from any more attempting it, was blessed in his disappointment; that to triumph in wickedness, and to continue in it and to prosper to the end, was the last, worst penalty inflicted by the divine vengeance. Ἰν' ἀθάνατος ᾖ ἄδικος ὤν—to go on with injustice through this world and through all eternity, uncleansed by any purgatorial fire, untaught by any untoward consequence to open his eyes and to see in its true accursed form the miserable demon to which he has sold himself,—this, of all catastrophes which could befall an evil man, was the deepest, lowest, and most savouring of hell, which the purest of the Grecian moralists could reason out for himself,—under which third hypothesis many an uneasy misgiving would vanish away, and Mr. Carlyle's broad aphorism be accepted by us with thankfulness.

It appeared, therefore, at any rate, to have come to this—that if we wanted a solution for our sphinx enigma, no Oedipus was likely to rise and find it for us ; and that if we wanted help, we must make it for ourselves. This only we found, that if we sinned in our regard for the unworthy animal, we shared our sin with the largest number of our own sex; and, comforted with the sense of good fellowship, we went boldly to work upon our consciousness; and the imperfect analysis which we succeeded in accomplishing, we here lay before you, whoever you may be, who have felt, as we have felt, a regard which was a moral disturbance to you, and which you will be pleased if we enable you to justify—

> Si quid novisti rectius istis,
> Candidus imperti; si non, his utere mecum.

Following the clue which was thrust into our hand by the marked difference of the feelings of men upon the subject from those of women, we were at once satisfied that Reineke's goodness, if he had any, must lay rather in the active than the passive department of life. The negative obedience to prohibitory precepts, under which women are bound as well as men, as was already too clear, we were obliged to surrender as hopeless. But it seemed as if, with respect to men whose business is to do, and to labour, and to accomplish, this negative test was a seriously imperfect one ; and it was quite as possible that a man who unhappily had broken many prohibitions might yet exhibit positive excellences, as that he might walk through life picking his way with the utmost assiduity, risking nothing and doing nothing, not committing a single sin, but keeping his talent carefully wrapped up in a napkin, and get sent, in the end, to outer darkness for his pains, as an unprofitable servant ; and this appeared the more important to us, as it was very little dwelt upon by religious or moral teachers ; and at the end of six thousand years, the popular notion of virtue, as far as it could get itself expressed, had not risen beyond the mere abstinence from certain specific bad actions.

The king of the beasts forgives Reineke on account of the substantial services which at various times he has rendered. His counsel was always the wisest, his hand the promptest in cases of difficulty ; and all that dexterity, and politeness, and courtesy, and exquisite culture had not been learnt without an effort or without conquering many undesirable tendencies in himself. Men are not born with any art in its perfection, and he had made himself valuable by his own sagacity and exertion. Now, on the human stage, a man who has made himself valuable is certain to be valued. However we may pretend to estimate men according to the wrong things which they have done, or abstained from doing, we in fact follow the example of Nobel, the king of the beasts, and give them their places among us according to the serviceableness and capability which they display. We might mention not a few eminent public servants, whom the world delights to honour—ministers, statesmen, lawyers, men of science, artists, poets, soldiers, who, if they were tried by the negative test, would show but a poor figure ; yet their value is too real to be dispensed with ; and we tolerate unquestionable wrong to secure the services of eminent ability. The world really does, and it always has really done so from the beginning of the human history ; and it is only indolence or cowardice which has left our ethical teaching halting so far behind the universal and necessary practice. Even questionable prima donnas, in virtue of their sweet voices, have their praises hymned in drawing-room and newspaper, and applause rolls over them, and gold and bouquets shower on them from lips and hands which, except for those said voices, would treat them to a ruder reward. In real fact, we take our places in this world not according to what we are not, but according to what we are. His Holiness Pope Clement, when his audience-room rang with furious outcries for justice on Benvenuto Cellini, who, as far as half a dozen murders could form a title, was as fair a candidate for the gallows as ever swung from that unlucky wood, replied, 'All this is very well, gentlemen: these murders are bad things, we know that. But where am I to get another Benvenuto, if you hang this one for me?'

Or, to take an acknowledged hero, one of the old Greek sort, the theme of the song of the greatest of human poets, whom it is less easy to refuse to admire than even our friend Reineke. Take Ulysses. It cannot be said that he kept his hands from taking what was not his, or his tongue from speaking what was not true ; and if Frau Ermelyn had to complain (as indeed there was too much reason for her complaining) of certain infirmities in her good husband, Penelope, too, might have urged a thing or two, if she had known as much about the matter as we know, which the modern moralist would find it hard to excuse.

After all is said, the capable man is the man to be admired. The man who tries and fails, what is the use of him ? We are in this world to do something—not to fail in doing it. Of your bunglers—helpless, inefficient persons, 'unfit alike for good or ill,' who try one thing, and fail because they are not strong enough, and another, because they have not energy enough, and a third, because they have no talent—inconsistent, unstable, and therefore never to excel, what shall we say of them ? what use is there in them ? what hope is there of them ? what can we wish for them ? *τὸ μήποτ' εἶναι πάντ' ἄριστον*. It were better for them they had never been born. To be able to do what a man tries to do, that is the first requisite ; and given that, we may hope all things for him. 'Hell is paved with good intentions,' the proverb says ; and the enormous proportion of bad successes in this life lie between the desire and the execution. Give us a man who is able to do what he settles that he desires to do, and we have the one thing indispensable. If he can succeed doing ill, much more he can succeed doing well. Show him better, and, at any rate, there is a chance that he will do better.

We are not concerned here with Benvenuto or

with Ulysses further than to show, through the position which we all consent to give them, that there is much unreality, against which we must be on our guard. And if we fling off an old friend, and take to affecting a hatred of him which we do not feel, we have scarcely gained by the exchange, even though originally our friendship may have been misplaced.

Capability no one will deny to Reineke. That is the very *differentia* of him. An 'animal capable' would be his sufficient definition. Here is another very genuinely valuable feature about him—his wonderful singleness of character. Lying, treacherous, cunning scoundrel as he is, there is a wholesome absence of humbug about him. Cheating all the world, he never cheats himself; and while he is a hypocrite, he is always a conscious hypocrite—a form of character, however paradoxical it may seem, a great deal more accessible than the other of the unconscious sort. Ask Reineke for the principles of his life, and if it suited his purpose to tell you, he could do so with the greatest exactness. There would be no discrepancy between the profession and the practice. He is most truly single-minded, and therefore stable in his ways, and therefore as the world goes, and in the world's sense, successful. Whether really successful is a question we do not care here to enter on; but only to say this—that of all unsuccessful men in every sense, either divine, or human, or devilish, there is none equal to old Bunyan's Mr. Facing-both-ways—the fellow with one eye on heaven and one on earth—who sincerely preaches one thing, and sincerely does another; and from the intensity of his unreality is unable either to see or feel the contradiction.

Serving God with his lips, and with the half of his mind which is not bound up in the world; and serving the devil with his actions, and with the other half, he is substantially trying to cheat both God and the devil, and is, in fact, only cheating himself and his neighbours. This, of all characters upon the earth, appears to us to be the one of whom there is no hope at all—a character becoming, in these days, alarmingly abundant; and the abundance of which makes us find even in a Reineke an inexpressible relief.

But what we most thoroughly value in him is his capacity. He can do what he sets to work to do. That blind instinct with which the world shouts and claps its hand for the successful man, is one of those latent forces in us which are truer than we know; it is the universal confessional to which Nature leads us, and, in her intolerance of disguise and hypocrisy, compels us to be our own accusers. Whoever can succeed in a given condition of society, can succeed only in virtue of fulfilling the terms which society exacts of him; and if he can fulfil them triumphantly, of course it rewards him and praises him. He is what the rest of the world would be, if their powers were equal to their desires. He has accomplished what they all are vaguely, and with imperfect consistency, struggling to accomplish; and the character of the conqueror—the means and appliances by which he has climbed up that great pinnacle on which he stands victorious, the observed of all observers, is no more than a very exact indicator of the amount of real virtue in the age, out of which he stands prominent.

We are forced to acknowledge that it was not

a very virtuous age in which Reineke made himself a great man; but that was the fault of the age as much as the fault of him. His nature is to succeed wherever he is. If the age had required something else of him, then he would have been something else. Whatever it had said to him 'do, and I will make you my hero', that Reineke would have done. No appetite makes a slave of him—no faculty refuses obedience to his will. His entire nature is under perfect organic control to the one supreme authority. And the one object for which he lives, and for which, let his lot have been cast in whatever century it might, he would always have lived, is to rise, to thrive, to prosper, and become great.

The world as he found it said to him—Prey upon us, we are your oyster; let your wit open us. If you will only do it cleverly—if you will take care that we shall not close upon your fingers in the process, you may devour us at your pleasure, and we shall feel ourselves highly honoured. Can we wonder at a fox of Reineke's abilities taking such a world at its word?

And let it not be supposed that society in this earth of ours is ever so viciously put together, is ever so totally without organic life, that a rogue, unredeemed by any merit, can prosper in it. There is no strength in rottenness; and when it comes to that, society dies and falls in pieces. Success, as it is called, even worldly success, is impossible, without some exercise of what is called moral virtue, without some portion of it, infinitesimally small, perhaps, but still some. Courage, for instance, steady self-confidence, self-trust, self-reliance—that only basis and foundation-stone on which a strong character can rear itself—do we not see this in Reineke. While he lives he lives for himself; but if it comes to dying, he can die like his betters; and his wit is not of that effervescent sort which will fly away at the sight of death and leave him panic-stricken. It is true there is a meaning to that word courage, which was perhaps not to be found in the dictionary in which Reineke studied. 'I hope I am afraid of nothing, Trim,' said my uncle Toby, 'except doing a wrong thing.' With Reineke there was no 'except'. His digestive powers shrank from no action, good or bad, which would serve his turn. Yet it required no slight measure of courage to treat his fellow creatures with the steady disrespect with which Reineke treats them. To walk along among them, regardless of any interest but his own; out of mere wantonness to hook them up like so many cockchafers, and spin them for his pleasure; not like Domitian, with an imperial army to hold them down during the operation, but with no other assistance but his own little body and large wit; it was something to venture upon. And a world which would submit to be so treated, what could he do but despise?

To the animals utterly below ourselves, external to our own species, we hold ourselves bound by no law.

We say to them, *vos non vobis*, without any uneasy misgivings. We rob the bees of their honey, the cattle of their lives, the horse and the ass of their liberty. We kill the wild animals that they may not interfere with our pleasures; and acknowledge ourselves bound to them by no terms except what are dictated by our own convenience. And why should Reineke have acknowledged an obligation any more than we, to creatures so utterly below himself? He was so clever, as our friend said, that he had a right. That he *could* treat them so, Mr. Carlyle would say, proves that he had a right.

But it is a mistake to say he is without a conscience. No bold creature is ever totally without one. Even Iago shows some sort of conscience. Respecting nothing else in heaven or earth, he respects and even reverences his own intellect. After one of those sweet interviews with Roderigo, his, what we must call, conscience takes him to account for his company; and he pleads to it in his own justification—

For I mine own gained knowledge should *profane*
Were I to waste myself with such a snipe
But for my sport and profit.

And Reineke, if we take the mass of his misdeeds, preyed chiefly, like our own Robin Hood, on rogues who were greater rogues than himself. If Bruin chose to steal Rusteviel's honey, if Hintze trespassed in the priest's granary, they were but taken in their own evil-doings. And what is Isegrim, the worst of Reineke's victims, but a great heavy, stupid, lawless brute?—fair type, we will suppose, of not a few Front-de-Bœufs and other so-called nobles of the poet's era, whose will to do mischief was happily limited by their obtuseness; or that French baron, Sir Gilbert de Retz, we believe, was his name, who, like Isegrim, had studied at the universities, and passed for learned, whose after-dinner pastime for many years, as it proved at last, was to cut children's throats for the pleasure of watching them die—we may well feel gratitude that a Reineke was provided to be the scourge of such monsters as they; and we have a thorough pure, exuberant satisfaction in seeing the intellect in that little weak body triumph over them and trample them down. This, indeed, this victory of intellect over brute force is one great secret of our pleasure in the poem, and goes far, in the Carlyle direction, to satisfy us that, at any rate, it is not given to mere base physical strength to win in the battle of life, even in times when physical strength is apparently the only recognized power.

We are insensibly falling from our self-assumed judicial office into that of advocacy; and sliding into what may be plausibly urged, rather than standing fast on what we can surely affirm. Yet there are cases when it is fitting for the judge to become the advocate of an undefended prisoner; and advocacy is only plausible when a few words of truth are mixed with what we say, like the few drops of wine which colour and faintly flavour the large draught of water. Such few grains or drops, whatever they may be, we must leave to the kindness of Reynard's friends to distil for him, while we continue a little longer in the same strain.

After all it may be said, what is it in man's nature which is really admirable? It is idle for us to waste our labour in passing Reineke through the moral crucible unless we shall recognize the results when we obtain them; and in these moral sciences our analytical tests can only be obtained by a study of our own internal experience. If we desire to know what we admire in Reineke we must look for what we admire in ourselves. And what is that? Is it what on Sundays, and on set occasions, and when we are mounted on our moral stilts, we are pleased to call goodness, probity, obedience, humility? Is it? Is it really? Is it not rather the face and form which Nature made—the strength which is ours, we know not how—our talents, our rank, our possessions? It appears to us that we most value in ourselves and most admire in our neighbour not acquisitions, but *gifts*. A man does not praise himself for being good. If he praise himself he is not good. The first condition of goodness is forgetfulness of self; and where self has entered, under however plausible a form, the health is but skin-deep, and underneath there is corruption—and so through everything. We value, we are vain of, proud of, or whatever you please to call it, not what we have done for ourselves, but what has been done for us—what has been given to us by the upper powers. We look up to high-born men, to wealthy men, to fortunate men, to clever men. Is it not so? Who do we choose for the county member, the magistrate, the officer, the minister? The good man we leave to the humble enjoyment of his goodness, and we look out for the able or the wealthy. And again of the wealthy, as if on every side to witness to the same universal law, the man who with no labour of his own has inherited a fortune, ranks higher in the world's esteem than his father who made it. We take rank by descent. Such of us as have the longest pedigree, and are therefore the farthest removed from the first who made the fortune and founded the family, we are the noblest. The nearer to the fountain the fouler the stream; and that first ancestor, who has soiled his fingers by labour, is no better than a parvenu.

And as it is with what we value, so it is with what we blame. It is an old story, that there is no one who would not in his heart prefer being a knave to being a fool; and when we fail in a piece of attempted roguery, as Coleridge has wisely observed, though reasoning unwisely from it, we lay the blame not on our own moral nature, for which we are responsible, but on our intellectual, for which we are not responsible. We do not say what knaves, we say what fools, we have been; perplexing Coleridge, who regards it as a phenomenon of some deep moral disorder; whereas it is but one more evidence of the universal fact that *gifts* are the true and proper object of appreciation, and as we admire men for possessing gifts, so we blame them for their absence. The noble man is the gifted man; the ignoble is the ungifted; and therefore we have only to state a simple law in simple language to have a full solution of the enigma of Reineke. He has gifts enough: of that, at least, there can be no doubt; and if he lacks the gift to use them in the way which we call good, at least he uses them successfully. His victims are less gifted than he, and therefore less noble; and therefore he has a right to use them as he pleases.

And after all, what are these victims? Among the heaviest charges which were urged against him was the killing and eating of that wretched Scharfenebbe—Sharpbeak—the crow's wife. It is well that there are two sides to every story. A poor weary fox, it seemed, was not to be allowed to enjoy a quiet sleep in the sunshine but what an unclean carrion bird must come down and take a peck at him. We can feel no sympathy with the outcries of the crow husband over the fate of the unfortunate Sharpbeak. Woefully, he says, he flew over the place where, a few moments before, in the glory of glossy plumage, a loving wife sat croaking out her passion for him, and found nothing—nothing but a little blood and a few torn feathers—all else clean gone and utterly abolished. Well, and if it was so, it was a blank prospect for him, but the earth was well rid of her; and for herself, it was a higher fate to be assimilated into the body of a Reineke than to remain in a miserable individuality to be a layer of carrion crows' eggs.

And then for Bellyn, and for Bruin, and for Hintze, and the rest, who would needs be meddling with what was no concern of theirs, what is there in them to challenge either regret or pity. They made love to their occupation.

> 'Tis dangerous when the baser nature falls
> Between the pass and fell incensed points
> Of mighty opposites:
> They lie not near our conscience:

Ah! if they were all.... But there is one misdeed, one which outweighs all others whatsoever—a crime which it is useless to palliate, let our other friend say what he pleased; and Reineke himself felt it so. It sat heavy, *for him*, on his soul, and alone of all the actions of his life we are certain that he wished it undone—the death and eating of that poor foolish Lampe. It was a paltry revenge in Reineke. Lampe had told tales of him; he had complained that Reineke, under pretence of teaching him his lesson, had seized him, and tried to murder him; and though he provoked his fate by thrusting himself, after such a warning, into the jaws of Malepartus, Reineke betrays an uneasiness about it in confession; and, unlike himself, feels it necessary to make some sort of an excuse.

Grimbart had been obliged to speak severely of

the seriousness of the offence. 'You see,' he answers :—

To help oneself out through the world is a queer sort of business : one can not
Keep, you know, quite altogether as pure as one can in the cloister.
When we are handling honey we now and then lick at our fingers.
Lampe sorely provoked me ; he frisked about this way and that way,
Up and down, under my eyes, and he looked so fat and so jolly,
Really I could not resist it. I entirely forgot how I loved him.
And then he was so stupid.

But even this acknowledgement does not satisfy Reineke. His mind is evidently softened, and it is on that occasion that he pours out his pathetic lamentation over the sad condition of the world—so fluent, so musical, so touching, that Grimbart listened with wide eyes, unable, till it had run to the length of a sermon, to collect himself. It is true that at last his office as ghostly confessor obliged him to put in a slight demurrer :—

Uncle, the badger replied, why these are the sins of your neighbours ;
Yours, I should think, were sufficient, and rather more now to the purpose.

But he sighs to think what a preacher Reineke would have made.

And now, for the present, farewell to Reineke Fuchs, and to the song in which his glory is enshrined—the Welt Bibel, Bible of this world, as Goethe called it, the most exquisite moral satire, as we will call it, which has ever been composed. It is not addressed to a passing mode of folly or of profligacy, but it touches the perennial nature of mankind, laying bare our own sympathies, and tastes, and weaknesses, with as keen and true an edge as when the living world of the old Swabian poet winced under its earliest utterance.

Humorous in the high pure sense, every laugh which it gives may have its echo in a sigh, or may glide into it as excitement subsides into thought; and yet, for those who do not care to find matter there either for thought or sadness, may remain innocently as a laugh.

Too strong for railing, too kindly and loving for the bitterness of irony, the poem is, as the world itself, a book where each man will find what his nature enables him to see, which gives us back each our own image, and teaches us each the lesson which each of us desires to learn.

JAMES RUSSELL LOWELL

1819–1891

IN THE MEDITERRANEAN

THE first sight of a shore so historical as that of Europe gives an American a strange thrill. What we always feel the artistic want of at home is background. It is all idle to say we are Englishmen, and that English history is ours too. It is precisely in this that we are *not* Englishmen, inasmuch as we only possess their history through our minds, and not by life-long association with a spot and an idea we call England. History without the soil it grew in is more instructive than inspiring—an acquisition, and not an inheritance. It is laid away in our memories, and does not run in our veins. Surely, in all that concerns aesthetics, Europeans have us at an immense advantage. They start at a point which we arrive at after weary years, for literature is not shut up in books, nor art in galleries: both are taken in by unconscious absorption through the finer pores of mind and character in the atmosphere of society. We are not yet out of our Crusoehood, and must make our own tools as best we may. Yet I think we shall find the good of it one of these days, in being thrown back more wholly on nature; and our literature, when we have learned to feel our own strength, and to respect our own thought because it is ours, and not because the European Mrs. Grundy agrees with it, will have a fresh flavour and a strong body that will recommend it, especially as what we import is watered more and more liberally with every vintage.

My first glimpse of Europe was the shore of Spain. Since we got into the Mediterranean, we have been becalmed for some days within easy view of it. All along are fine mountains, brown all day, and with a bloom on them at sunset like that of a ripe plum. Here and there at their feet little white towns are sprinkled along the edge of the water, like the grains of rice dropped by the princess in the story. Sometimes we see larger buildings on the mountain slopes, probably convents. I sit and wonder whether the farther peaks may not be the Sierra Morena (the rusty saw) of Don Quixote. I resolve that they shall be, and am content. Surely latitude and longitude never showed me any particular respect, that I should be over-scrupulous with them.

But, after all, Nature, though she may be more beautiful, is nowhere so entertaining as in man, and the best thing I have seen and learned at sea is our Chief Mate. My first acquaintance with him was made over my knife, which he asked to look at, and, after a critical examination, handed back to me, saying, 'I shouldn't wonder if that 'ere was a good piece o' stuff.' Since then he has transferred a part of his regard for my knife to its owner. I like folks who like an honest piece of steel, and take no interest whatever in 'your Raphaels, Correggios, and stuff.' There is always more than the average human nature in a man who has a hearty sympathy with iron. It is a manly metal, with no sordid associations like gold and silver. My sailor fully came up to my expectation on further acquaintance. He might well be called an old salt who had been wrecked on Spitzbergen before I was born. He was not an American, but I should never have guessed it by his speech, which was the purest Cape Cod, and I reckon myself a good taster of dialects. Nor was he less Americanized in all his thoughts and feelings, a singular proof of the ease with which our omnivorous country assimilates foreign matter, provided it be Protestant, for he was a man ere he became an American citizen. He used to walk the deck with his hands in his pockets, in seeming abstraction, but nothing escaped his eye. *How* he saw, I could never make out, though I had a theory that it was with his elbows. After he had taken me (or my knife) into his confidence, he took care that I should see whatever he deemed of interest to a landsman. Without looking up, he would say, suddenly, 'There's a whale blowin' clearn up to win'ard,' or, 'Them's porpises to leeward: that means change o' wind.' He is as impervious to cold as the polar bear, and paces the deck during his watch much as one of those yellow hummocks goes slumping up and down his cage. On the Atlantic, if the wind blew a gale from the north-east, and it was cold as an English summer, he was sure to turn out in a calico shirt and trousers, his furzy brown chest half bare, and slippers, without stockings. But lest you might fancy this to have chanced by defect of wardrobe, he comes out in a monstrous pea-jacket here in the Mediterranean when the evening is so hot that Adam would have been glad to leave off his fig-leaves. 'It's a kind o' damp and unwholesome in these 'ere waters,' he says, evidently regarding the Midland Sea as a vile standing pool, in comparison with the bluff ocean. At meals he is superb, not only for his strengths, but his weaknesses. He has somehow or other come to think me a wag, and if I ask him to pass the butter, detects an occult joke, and laughs as much as is proper for a mate. For you must know that our social hierarchy on shipboard is precise, and the second mate, were he present, would only laugh half as much as the first. Mr. X. always combs his hair, and works himself into a black frock-coat (on Sundays he adds a waistcoat) before he comes to meals, sacrificing himself nobly and painfully to the social proprieties. The second mate, on the other hand, who eats after us, enjoys the privilege of shirt-sleeves, and is, I think, the happier man of the two. We do not have seats above and below the salt, as in old time, but above and below the white sugar. Mr. X. always takes brown sugar, and it is delightful to see how he ignores the existence of certain delicates which he considers above his grade, tipping his head on one side with an air of abstraction, so that he may seem not to deny himself, but to omit helping himself from inadvertence or absence of mind. At such times he wrinkles his forehead in a peculiar manner, inscrutable at first as a cuneiform inscription, but as easily read after you once get the key. The sense of it is something like this: 'I, X., know my place, a height of wisdom attained by few. Whatever you may think, I do *not* see that currant jelly, nor that preserved grape. Especially, a kind Providence has made me blind to bowls of white sugar, and deaf to the pop of champagne corks. It is much that a merciful compensation gives me a sense of the dingier hue of Havanna, and the muddier gurgle of beer. Are there potted meats? My physician has ordered me three pounds of minced salt-junk at every meal.' There is such a thing, you know, as a ship's husband: X. is the ship's poor relation.

As I have said, he takes also a below-the-white-sugar interest in the jokes, laughing by precise point of compass, just as he would lay the ship's course, all *yawing* being out of the question with his scrupulous decorum at the helm. Once or twice I have got the better of him, and touched him off into a kind of compromised explosion, like that of damp fireworks, that splutter and simmer a little, and then go out with painful slowness and occasional relapses. But his fuse is always of the unwillingest, and you must blow your match, and touch him off again and again with the same joke. Or rather, you must magnetize him many times to get him *en rapport* with a jest. This once accomplished, you have him, and one bit of fun will last the whole voyage. He prefers those of one syllable, the *a-b abs* of humour. The gradual fattening of the steward, a benevolent mulatto with whiskers and ear-rings, who looks as if he had been meant for a woman, and had become a man by accident, as in some of those stories of the elder physiologists, is an abiding topic of humorous comment with Mr. X. 'That 'ere stooard,' he says, with a brown grin like what you might fancy on the face of a serious and aged seal, ''s agittin' as fat 's a porpis. He was as thin 's a shingle when he come aboord last v'yge. Them trousis'll bust yit. He don't darst take 'em off nights, for the whole ship's company couldn't git him into 'em agin.' And then he turns aside to enjoy the intensity of his emotion by himself, and you hear at intervals low rumblings, an indigestion of laughter. He tells me of St. Elmo's fires, Marvell's *corposants*, though with him the original *corpos santos* has suffered a sea change, and turned to *comepleasants*, pledges of fine weather. I shall not soon find a pleasanter companion. It is so delightful to meet a man who knows just what you do *not*. Nay, I think the tired mind finds something in plump ignorance like what the body feels in cushiony moss. Talk of the sympathy of kindred pursuits! It is the sympathy of the upper and nether millstones, both for ever grinding the same grist, and wearing each other smooth. One has not far to seek for book-nature, artist-nature, every variety of superinduced nature, in short, but genuine human-nature is hard to find. And how good it is! Wholesome as a potato, fit company for any dish. The free-masonry of cultivated men is agreeable, but artificial, and I like better the natural grip with which manhood recognizes manhood.

X. has one good story, and with that I leave him, wishing him with all my heart that little inland farm at last which is his calenture as he paces the windy deck. One evening, when the clouds looked wild and whirling, I asked X. if it was coming on to blow. 'No, I guess not,' said he; 'bumby the moon'll be up, and scoff away that 'ere loose stuff.' His intonation set the phrase 'scoff away' in quotation marks as plain as print. So I put a query in each eye, and he went on. 'Ther' was a Dutch cappen onct, an' his mate come to him in the cabin, where he sot takin' his schnapps, an' says, "Cappen, it's agittin' thick, an' looks kin' o' squally; hedn't we's good 's shorten sail?" "Gimmy my alminick," says the cappen. So he looks at it a spell, an' says he, "The moon's due in less 'n half an hour, an' she'll scoff away ev'ythin' clare agin." So the mate he goes, an' bumby down he comes agin', an' says, "Cappen, this 'ere's the allfiredest, powerfullest moon 't ever you *did* see. She's scoffed away the maintogallants'l, an' she's to work on the foretops'l now. Guess you'd better look in the alminick agin, an' fin' out when *this* moon sets." So the cappen thought 'twas 'bout time to go on deck. Dreadful slow them Dutch cappens be.' And X. walked away, rumbling inwardly like the rote of the sea heard afar.

And so we arrived at Malta. Did you ever hear of one of those eating-houses where, for a certain fee, the guest has the right to make one thrust with a fork into a huge pot, in which the whole dinner is bubbling, getting perhaps a bit of boiled meat, or a potato, or else nothing? Well, when the great cauldron of war is seething, and the nations stand around it striving to fish out something to their purpose from the mess, Britannia always has a great advantage in her trident. Malta is one of the tit-bits she has impaled with that awful implement. I was not sorry for it, when I reached my clean inn, with its kindly English landlady.

JOHN RUSKIN

1819–1900

THE EXTENSION OF RAILWAYS IN THE LAKE DISTRICT[1]

A PROTEST

THE evidence collected in the following pages, in support of their pleading, is so complete, and the summary of his cause given with so temperate mastery by Mr. Somervell, that I find nothing to add in circumstance, and little to reinforce in argument. And I have less heart to the writing even of what brief preface so good work might by its author's courtesy be permitted to receive from me, occupied as I so long have been in efforts tending in the same direction, because, on that very account, I am far less interested than my friend in this local and limited resistance to the elsewhere fatally victorious current of modern folly, cruelty, and ruin. When the frenzy of avarice is daily drowning our sailors, suffocating our miners, poisoning our children, and blasting the cultivable surface of England into a treeless

[1] Preface to a pamphlet compiled (1876) by Robert Somervell, entitled 'A Protest against the Extension of Railways in the Lake District' (Windermere, J. Garnett; London, Simpkin, Marshall & Co.).

waste of ashes,[1] what does it really matter whether a flock of sheep, more or less, be driven from the slopes of Helvellyn, or the little pool of Thirlmere filled with shale, or a few wild blossoms of St. John's vale lost to the coronal of English spring? Little to any one; and—let me say this, at least, in the outset of all saying—*nothing* to *me*. No one need charge me with selfishness in any word or action for defence of these mossy hills. I do not move, with such small activity as I have yet shown in the business, because I live at Coniston (where no sound of the iron wheels by Dunmail Raise can reach me), nor because I can find no other place to remember Wordsworth by, than the daffodil margin of his little Rydal marsh. What thoughts and work are yet before me, such as he taught, must be independent of any narrow associations. All my own dear mountain grounds and treasure-cities, Chamouni, Interlachen, Lucerne, Geneva, Venice, are long ago destroyed by the European populace; and now, for my own part, I don't care what more they do; they may drain Loch Katrine, drink Loch Lomond, and blow all Wales and Cumberland into a heap of slate shingle; the world is wide enough yet to find me some refuge during the days appointed for me to stay in it. But it is no less my duty, in the cause of those to whom the sweet landscapes of England are yet precious, and to whom they may yet teach what they taught me, in early boyhood, and would still

[1] See—the illustration being coincidently given as I correct this page for press—the description of the horrible service, and history of the fatal explosion of dynamite, on the once lovely estates of the Duke of Hamilton, in the *Hamilton Advertiser* of 10th and 17th June.

if I had it now to learn,—it is my duty to plead with what earnestness I may, that these sacred sibylline books may be redeemed from perishing.

But again, I am checked, because I don't know how to speak to the persons who *need* to be spoken to in this matter.

Suppose I were sitting, where still, in much-changed Oxford, I am happy to find myself, in one of the little latticed cells of the Bodleian Library, and my kind and much-loved friend, Mr. Coxe, were to come to me with news that it was proposed to send nine hundred excursionists through the library every day, in three parties of three hundred each; that it was intended they should elevate their minds by reading all the books they could lay hold of while they stayed;—and that practically scientific persons accompanying them were to look out for and burn all the manuscripts that had any gold in their illuminations, that the said gold might be made of practical service; but that he, Mr. Coxe, could not, for his part, sympathize with the movement, and hoped I would write something in deprecation of it! As I should then feel, I feel now, at Mr. Somervell's request that I would write him a preface in defence of Helvellyn. What could I say for Mr. Coxe? Of course, that nine hundred people should see the library daily, instead of one, is only fair to the nine hundred, and if there is gold in the books, is it not public property? If there is copper or slate in Helvellyn, shall not the public burn or hammer it out—and they say they will, of course—in spite of us? What does it signify to *them* how we poor old quiet readers in this mountain library feel? True, we know well enough,—what the nine hundred excursionist scholars don't—that the library can't be read quite through in a quarter of an hour; also, that there is a pleasure in real reading, quite different from that of turning pages; and that gold in a missal, or slate in a crag, may be more precious than in a bank or a chimney-pot. But how are these practical people to credit us,—these, who cannot read, nor ever will; and who have been taught that nothing is virtuous but care for their bellies, and nothing useful but what goes into them?

Whether to be credited or not, the real facts of the matter, made clear as they are in the following pages, can be briefly stated for the consideration of any candid person.

The arguments in favour of the new railway are in the main four, and may be thus answered.

1. 'There are mineral treasures in the district capable of development.'

Answer. It is a wicked fiction, got up by whosoever has got it up, simply to cheat shareholders. Every lead and copper vein in Cumberland has been known for centuries; the copper of Coniston does not pay; and there is none so rich in Helvellyn. And the main central volcanic rocks, through which the track lies, produce neither slate nor haematite, while there is enough of them at Llanberis and Dalton to roof and iron-grate all England into one vast Bedlam, if it honestly perceives itself in need of that accommodation.

2. 'The scenery must be made accessible to the public.'

Answer. It is more than accessible already; the public are pitched into it head-foremost, and necessarily miss two-thirds of it. The Lake scenery really begins, on the south, at Lancaster, where the Cumberland hills are seen over Morecambe Bay; on the north, at Carlisle, where the moors of Skiddaw are seen over the rich plains between them and the Solway. No one who loves mountains would lose a step of the approach, from these distances, on either side. But the stupid herds of modern tourists let themselves be emptied, like coals from a sack, at Windermere and Keswick. Having got there, what the new railway has to do is to shovel those who have come to Keswick to Windermere, and to shovel those who have come to Windermere to Keswick. And what then?

3. 'But cheap and swift transit is necessary for the working population, who otherwise could not see the scenery at all.'

Answer. After all your shrieking about what the operatives spend in drink, can't you teach them to save enough out of their year's wages to pay for a chaise and pony for a day, to drive Missis and the Baby that pleasant twenty miles, stopping when they like, to unpack the basket on a mossy bank? If they can't enjoy the scenery that way, they can't any way; and all that your railroad company can do for them is only to open taverns and skittle grounds round Grasmere, which will soon, then, be nothing but a pool of drainage, with a beach of broken gingerbeer bottles; and their minds will be no more improved by contemplating the scenery of such a lake than of Blackpool.

4. What else is to be said? I protest I can find nothing, unless that engineers and contractors must live. Let them live, but in a more useful and honourable way than by keeping Old Bartholomew Fair under Helvellyn, and making a steam merry-go-round of the lake country.

There are roads to be mended, where the parish will not mend them, harbours of refuge needed, where our deck-loaded ships are in helpless danger; get your commissions and dividends where you know that work is needed, not where the best you can do is to persuade pleasure-seekers into giddier idleness.

The arguments brought forward by the promoters of the railway may thus be summarily answered. Of those urged in the following pamphlet in defence of the country as it is, I care only myself to direct the reader's attention to one (see pp. 27, 28), the certainty, namely, of the deterioration of moral character in the inhabitants of every district penetrated by a railway. Where there is little moral character to be lost, this argument has small weight. But the Border peasantry of Scotland and England, painted with absolute fidelity by Scott and Wordsworth (for leading types out of this exhaustless portraiture, I may name Dandie Dinmont and Michael), are hitherto a scarcely injured race, whose strength and virtue yet survive to represent the body and soul of England before her days of mechanical decrepitude and commercial dishonour. There are men working in my own fields who might have fought with Henry the Fifth at Agincourt without being discerned from among his knights; I can take my tradesmen's word for a thousand pounds; my garden gate opens on the latch to the public road, by day and night, without fear of any foot entering but my own, and my girl-guests may wander by road, or moorland, or through every bosky dell of this wild wood, free as the heather bees or squirrels.

What effect, on the character of such a population, will be produced by the influx of that of the suburbs of our manufacturing towns, there is evidence enough, if the reader cares to ascertain the facts, in every newspaper on his morning table.

And now one final word concerning the proposed beneficial effect on the minds of those whom you send to corrupt us.

I have said I take no selfish interest in this resistance to the railroad. But I do take an unselfish one. It is precisely because I passionately wish to improve the minds of the populace, and because I am spending my own mind, strength, and fortune, wholly on that object, that I don't want to let them see Helvellyn while they are drunk. I suppose few men now living have so earnestly felt—none certainly have so earnestly declared—that the beauty of nature is the blessedest and most necessary of lessons for men; and that all other efforts in education are futile till you have taught your people to love fields, birds, and flowers. Come then, my benevolent friends, join with me in that teaching. I have been at it all my life, and without pride, do solemnly assure you that I know how it is to be managed. I cannot indeed tell you, in this short preface, how, completely, to fulfil so glorious a task. But I can tell you clearly, instantly, and emphatically, in what temper you must set about it. *Here* are you, a Christian, a gentleman, and a trained scholar; *there* is your subject of education—a Godless clown, in helpless ignorance. You can present no more blessed offering to God than that human creature, raised into faith, gentleness, and the knowledge of the works of his Lord. But observe this—you must not hope to make so noble an offering to God of that which doth cost you nothing! You must be resolved to labour, and to lose, yourself, before you can rescue this overlaboured lost sheep, and offer it alive to its Master. If then, my benevolent friend, you are prepared to take OUT your two pence, and to give them to the hosts here in Cumberland, saying—'Take care of him, and whatsoever thou spendest more, I will repay thee when I come to Cumberland myself,' on *these* terms—oh my benevolent friends, I am with you, hand and glove, in every effort you wish to make for the enlightenment of poor men's eyes. But if your motive is, on the contrary, to put two pence into your own purse, stolen between the Jerusalem and Jericho of Keswick and Ambleside, out of the poor drunken traveller's pocket;—if your real object, in your charitable offering, is, not even to lend unto the Lord by *giving* to the poor, but to lend unto the Lord by making a dividend out of the poor;—then, my pious friends, enthusiastic Ananias, pitiful Judas, and sanctified Korah, I will do my best, in God's name, to stay your hands, and stop your tongues.

BRANTWOOD, 22*nd June*, 1876.

GEORGE ELIOT (MARY ANN EVANS)

1819–1880

AUTHORSHIP

To lay down in the shape of practical moral rules courses of conduct only to be made real by the rarest states of motive and disposition, tends not to elevate but to degrade the general standard, by turning that rare attainment from an object of admiration into an impossible prescription, against which the average nature first rebels and then flings out ridicule. It is for art to present images of a lovelier order than the actual, gently winning the affections, and so determining the taste. But in any rational criticism of the time which is meant to guide a practical reform, it is idle to insist that action ought to be this or that, without considering how far the outward conditions of such change are present, even supposing the inward disposition towards it. Practically, we must be satisfied to aim at something short of perfection—and at something very much further off it in one case than in another. While the fundamental conceptions of morality seem as stationary through ages as the laws of life, so that a moral manual written eighteen centuries ago still admonishes us that we are low in our attainments, it is quite otherwise with the degree to which moral conceptions have penetrated the various forms of social activity, and made what may be called the special conscience of each calling, art, or industry. While on some points of social duty public opinion has reached a tolerably high standard, on others a public opinion is not yet born; and there are even some functions and practices with regard to which men far above the line in honourableness of nature feel hardly any scrupulosity, though their consequent behaviour is easily shown to be as injurious as bribery, or any other slowly poisonous procedure which degrades the social vitality.

Among those callings which have not yet acquired anything near a full-grown conscience in the public mind is Authorship. Yet the changes brought about by the spread of instruction and the consequent struggles of an uneasy ambition, are, or at least might well be, forcing on many minds the need of some regulating principle with regard to the publication of intellectual products, which would override the rule of the market: a principle, that is, which should be derived from a fixing of the author's vocation according to those characteristics in which it differs from the other bread-winning professions. Let this be done, if possible, without any cant, which would carry the subject into Utopia away from existing needs. The guidance wanted is a clear notion of what should justify men and women in assuming public authorship, and of the way in which they should be determined by what is usually called success. But the forms of authorship must be distinguished; journalism, for example, carrying a necessity for that continuous production which in other kinds of writing is precisely the evil to be fought against, and judicious careful compilation, which is a great public service, holding in its modest diligence a guarantee against those deductions of vanity and idleness which draw many a young gentleman into reviewing, instead of the sorting and copying which his small talents could not rise to with any vigour and completeness.

A manufacturer goes on producing calicoes as long and as fast as he can find a market for them; and in obeying this indication of demand he gives his factory its utmost usefulness to the world in general and to himself in particular. Another manufacturer buys a new invention of some light kind likely to attract the public fancy, is successful in finding a multitude who will give their testers for the transiently desirable commodity, and before the fashion is out, pockets a considerable sum: the commodity was coloured with a green which had arsenic in it that damaged the factory workers and the purchasers. What then? These, he contends (or does not know or care to contend), are superficial effects, which it is folly to dwell upon while we have epidemic diseases and bad government.

The first manufacturer we will suppose blameless. Is an author simply on a par with him, as to the rules of production?

The author's capital is his brain-power—power of invention, power of writing. The manufacturer's capital, in fortunate cases, is being continually reproduced and increased. Here is the first grand difference between the capital which is turned into calico and the brain capital which is turned into literature. The calico scarcely varies in appropriateness of quality, no consumer is in danger of getting too much of it, and neglecting his boots, hats, and flannel-shirts in consequence. That there should be large quantities of the same sort in the calico manufacture is an advantage: the sameness is desirable, and nobody is likely to roll his person in so many folds of calico as to become a mere bale of cotton goods, and nullify his senses of hearing and touch, while his morbid passion for Manchester shirtings makes him still cry 'More!' The wise manufacturer gets richer and richer, and the consumers he supplies have their real wants satisfied and no more.

Let it be taken as admitted that all legitimate social activity must be beneficial to others besides the agent. To write prose or verse as a private exercise and satisfaction is not social activity; nobody is culpable for this any more than for learning other people's verse by heart if he does not neglect his proper business in consequence. If the exercise made him sillier or secretly more self-satisfied, that, to be sure, would be a roundabout way of injuring society; for though a certain mixture of silliness may lighten existence, we have at present more than enough.

But man or woman who publishes writings inevitably assumes the office of teacher or influencer of the public mind. Let him protest as he will that he only seeks to amuse, and has no pretension to do more than while away an hour of leisure or weariness—'the idle singer of an empty day'—he can no more escape influencing the moral taste, and with it the action of the intelligence, than a setter of fashions in furniture and dress can fill the shops with his designs and leave the garniture of persons and houses unaffected by his industry.

For a man who has a certain gift of writing to say, 'I will make the most of it while the public likes my wares—as long as the market is open and I am able to supply it at a money profit—such profit being the sign of liking'—he should have a belief that his wares have nothing akin to the arsenic green in them, and also that his continuous supply is secure from a degradation in quality which the habit of consumption encouraged in the buyers may hinder them from marking their sense of by rejection; so that they complain, but pay, and read while they complain. Unless he has that belief, he is on a level with the manufacturer who gets rich by fancy-wares coloured with arsenic green. He really cares for nothing but his income. He carries on authorship on the principle of the gin-palace.

And bad literature of the sort called amusing is spiritual gin.

A writer capable of being popular can only escape this social culpability by first of all getting a profound sense that literature is good-for-nothing, if it is not admirably good: he must detest bad literature too heartily to be indifferent about producing it if only other people don't detest it. And if he has this sign of the divine afflatus within him, he must make up his mind that he must not pursue authorship as a vocation with a trading determination to get rich by it. It is in the highest sense lawful for him to get as good a price as he honourably can for the best work he is capable of; but not for him to force or hurry his production, or even do over again what has already been done, either by himself or others, so as to render his work no real contribution, for the sake of bringing up his income to the fancy pitch. An author who would keep a pure and noble conscience, and with that a developing instead of degenerating intellect and taste, must cast out of his aims the aim to be rich. And therefore he must keep his expenditure low—he must make for himself no dire necessity to earn sums in order to pay bills.

In opposition to this, it is common to cite Walter Scott's case, and cry, 'Would the world have got as much innocent (and therefore salutary) pleasure out of Scott, if he had not brought himself under the pressure of money-need?' I think it would—and more; but since it is impossible to prove what would have been, I confine myself to replying that Scott was not justified in bringing himself into a position where severe consequences to others depended on his retaining or not retaining his mental competence. Still less is Scott to be taken as an example to be followed in this matter, even if it were admitted that money-need served to press at once the best and the most work out of him; any more than a great navigator who has brought his ship to port in spite of having taken a wrong and perilous route, is to be followed as to his route by navigators who are not yet ascertained to be great.

But after the restraints and rules which must guide the acknowledged author, whose power of making a real contribution is ascertained, comes the consideration, how or on what principle are we to find a check for that troublesome disposition to authorship arising from the spread of what is called Education, which turns a growing rush of vanity and ambition into this current? The well-taught, an increasing number, are almost all able to write essays on given themes, which demand new periodicals to save them from lying in cold obstruction. The ill-taught—also an increasing number—read many books, seem to themselves able to write others surprisingly like what they read, and probably superior, since the variations are such as please their own fancy, and such as they would have recommended to their favourite authors: these ill-taught persons are perhaps idle and want to give themselves 'an object'; or they are short of money, and feel disinclined to get it by a commoner kind of work; or they find a facility in putting sentences together which gives them more than a suspicion that they have genius, which, if not very cordially believed in by private confidants, will be recognized by an impartial public; or finally, they observe that writing is sometimes well paid, and sometimes a ground of fame or distinction, and without any use of punctilious logic, they conclude to become writers themselves.

As to these ill-taught persons, whatever medicines of a spiritual sort can be found good against mental emptiness and inflation—such medicines are needful for *them*. The contempt of the world for their productions only comes after their disease has wrought its worst effects. But what is to be said to the well-taught, who have such an alarming equality in their power of writing 'like a scholar and a gentleman'? Perhaps they, too, can only be cured by the medicine of higher ideals in social duty, and by a fuller representation to themselves of the processes by which the general culture is furthered or impeded.

MATTHEW ARNOLD

1822–1888

DANTE AND BEATRICE

Those critics who allégorize the *Divine Comedy*, who exaggerate, or, rather, who mistake the supersensual element in Dante's work, who reduce to nothing the sensible and human element, are hardly worth refuting. They know nothing of the necessary laws under which poetic genius works, of the inevitable conditions under which the creations of poetry are produced. But, in their turn, those other critics err hardly less widely, who exaggerate, or, rather, who mistake the human and real element in Dante's poem; who see, in such a passion as that of Dante for Beatrice, an affection belonging to the sphere of actual domestic life, fitted to sustain the wear and tear of our ordinary daily existence. Into the error of these second critics an accomplished recent translator of Dante, Mr. Theodore Martin, seems to me to have fallen. He has ever present to his mind, when he speaks of the Beatrice whom Dante adored, Wordsworth's picture of

> The perfect woman, nobly planned
> To warn, to comfort, and command;
> And yet a spirit still, and bright
> With something of an angel light.

He is ever quoting these lines in connexion with Dante's Beatrice; ever assimilating to this picture Beatrice as Dante conceived her; ever attributing to Dante's passion a character identical with that of the affection which Wordsworth, in the poem from which these lines are taken, meant to portray. The affection here portrayed by Wordsworth is, I grant, a substantial human affection, inhabiting the domain of real life, at the same time that it is poetical and beautiful. But in order to give this flesh-and-blood character to Dante's passion for Beatrice, what a task has Mr. Martin to perform! how much to shut his eyes to, or to disbelieve! Not perceiving that the vital impulse of Dante's soul is towards reverie and spiritual vision; that the task Dante sets himself is not the task of reconciling poetry and reality, of giving to each its due part, of supplementing the one by the other; but the task of sacrificing the world to the spirit, of making the spirit all in all, of effacing the world in the presence of the spirit—Mr. Martin seeks to find a Dante admirable and complete in the life of the world as well as in the life of the spirit; and when he cannot find him, he invents him. Dante saw the world, and used in his poetry what he had seen; for he was a born artist. But he was essentially aloof from the world, and not complete in the life of the world; for he was a born spiritualist and solitary. Keeping in our minds this, his double character, we may seize the exact truth as to his relations with Beatrice, and steer a right course between the error of those who deliteralize them too much, on the one hand, and that of those who literalize them too much, on the other.

The *Divine Comedy*, I have already said, is no allegory, and Beatrice no mere personification of theology. Mr. Martin is quite right in saying that Beatrice is the Beatrice whom men turned round to gaze at in the streets of Florence; that she is no 'allegorical phantom', no 'fiction purely ideal'. He is quite right in saying that Dante 'worships no phantoms', that his passion for Beatrice was a real passion, and that his love-poetry does not deal 'in the attributes of celestial charms'. He was an artist—one of the greatest artists; and art abhors what is vague, hollow, and impalpable.

Enough to make this fully manifest we have in the *Vita Nuova*. Dante there records how, a boy of ten, he first saw Beatrice, a girl of nine, dressed in crimson; how, a second time, he saw her, nine years later, passing along the street, dressed in white, between two ladies older than herself, and how she saluted him. He records how afterwards she once denied him her salutation; he records the profound impression which, at her father's death, the grief and beauty of Beatrice made on all those who visited her; he records his meeting with her at a party after her marriage, his emotion, and how some ladies present, observing his emotion, 'made a mock of him to that most gentle being'; he records her death, and how, a year afterwards, some gentlemen found him, on the anniversary of her death, 'sketching an angel on his tablets'. He tells us how, a little later, he had a vision of the dead Beatrice 'arrayed in the same crimson robe in which she had originally appeared in my eyes and she seemed as youthful as on the day I saw her first'. He mentions how, one day, the sight of some pilgrims passing along a particular street in Florence brought to his mind the thought that perhaps these pilgrims, coming from a far country, had never even heard the name of her who filled his thoughts so entirely.

And even in the *Divine Comedy*, composed many

years afterwards, and treating of the glorified Beatrice only, one distinct trait of the earthly Beatrice is still preserved—her smile; the *santo riso* of the *Purgatory*, the *dolce riso* of the *Paradise.*

Yes, undoubtedly there was a real Beatrice, whom Dante had seen living and moving before him, and for whom he had felt a passion. This basis of fact and reality he took from the life of the outward world: this basis was indispensable to him, for he was an artist.

But this basis was enough for him as an artist: to have seen Beatrice two or three times, to have felt her beauty, her charm; to have had the emotion of her marriage, her death—this was enough. Art requires a basis of fact, but it also desires to treat this basis of fact with the utmost freedom; and this desire for the first handling of its object is even thwarted when its object is too near, and too real. To have had his relations with Beatrice more positive, intimate, and prolonged, to have had an affection for her into which there entered more of the life of this world, would have even somewhat impeded, one may say, Dante's free use of these relations for the purpose of art. And the artist nature in him was in little danger of being thus impeded; for he was a born solitary.

Thus the conditions of art do not make it necessary that Dante's relations with Beatrice should have been more close and real than the *Vita Nuova* represents them; and the conditions of Dante's own nature do not make it probable. Not the less do such admirers of the poet as Mr. Martin —misconceiving the essential characteristic of chivalrous passion in general, and of Dante's divinization of Beatrice in particular, misled by imagining this 'worship for woman', as they call it, to be something which it was not, something involving modern relations in social life between the two sexes—insist upon making out of Dante's adoration of Beatrice a substantial modern love-story, and of arranging Dante's real life so as to turn it into the proper sort of real life for a 'worshipper of woman' to lead. The few real incidents of Dante's passion, enumerated in the *Vita Nuova*, sufficient to give to his great poem the basis which it required, are far too scanty to give to such a love-story as this the basis which it requires; therefore they must be developed and amplified. Beatrice was a living woman, and Dante had seen her; but she must become

> The creature not too bright and good
> For human nature's daily food,

of Wordsworth's poem: she must become 'pure flesh and blood—beautiful, yet substantial', and 'moulded of that noble humanity wherewith Heaven blesses not unfrequently our common earth'. Dante had saluted Beatrice, had spoken to her; but this is not enough: he has surely omitted to 'record particulars': it is 'scarcely credible that he should not have found an opportunity of directly declaring his attachment'; for 'in position, education, and appearance he was a man worth any woman', and his face 'at that time of his life must have been eminently engaging'. Therefore 'it seems strange that his love should not have found its issue in marriage'; for 'he loved Beatrice as a man loves, and with the passion that naturally perseveres to the possession of its mistress'.

However, his love did *not* find its issue in marriage.

Beatrice married Messer Simone dei Bardi, to whom, says Mr. Martin, 'her hand had been, perhaps lightly or to please her parents, pledged in ignorance of the deep and noble passion which she had inspired in the young poet's heart'. But she certainly could not 'have been insensible to his profound tenderness and passion'; although whether 'she knew of it before her marriage', and whether 'she, either then or afterwards, gave it her countenance and approval, and returned it in any way, and in what degree'—questions which, Mr. Martin says, 'naturally suggest themselves'—are, he confesses, questions for solving which 'the materials are most scanty and unsatisfactory'. 'Unquestionably,' he adds, 'it startles and grieves us to find Beatrice taking part with her friends "in laughing at Dante when he was overcome at first meeting her after her marriage". But there may,' he thinks, 'have been causes for this—causes for which, in justice to her, allowance must be made, even as we see that Dante made it.' Then, again, as to Messer Simone dei Bardi's feelings about this attachment of Dante to his wife. 'It is true,' says Mr. Martin, 'that we have no direct information on this point;' but 'the love of Dante was of an order too pure and noble to occasion distrust, even if the purity of Beatrice had not placed her above suspicion'; but Dante 'did what only a great and manly nature could have done—he triumphed over his pain; he uttered no complaint, his regrets were buried within his own heart'. 'At the same time,' Mr. Martin thinks, 'it is contrary to human nature that a love unfed by any tokens of favour should retain all its original force; and without wrong either to Beatrice or Dante, we may conclude that an understanding was come to between them, which in some measure soothed his heart, if it did not satisfy it.' And 'sooner or later, before Beatrice died, we cannot doubt that there came a day when words passed between them which helped to reconcile Dante to the doom that severed her from his side during her all too brief sojourn on earth, when the pent-up heart of the poet swept down the barriers within which it had so long struggled, and he

> Caught up the whole of love, and utter'd it,
> Then bade adieu for ever,

if not to her, yet to all those words which it was no longer meet should be spoken to another's wife '.

But Dante married, as well as Beatrice ; and so Dante's married life has to be *arranged* also. 'It is,' says Mr. Martin, 'only those who have observed little of human nature, or of their own hearts, who will think that Dante's marriage with Gemma Donati argues against the depth of sincerity of his first love. Why should he not have sought the solace and the support of a generous woman's nature, who, knowing all the truth, was yet content with such affection as he was able to bring to a second love ? Nor was that necessarily small. Ardent and affectionate as his nature was, the sympathies of such a woman must have elicited from him a satisfactory response ; while, at the same time, without prejudice to the wife's claim on his regard, he might entertain his heavenward dream of the departed Beatrice.' The tradition is, however, that Dante did not live happily with his wife ; and some have thought that he means to cast a disparaging reflection on his marriage in a passage of the *Purgatory*. I need not say that this sort of thing would never do for Mr. Martin's hero—that hero who can do nothing 'inconsistent with the purest respect to her who had been the wedded wife of another, on the one hand, or with his regard for the mother of his children, on the other'. Accordingly, 'are we to assume,' Mr. Martin cries, 'that the woman who gave herself to him in the full knowledge that she was not the bride of his imagination, was not regarded by him with the esteem which her devotion was calculated to inspire?' It is quite impossible. 'Dante was a true-hearted gentleman, and could never have spoken slightingly of her on whose breast he had found comfort amid many a sorrow, and who had borne to him a numerous progeny—the last a Beatrice.' Donna Gemma was a 'generous and devoted woman, and she and Dante thoroughly understood each other'.

All this has, as applied to real personages, the grave defect of being entirely of Mr. Martin's own imagining. But it has a still graver defect, I think, as applied to Dante, in being so singularly inappropriate to his object. The grand, impracticable Solitary, with keen senses and ardent passions—for nature had made him an artist, and art must be, as Milton says, 'sensuous and impassioned'—but with an irresistible bent to the inward life of imagination, vision, and ecstasy; with an inherent impatience of the outward life; the life of distraction, jostling, mutual concession, this man 'of a humour which made him hard to get on with', says Petrarch; 'melancholy and pensive,' says Boccaccio; 'by nature abstracted and taciturn, seldom speaking unless he was questioned, and often so absorbed in his own reflections that he did not hear the questions which were put to him'; who could not live with the Florentines, who could not live with Gemma Donati, who could not live with Can Grande della Scala; this lover of Beatrice, but of Beatrice a vision of his youth, hardly at all in contact with him in actual life, vanished from him soon, with whom his imagination could deal freely, whom he could divinize into a fit object for the spiritual longing which filled him—this Dante is transformed, in Mr. Martin's hands, into the hero of a sentimental, but strictly virtuous, novel! To make out Dante to have been eminent for a wise, complete conduct of his outward life, seems to me as unimportant as it is impossible. I can quite believe the tradition, which represents him as not having lived happily with his wife, and attributes her not having joined him in his exile to this cause. I can even believe, without difficulty, an assertion of Boccaccio which excites Mr. Martin's indignation, that Dante's conduct, even in mature life, was at times exceedingly irregular. We know how the followers of the spiritual life tend to be antinomian in what belongs to the outward life: they do not attach much importance to such irregularity themselves; it is their fault, as complete men, that they do not; it is the fault of the spiritual life, as a complete life, that it allows this tendency: by dint of despising the outward life, it loses the control of this life, and of itself when in contact with it. My present business, however, is not to praise or blame Dante's practical conduct of his life, but to make clear his peculiar mental and spiritual constitution. This, I say, disposed him to absorb himself in the inner life, wholly to humble and efface before this the outward life. We may see this in the passage of the *Purgatory* where he makes Beatrice reprove him for his backslidings after she, his visible symbol of spiritual perfection, had vanished from his eyes.

'For a while'—she says of him to the 'pious substances', the angels—'for a while with my countenance I upheld him; showing to him my youthful eyes, with me I led him turned towards the right way.

'Soon as I came on the threshold of my second age, and changed my life, this man took himself from me and gave himself to others.

'When that I had mounted from flesh to spirit, and beauty and spirit were increased unto me, I was to him less dear and less acceptable.

'He turned his steps to go in a way not true, pursuing after false images of good, which fulfil nothing of the promises which they give.

'Neither availed it me that I obtained inspirations to be granted me, whereby, both in dream and otherwise, I called him back; so little heed paid he to them.

'So deep he fell, that, for his salvation all means came short, except to show him the people of perdition.

'The high decree of God would be broken, could Lethe be passed, and that so fair aliment tasted, without some scot paid of repentance, which pours forth tears.'

Here, indeed, and in a somewhat similar passage of the next canto, Mr. Martin thinks that the 'obvious allusion' is to certain moral shortcomings, occasional slips, of which (though he treats Boccaccio's imputation as monstrous and incredible) 'Dante, with his strong and ardent passions, having, like meaner men, to fight the perennial conflict between flesh and spirit', had sometimes, he supposes, been guilty. An Italian commentator gives at least as true an interpretation of these passages when he says that 'in them Dante makes Beatrice, as the representative of theology, lament that he should have left the study of divinity—in which by the grace of Heaven, he might have attained admirable proficiency—to immerse himself in civil affairs with the parties of Florence'. But the real truth is, that all the life of the world, its pleasures, its business, its parties, its politics, all is alike hollow and miserable to Dante in comparison with the inward life, the ecstasy of the divine vision; every way which does not lead straight towards this is for him a *via non vera*; every good thing but this is for him a false image of good, fulfilling none of the promises which it gives; for the excellency of the knowledge of this he counts all things but loss. Beatrice leads him to this; herself symbolizes for him the ineffable beauty and purity for which he longs. Even to Dante at twenty-one, when he yet sees the living Beatrice with his eyes, she already symbolizes this for him, she is already not the 'creature not too bright and good' of Wordsworth, but a spirit far more than a woman; to Dante at twenty-five composing the *Vita Nuova* she is still more a spirit; to Dante at fifty, when his character has taken its bent, when his genius is come to its perfection, when he is composing his immortal poem, she is a spirit altogether.

WALTER BAGEHOT

1826–1877

BOSCASTLE

WHATEVER doubt there may be as to the truth of Mr. Darwin's speculations on other points, there is no doubt that they are applicable to the coast cliffs of north Cornwall. No doubt every cliff owes its being to natural selection. All the weak rocks have been worn away by ages of conflict with the whole Atlantic, and only the strong rocks are left. They often are worn, too, into shapes resembling the spare and gigantic veterans of many wars; wherever the subtle ocean detected a bit of soft stone, it set to and wore it away, so that the grim masses which stand are all granite—the 'bones and sinews' of geology. The peculiarity of the coast, among other beautiful ones, is that it is a mere coast;—the picturesque stops at the cliff line. In the adjacent coast of north and west the high hills of the interior send down many streams, which in the course of ages have hollowed out deep valleys and softened with woody banks the wild and stony fields. But Cornwall is a thin county, has no deep interior to be a source of big streams, and the little ones which trickle forth have to rush over a rock too hard and too bleak for them to wear it into delicate valleys. But the shore line is charming, not only because the waves swell with the force of the full ocean, while the bays are scooped and the rocks scarred by its incessant hand—its careful hand, I had almost said, so minute and pervading are its touches—but the hard grey rock of the shore also contributes much to make *clean foam.* The softer rocks always mix something of their own alloy with the pure sea, but the grey grit here has no discolouring power; the white line of spray dances from headland to headland as pure and crystal-like as if it had not touched the earth.

But I have no intention of wearying you with a description of scenery. The seashore is a pretty thing, but it is not a discovery of my own. The coast is very curious, I do not mean in those ante-Roman remains which your most learned contributor has so well described. I cannot presume to tell you whether in truth in this place, as in so many others, according to the last ideas and perhaps the hardest terms of ethnology, the dolichocephalic race of men attacked and extirpated the brachycephalic, or short-headed, ten thousand years before history began. Anyhow, if the theory is true, it must have been cold work on these cliffs and moors, when you picked up mussels and (if possible) cray-fish, and cut skins, if you had any, into clothes with a blunt flint, when fire had just come in as a new and (Conservative thought!) suspicious thing, and tattooing was still the best of the fine arts. The year A.D. 1866 has defects, but it is better certainly than the B.C. 18,660, if the human races were really about then. But, as I said, I cannot deal with such matters; I have only a little to say about the changes of life and civilization which this coast marks in the last century or two.

We are familiar with the present state of trade,

and with the phenomena it creates and the conditions it requires. It shows itself to the eye at once in immense warehouses, cities spreading over miles and miles, and not seeming even to anticipate a boundary, a population daily streaming from the thinly inhabited outskirts, and daily concentrating itself more and more in the already thronged cities. Commerce gives much to those who have much, and from such as have little it takes that little away. But the pre-requisites of our commerce are of recent growth, and our ancestors even lately did not possess them. They are—large and ready capital, rapid and cheap land-carriage, the power of making great breakwaters to keep out storms, the power of making large docks to hold many vessels, the ability to protect and the confidence to amass great wealth close to the seashore. But a very few generations ago these gifts were wanting. It was useless to bring all merchandise to one port, for when there you could not use it; no railway and no canal distributed bulky articles; they had to be brought by water to the nearest possible market; they might nearly as well have stayed where they were grown, if they had to be conveyed a hundred or two hundred miles when here. All our great protective works against the sea, all our great accumulative works at the great ports, are modern in the strictest sense, post-modern, as geologists would say, part of the 'drift' of this age.

But though in theory we know these things, yet they come upon us with a sudden completeness when we see the sort of place our ancestors thought a port. Boscastle is as good an example of their idea as can be found. It is a creek shaped like a capital *S*, with, I should think, the earliest and smallest breakwater on record just about the middle. The sea runs with great violence on all this coast, and no open bay is safe for a moment. But the turn or crook of the Boscastle creek, which I have endeavoured to describe by likening it to the letter *S*, in a great measure protects it, and even early masons were able to run out on the solid rock some few feet of compact stones, which help to add to the shelter. The whole creek is never nearly as broad as Regent Street, and it gradually runs away to be narrower than the Strand, while at the point of the breakwater there is a real Temple Bar, which hardly seems wide enough for a ship at all. The whole thing, when you first look down on it, gives you the notion that you are looking at a big port through a diminishing glass, so complete is the whole equipment, and yet so absurdly disproportionate, according to our notions, is the size. The principal harbour of Lilliput probably had just this look. But though its size across is small, the rocks which make its jaws are very formidable, and the sea foams against them in an unpleasant manner. I suppose we ought to think much of the courage with which sailors face such dangers, and of the feelings of their wives and families when they wait the return of their husbands and fathers; but my City associations at once carried me away to the poor underwriter who should insure against loss at such a place. How he would murmur, 'Oh! my premium,' as he saw the ship tossing up to the great black rock and the ugly breakwater, and seeming likely enough to hit both. I shall not ask at Lloyd's what is the rate for Boscastle rocks, for I remember the grave rebuke I once got from a serious underwriter when I said some other such place was pretty. 'Pretty! I should think it was,' he answered; 'why it is lined with our money!'

But our ancestors had no choice but to use such places. They could not make London and Liverpool; they had not the money; what wealth existed was scattered all over the country; the central money-market was not. There was no use in going to the goldsmiths who made Lombard Street to ask for a couple of millions to make docks or breakwaters, even if our science could have then made large specimens of the latter, which it could not. And, as I said before, these large emporia when made would have been quite useless; the auxiliary facilities which alone make such places serviceable did not exist. The neighbourhoods of Bideford and Boscastle had then to trust to Bideford and Boscastle; they had no access to London or Liverpool; they relied on their local port, and if that failed them had no resource or substitute.

The fringe of petty ports all over our coasts serves to explain the multitudes of old country houses, in proportion to the populations of old times, which are mouldering in out-of-the-way and often very ugly places. The tourist thinks—how did people come to build in such an inaccessible and unpicturesque place? But few of our old gentry cared for what we now call the beauties of nature; they built on their own estates when they could, and if those estates were near some wretched little haven they were much pleased. The sea was the railway of those days; it brought, as it did to Ellangowan in Dirk Hatterick's time, brandy for the men and 'pinners' for the women to the lonest of coast castles. According to popular belief, King Arthur himself thus lived. The famous castle of Tintagel hangs over the edge of a cliff, right over the next little bay to that of Boscastle—a very lone place, where a boat could get out to sea if the pilot knew the place, but where no stranger or pirate could get in with the tiniest craft, under peril of his life. By land, too, the Saxon must have had many a weary mile of bog and moorland to cross before he reached the crag's edge, and had very tough walls to deal with there, for they have not been repaired these thousand years, and at perhaps the most windy point in England some of them are standing still. King Arthur is out of luck just now. The sceptical, prosaic historians disbelieve in him, and the ethnologists despise him. What indeed is the interest of a dubious antiquity of thirteen hundred years, if we really can get to the people who dwelt 'near Bedford' side by side in daily life with the long-horned rhinoceros and the woolly-haired mammoth? So between the literati who think him too far off to believe in, and the literati who consider him too modern to take an interest in, King Arthur is at his nadir. But how singular was his zenith before! Whatever may be the doubt as to the existence of his person, there is no doubt as to the existence of his reputation, and it is the queerest perhaps even in legend. If he was anything, he was a Celt who resisted the Teutonic invaders, and yet years after, when these very Teutons created their own chivalry, they made into a fancied model of it this Celt, who never dreamed of it, who could not have understood an iota of it, who hated and perhaps slew the ancestors of those who made it. There are hundreds of kings whose reality is as uncertain as Arthur's, and some, though not many, whose fame has been as great as his; but there is no king or hero perhaps whose reality, if it were proved, *must* be so inconsistent with his fame.

I did not intend to have gone into this matter, but the 'strong' legend of the place was too much for me. I meant only to have said that it was in the ruined small ports and coast granges and castles of Queen Elizabeth's time that our Raleighs, and Drakes, and Frobishers were formed. In the ante-Lancashire period, now forgotten, Devon was a great mercantile county, and adjacent Cornwall shared, though somewhat less, in its power and its celebrity. It was 'Devonshire', local enthusiasts have said, 'which beat the Spanish Armada.' I am not sure of the history; according to my memory, the Armada was beaten by the waves; but Devonshire is right in this—she bred a main part of those who would have resisted the Armada, and who in that age fought the Spaniards whenever, in either hemisphere, propitious fate sent an opportunity.

Mr. Arnold has lately been writing on the influence of the Celtic character on the English. I wish he would consider whether the predominance of Southern England in old times, say in the Tudor period, had nothing to do with the largely romantic elements in the characters of those times. 'North of the Trent' the population was always thin till the manufacturing times, and there must have been a much scantier subjacent race of Celts there than in Devon and the South. It may be accident, but certainly the Tudor Englishman tends to crop up hereabouts. There is Mr. Kingsley, who was born, I believe, at Clovelly, and has drunk into his very nature all the life of this noble coast. There is in his style a vigour, softened, yet unrelaxed, which is like the spirit of these places. If he is not more like a Tudor Englishman than a nineteenth-century Englishman, then words have no meaning, and Mr. Arnold may be able to prove, though I can but suggest, that the source of all this compacted energy, fancy, and unsoundness lies in the universal local predominance of the Celtic nature. The datum is certain at least; we can all see that Mr. Kingsley is not like the pure Goth of Lancashire, for there can be little of the Celt there.

I do not feel able to confirm these ethnological speculations by any personal observations of my own upon the Boscastle natives. Their principal feature, to a stranger at least, is a theory they have that their peculiar pronunciation of the English language is the most correct. I asked a native the way to the chemist's, pronouncing *ch*, as is usual, like a *k*. The man looked at me wondering, then I repeated, when he said with pity, 'You mean the *tch*emist's.' Is this the last soft remnant of a Celtic guttural, or only the outcome of the inbred pragmaticalness of the natural rural mind?

ALGERNON CHARLES SWINBURNE

1837-1909

MORRIS'S *LIFE AND DEATH OF JASON*

The hardest work and the highest that can be done by a critic studious of the right is first to discern what is good, and then to discover how and in what way it is so. To do this office for any man during his life is a task always essentially difficult, sometimes seemingly ungracious. We demand of the student who stands up as a judge to show us as he best may how and why this man excels that, what are the stronger and what the weaker sides of his attempted or achieved work when set fairly by the work of others. For if in some one point at least it does not exceed theirs, it is not work of a high kind, and worthy of enduring study. Who is to say this, who is to prove it, we have first to find out; and found out it must be, if criticism is to be held of more account than the ephemeral cackle of casual praisers and blamers; if it is to be thoughtful and truthful, worthy the name of an art, handmaid of higher arts. Now, as a rule, men are mistrustful of one who takes leave to judge the work of a fellow workman. And not without reason or show of reason; for no verdicts more foolish or more false have been delivered than some of those passed by poet upon poet, by painter upon painter. Nor need this be taken as proof of anything base or partial or jealous in the speaker's mind. It is not easy to see at once widely and well. For example, could Byron and Wordsworth have judged better of each other's work, each might have lost something of fitness for his own. It is a hard law, but a law it is. Against this, however, a counter truth not less grave than this must be weighed. We do not appeal to men ignorant of politics for a verdict on affairs of state, to men unskilled in science on a scientific question. And no matter of science or of state is more abstruse and hard to settle than a question of art; nor is any more needful to have settled for us in good time, if only lest accident or neglect, ignorance or violence, rob us unaware of some precious and irrecoverable thing, not known of or esteemed while safely with us. Consider what all men have lost already and for ever, merely by such base means as these; how much of classic work and mediaeval, how much of Greece, of Italy, of England, has gone from us that we might have kept. For this and other reasons it may be permissible, or pardonable at least, for a student of art to speak now and then on art; so long only as he shall speak honestly and carefully, without overmuch of assumption or deprecation.

Over the first fortunes of a newly-born work of art accident must usually preside for evil or for good. Over the earliest work of the artist whom we are here to take note of, that purblind leader of the blind presided on the whole for evil. Here and there it met with eager recognition and earnest applause; nowhere, if I err not, with just praise or blame worth heeding. It seems to have been now lauded and now decried as the result and expression of a school rather than a man, of a theory or tradition rather than a poet or student.

Those who so judged were blind guides of the purblind; reversing thus the undivine office of their god Accident. Such things as were in this book are taught and learnt in no school but that of instinct. Upon no piece of work in the world was the impress of native character ever more distinctly stamped, more deeply branded. It needed no exceptional acuteness of ear or eye to see or hear that this poet held of none, stole from none, clung to none, as tenant or as beggar or as thief. Not as yet a master, he was assuredly no longer a pupil.

A little later than this one appeared another volume of poems, not dissimilar in general choice of stories and subjects, perfect where this was imperfect, strong where this was weak; but strong and perfect on that side alone. All that was wanting here was there supplied, but all that was here supplied was wanting there. In form, in structure, in composition, few poems can be more faultless than those of Mr. Tennyson, few faultier than those of Mr. Morris, which deal with the legend of Arthur and Guenevere. I do not speak here of form in the abstract and absolute sense; for where this is wanting, all is wanting; without this there can be no work of art at all. I speak of that secondary excellence always necessary to the perfection, but not always indispensable to the existence of art. These first poems of Mr. Morris were not malformed; a misshapen poem is no poem; as well might one talk of unnatural nature or superhuman manhood; but they are not well clad; their attire now and then has been huddled on; they have need sometimes of combing and trimming. Take that one, for example, called

'King Arthur's Tomb'. It has not been constructed at all; the parts hardly hold together; it has need of joists and screws, props and rafters. Many able writers of verse whom no miracle could endow with competence to do such work would have missed the faults as surely as the merits; would have done something where the poet has cared to do nothing. There is scarcely connexion here, and scarcely composition. There is hardly a trace of narrative power or mechanical arrangement. There is a perceptible want of tact and practice, which leaves the poem in parts indecorous and chaotic. But where among other and older poets of his time and country is one comparable for perception and expression of tragic truth, of subtle and noble, terrible and piteous things? where a touch of passion at once so broad and so sure? The figures here given have the blood and breath, the shape and step of life; they can move and suffer; their repentance is as real as their desire; their shame lies as deep as their love. They are at once remorseful for the sin and regretful of the pleasure that is past. The retrospective vision of Launcelot and of Guenevere is as passionate and profound as life. Riding towards her without hope, in the darkness and the heat of the way, he can but divert and sustain his spirit by recollection of her loveliness and her love, seen long since asleep and waking, in another place than this, on a distant night.

> Pale in the green sky were the stars, I ween,
> Because the moon shone like a tear she shed
> When she dwelt up in heaven a while ago
> And ruled all things but God.

Retrospect and vision, natural memories and

spiritual, here coalesce; and how exquisite is the retrospect, and how passionate the vision, of past light and colour in the sky, past emotion and conception in the soul! Not in the idyllic school is a chord ever struck, a note ever sounded, so tender and subtle as this. Again, when Guenevere has maddened herself and him with wild words of reproach and remorse, abhorrence and attraction, her sharp and sudden memory of old sights and sounds and splendid irrevocable days finds word and form not less noble and faithful to fact and life. The first words of Arthur bidding her cherish the knight 'whom all the land called his banner, sword, and shield'; the long first pressure of Launcelot's lips on her hand; the passionate and piteous course of love here ended (if ended at all) above the king's grave dug in part and unwittingly by their wrong-doing; the solitary sound of birds singing in her gardens, while in the lists the noise went on of spears and shouts telling which knight of them all rode here or there; the crying of ladies' names as men and horses clashed one against another, names that bit like the steel they impelled to its mark; the agony of anger and horror which gives edge and venom to her memory—

> Banner of Arthur—with black-bended shield
>
> Sinister-wise across the fair gold ground!
>   Here let me tell you what a knight you are,
> O sword and shield of Arthur! you are found
>   A crooked sword, I think, that leaves a scar
>
> On the bearer's arm so be he thinks it straight—
>   Twisted Malay's crease, beautiful blue-grey,
> Poisoned with sweet fruit—as he found too late,
>   My husband Arthur, on some bitter day!

O sickle cutting harvest all day long,
  That the husbandman across his shoulder hangs,
And going homeward about evensong,
  Dies the next morning, struck through by the fangs![1]

—all these points and phases of passion are alike truly and nobly rendered. I have not read the poem for years, I have not the book at hand, and I cite from memory; but I think it would be safe to swear to the accuracy of my citation. Such verses are not forgettable. They are not, indeed—as are the 'Idylls of the King'—the work of a dexterous craftsman in full practice. Little beyond dexterity, a rare eloquence, and a laborious patience of hand, has been given to the one or denied to the other.[2] These are good gifts and great; but it is better to want clothes than limbs.

The shortcomings of this first book are nowhere

[1] Perhaps in all this noble passage of poetry there is nothing nobler than this bitter impulse of irony, this fiery shame and rage of repentance, which here impels Guenevere to humiliate herself through her lover, and thus consummate the agony of abasement. 'False and fatal as banner, or shield, or sword, wherein is he better than a peasant's dangerous and vulgar implement, as fatal to him it may be, by carelessness or chance, as a king's weapon to the king if handled amiss?' And yet for all this she cannot but cleave to him; through her lover she scourges herself; it is suicide in her to slay him; but even so his soul must needs be saved—'so as by fire.' No poet about to start on his course ever saw for himself or showed to others a thing more tragic and more true than this study of noble female passion, half selfless and half personal, half mad and half sane.

[2] The comparison here made is rather between book and book than between man and man. Both poets have done better elsewhere, each after his kind; and except by his best work no workman can be fairly judged. A critic who should underrate either would be condemnable on both hands.

traceable in the second now lying before us. A nine years' space does not lie between them in vain; enough has been learned and unlearned, rejected and attained. Here indeed there is not the stormy variety, the lyric ardour of the first book; there is not the passion of the ballads, the change of note and diversity of power, all that fills with life and invigorates with colour the artist's earlier designs; for not all of this is here needed. Of passion and humour, of impulse and instinct, he had given noble and sufficient proof in manifold ways. But this 'Jason' is a large and coherent poem, completed as conceived; the style throughout on a level with the invention. In direct narrative power, in clear forthright manner of procedure, not seemingly troubled to select, to pick and sift and winnow, yet never superfluous or verbose, never straggling or jarring; in these high qualities it resembles the work of Chaucer. Even against the great master his pupil may fairly be matched for simple sense of right, for grace and speed of step, for purity and justice of colour. In all the noble roll of our poets there has been since Chaucer no second teller of tales, no second rhapsode comparable to the first, till the advent of this one. As with the Greeks, so with us; we have had in lieu of these a lyric and a tragic school; we have also had the subordinate schools, gnomic and idyllic, domestic and didactic. But the old story-singers, the old 'Saga-men', we have no more heard of. As soon might we have looked for a fresh Odyssey from southward, a fresh Njala from northward. And yet no higher school has brought forth rarer poets than this. 'But,' it is said, 'this sort of poetry is a March flower, a child of the first winds and suns of a nation; in May even, much more in August, you cannot have it except by forcing; and forcing it will not bear. A late romance is a hothouse daffodil.' And so indeed it must usually be. But so it is not here; and the proof is the poem. It could not be done, no doubt, only it has been. Here is a poem sown of itself, sprung from no alien seed, cast after no alien model; fresh as wind, bright as light, full of the spring and the sun. It shares of course the conditions of its kind; it has no time for the subtleties and hardly room for the ardours of tragic poetry. Passion in romance is of its nature subordinate to action; the flowing stream of story hushes and lulls the noise of its gurgling and refluent eddies with a still predominance of sound. To me it seems that there has here been almost too much of this. Only by rare and brief jets does the poet let out the fire of a potent passion which not many others can kindle and direct. For the most part, the river of romance flows on at full, but keeping well to its channel, unvexed by rains and undisturbed by whirlpools. In a word, through great part of this poem there is no higher excellence attempted than that of adventurous or romantic narrative couched in the simplest and fittest forms of poetry. This abstinence is certainly not due to impotence, possibly not to intention, more probably to distaste. Mr. Morris has an English respect for temperance and reserve; good things as drags, but not as clogs. He is not afraid to tackle a passion, but he will not move an inch from his way to tackle it. Tragedy can never be more than the episode of a romance, and romance is rather to his taste than naked tragedy. He reminds us of the knight in Chaucer cutting sharply short the monk's tragic histories as too piteous for recital, or the very monk himself breaking off the detail of Ugolino's agony with a reference to Dante for those who can endure it.

The descriptive and decorative beauties of this romance of 'Jason' are excellent above all in this, that numberless though they be they are always just and fit. Not a tone of colour, not a note of form, is misplaced or dispensable. The pictures are clear and chaste, sweet and lucid, as early Italian work. There are crowds and processions, battle-pieces and merry-makings, worthy of Benozzo or Carpaccio; single figures or groups of lovers in flowery watery land, worthy of Sandro or Filippo. The sea-pieces are like the younger Lippi's; the best possible to paint from shore. They do not taste salt or sound wide; but they have all the beauty of the beach. The romance poets have never loved the sea as have the tragic poets; Chaucer simply ignores it with a shiver; even Homer's men are glad to be well clear of it. Ulysses has no sea-king's impulse; he fights and beats it, and is glad, and there an end; necessity alone ever drives him off shore. But Aeschylus loves the Oceanides; and Shakespeare, landsman though he were, rejoices in the roll and clash of breakers.

For examples of the excellences we have noted—the chastity of colour and noble justice of composition, the fruitful and faithful touches of landscape incident—almost any page of the poem might be turned up. Compare the Hesperian with the Circean garden, the nameless northern desert lands with the wood of Medea's transformation, or the seaward bent where Jason 'died strangely'. No flower of the landscape is slurred, but no flower is obtrusive; the painting is broad and minute at once, large and sure by dint of accuracy. And there are wonderful touches on it of fairy mystery; weird lights pass over it and wafts of mystical wind; as here:—

> There comes a murmur from the shore,
> And in the place two fair streams are,
> Drawn from the purple hills afar,
> Drawn down unto the restless sea,
> *The hills whose flowers ne'er fed the bee,*
> *The shore no ship has ever seen,*
> Still beaten by the billows green,
> Whose murmur comes unceasingly
> Unto the place for which I cry.

All this song of a nymph to Hylas is full of the melody which involves colour and odour, but the two lines marked have in them the marvel and the music of a dream. Nor is any passage in the poem pitched in a higher and clearer key than the first hymn of Orpheus as Argo takes the sea. As noble is the song of triumph at page 217, which should be set by the side of this, to which it is in some sort antiphonal.

But the root of the romance lies of course in the character of Medea; and here, where it was needfullest to do well, the poet has done best. At her first entrance the poem takes new life and rises out of the atmosphere of mere adventure and incident. The subdued and delicate ardour of the scene in Jason's chamber, following as it does on the ghastly beauty of that in the wood of the Three-formed, is proof enough and at once with how strong and soft a touch the picture will be completed. Her incantations, and her flight with Jason, have no less of fanciful and tender power. The fifteenth book, where she beguiles Pelias to death at the hands of his daughters, is a sample of flawless verse and noble imagination unsurpassed by any here. For dramatic invention and vivid realism of the impossible, which turns to fair and sensible truth the wildest dreams of legend, there has been no poet for centuries comparable. But the very flower and crest of this noble poem is the final tragedy at Corinth. Queen, sorceress, saviour, she has sunk or risen to mere woman; and not in vain before entering the tragic lists has the poet called on that great poet's memory who has dealt with the terrible and pitiful passion of women like few but Shakespeare since.

Worthy, indeed, even of the master-hand is all that follows. Let the student weigh well the slight but great touches in which the fitful fury and pity and regret of the sufferer are given; so delicate and accurate that only by the entire and majestic harmony of tragedy will he discern the excellence and justice of every component note. To come upon this part of the poem is as the change from river to sea (Book XII), when wind and water had a larger savour in lip and nostril of the Argonauts. Note well the new and piteous beauty of this:—

Kindly I deal with thee, mine enemy;
Since swift forgetfulness to thee I send.
But thou shalt die—his eyes shall see thine end—
Ah! if thy death alone could end it all.

But ye—shall I behold you when leaves fall,
In some sad evening of the autumn-tide?
Or shall I have you sitting by my side
Amidst the feast, so that folk stare and say,
'Sure the grey wolf has seen the queen to-day'?

What! when I kneel in temples of the Gods
Must I bethink me of the upturned sods,
And hear a voice say: 'Mother, wilt thou come
And see us resting in our new-made home,
Since thou wert used to make us lie full soft,
Smoothing our pillows many a time and oft?
O mother, now no dainty food we need,
Whereof of old thou usedst to have such heed.
O mother, now we need no gown of gold,
Nor in the winter-time do we grow cold;
Thy hands would bathe us when we were thine own,
Now doth the rain wash every shining bone.
No pedagogue we need, for surely heaven
Lies spread above us, with the planets seven,
To teach us all its lore.

Rarely but in the ballad and romance periods has such poetry been written, so broad and sad and simple, so full of deep and direct fire, certain of its aim, without finish, without fault. The passion from hence fills and burns to a close; the verse for a little is as the garment of Medea steeped in strange moisture as of tears and liquid flame to be kindled by the sun.

O sons, with what sweet counsels and what tears
Would I have hearkened to the hopes and fears
Of your first loves: what rapture had it been
Your dear returning footsteps to have seen
Amidst the happy warriors of the land;
But now—but now—this is a little hand,
Too often kissed since love did first begin
To win such curses as it yet shall win,
When after all bad deeds there comes a worse;
Praise to the Gods! ye know not how to curse.

It should now be clear, or never, that in this poem a new thing of great price has been cast into the English treasure-house. Nor is the cutting or the setting of the jewel unworthy of it; art and instinct have wrought hand in hand to its perfection. Other and various fields await the workman who has here approved himself a master, acceptable into the guild of great poets on a footing of his own to be shared or disputed by no other. Strained clear and guided straight as now, his lofty lyrical power must keep all its promise to us. Diffusion is in the nature of a romance, and it cannot be said that here the stream has ever overflowed into marshland or stagnated in lock or pool. Therefore we do not blame the length and fullness of so fair a river ; but something of barrier or dam may serve to concentrate and condense the next. Also, if we must note the slightest ripples of the water-flies that wrinkle it, let us set down in passing that there are certain slight laxities or perversities of metre which fret the ear and perplex the eye, noticeable only as the least shortcoming is noticeable in great work. Elision, for example, is a necessity, not a luxury, of metre. This law Chaucer, a most loyal versifier, never allows himself to slight after the fashion of his follower. But into these straits of technical art we need not now steer. So much remains unremarked, so much unsaid ; so much of beauty slighted, of uncommended excellence ; that I close these inadequate and hurried notes with a sense of grave injustice done. To the third book of Mr. Morris we look now, not for the seal of our present judgement, but for the accomplishment of our highest hopes ; for a fresh honour done to English art, a fresh delight to us, and a fresh memory for the future.

WALTER HORATIO PATER

1839–1894

NOTES ON LEONARDO DA VINCI

IN Vasari's life of Leonardo da Vinci, as we now read it, there are some variations from the first edition. There, the painter who has fixed the outward type of Christ for succeeding centuries was a bold speculator, holding lightly by other men's beliefs, setting philosophy above Christianity. Words of his, trenchant enough to justify this impression, are not recorded, and would have been out of keeping with a genius of which one characteristic is a tendency to lose itself in a refined and graceful mystery. The suspicion was but the time-honoured form in which the world stamps its appreciation of one who has thoughts for himself alone, his high indifferentism, his intolerance of the common forms of things; and in the second edition the image was changed into something fainter and more conventional. But it is still by a certain mystery in his work, and something enigmatical beyond the usual measure of great men, that he fascinates, or perhaps half repels. His life is one of sudden revolts, with intervals in which he works not at all, or apart from the main scope of his work. By a strange fortune the works on which his more popular fame rested disappeared early from the world, as the Battle of the Standard; or are mixed obscurely with the work of meaner hands, as the Last Supper. His type of beauty is so exotic that it fascinates a larger number than it delights, and seems more than that of any other artist to reflect ideas and views and some scheme of the world within, so that he seemed to his contemporaries to be the possessor of some unsanctified and secret wisdom, as to Michelet and others to have anticipated modern ideas. He trifles with his genius, and crowds all his chief work into a few tormented years of later life; yet he is so possessed by his genius that he passes unmoved through the most tragic events, overwhelming his country and friends, like one who comes across them by chance on some secret errand.

His *legend*, as the French say, with the anecdotes which every one knows, is one of the most brilliant in Vasari. Later writers merely copied it, until, in 1804, Carlo Amoretti applied to it a criticism which left hardly a date fixed, and not one of those anecdotes intact. And now a French writer, M. Arsène Houssaye, gathering all that is known about Leonardo in an easily accessible form, has done for the third of the three great masters what Grimm has done for Michelangelo, and Passavant, long since, for Raphael. Antiquarianism has no more to do. For others remain the editing of the thirteen books of his manuscripts, and the separation by technical criticism of what in his reputed works is really his, from what is only half his or the work of his pupils. But a lover of strange souls may still analyse for himself the impression made on him by those works, and try to reach through it a definition of the chief elements of Leonardo's genius. The legend, corrected and enlarged by its critics, may now and then intervene to support the results of this analysis.

His life has three divisions,—thirty years at Florence, nearly twenty years at Milan, then nineteen years of wandering, till he sinks to rest under the protection of Francis I at the Château de Clou. The dishonour of illegitimacy hangs over his birth. Piero Antonio, his father, was of a noble Florentine house, of Vinci in the Val d'Arno, and Leonardo, brought up delicately among the true children of that house, was the love-child of his youth, with the keen puissant nature such children often have. We see him in his youth fascinating all men by his beauty, improvising music and songs, buying the caged birds and setting them free as he walked the streets of Florence, fond of odd bright dresses and spirited horses.

From his earliest years he designed many objects, and constructed models in relief, of which Vasari mentions some of women smiling. Signor Piero, thinking over this promise in the child, took him to the workshop of Andrea del Verrocchio, then the most famous artist in Florence. Beautiful objects lay about there—reliquaries, pyxes, silver images for the Pope's chapel at Rome, strange fancy-work of the Middle Age keeping odd company with fragments of antiquity, then but lately discovered. Another student Leonardo may have seen there—a boy into whose soul the level light and aerial illusions of Italian sunsets had passed, in after days famous as Perugino. Verrocchio was an artist of the earlier Florentine type, carver, painter, and worker in metals in one; designer, not of pictures only, but of all things, for sacred or household use, drinking-vessels, ambries, instruments of music, making them all fair to look upon, filling the common ways of life with the reflection of some far-off brightness; and years of patience had refined his hand till his work was now sought after from distant places.

It happened that Verrocchio was employed by the brethren of Vallombrosa to paint the Baptism of Christ, and Leonardo was allowed to finish an angel in the left-hand corner. It was one of those moments in which the progress of a great thing—here that of the art of Italy—presses hard and sharp on the happiness of an individual, through whose discouragement and decrease humanity, in more fortunate persons, comes a step nearer to its final success.

For beneath the cheerful exterior of the mere well-paid craftsman, chasing brooches for the copes of Santa Maria Novella, or twisting metal screens for the tombs of the Medici, lay the ambitious desire of expanding the destiny of Italian art by a larger knowledge and insight into things—a purpose in art not unlike Leonardo's still unconscious purpose; and often, in the modelling of drapery, or of a lifted arm, or of hair cast back from the face, there came to him something of the freer manner and richer humanity of a later age. But in this Baptism the pupil had surpassed the master; and Verrocchio turned away as one stunned, and as if his sweet earlier work must thereafter be distasteful to him, from the bright animated angel of Leonardo's hand.

The angel may still be seen in Florence, a space of sunlight in the cold, laboured old picture; but the legend is true only in sentiment, for painting had always been the art by which Verrocchio set least store. And as in a sense he anticipates

Leonardo, so to the last Leonardo recalls the studio of Verrocchio, in the love of beautiful toys, such as the vessel of water for a mirror and lovely needlework about the implicated hands in the Modesty and Vanity, and of reliefs, like those cameos which in The Virgin of the Balances hang all round the girdle of St. Michael, and of bright variegated stones, such as the agates in the Saint Anne, and in a hieratic preciseness and grace, as of a sanctuary swept and garnished. Amid all the cunning and intricacy of his Lombard manner this never left him. Much of it there must have been in that lost picture of Paradise, which he prepared as a cartoon for tapestry to be woven in the looms of Flanders. It was the apex of the older Florentine style of miniature painting, with patient putting of each leaf upon the trees and each flower in the grass, where the first man and woman were standing.

And because it was the perfection of that style, it awoke in Leonardo some seed of discontent which lay in the secret places of his nature. For the way to perfection is through a series of disgusts; and this picture—all that he had done so far in his life at Florence—was after all in the old slight manner. His art, if it was to be something in the world, must be weighted with more of the meaning of nature and purpose of humanity. Nature was 'the true mistress of higher intelligences'. So he plunged into the study of nature. And in doing this he followed the manner of the older students; he brooded over the hidden virtues of plants and crystals, the lines traced by the stars as they moved in the sky, over the correspondences which exist between the different orders of living things, through which, to eyes opened, they interpret each other; and for years he seemed to those about him as one listening to a voice silent for other men.

He learned here the art of going deep, of tracking the sources of expression to their subtlest retreats, the power of an intimate presence in the things he handled. He did not at once or entirely break with art; only he was no longer the cheerful objective painter, through whose soul, as through clear glass, the bright figures of Florentine life, only made a little mellower and more pensive by the transit, passed on to the white wall. He wasted many days in curious tricks of design, seeming to lose himself in the spinning of intricate devices of lines and colours. He was smitten with a love of the impossible—the perforation of mountains, changing the course of rivers, raising great buildings, such as Giovanni Church, in the air; all those feats for the performance of which natural magic professes to have the key. Later writers, indeed, see in these efforts an anticipation of modern mechanics; in him they were rather dreams, thrown off by the overwrought and labouring brain. Two ideas were especially fixed in him, as reflexes of things that had touched his brain in childhood beyond the measure of other impressions—the smiling of women and the motion of great waters.

And in such studies some interfusion of the extremes of beauty and terror shaped itself, as an image that might be seen and touched, in the mind of this gracious youth, so fixed, that for the rest of his life it never left him; and as catching glimpses of it in the strange eyes or hair of chance people, he would follow such about the streets of

Florence till the sun went down, of whom many sketches of his remain. Some of these are full of a curious beauty, that remote beauty apprehended only by those who have sought it carefully; who, starting with acknowledged types of beauty, have refined as far upon these as these refine upon the world of common forms. But mingled inextricably with this there is an element of mockery also; so that, whether in sorrow or scorn, he caricatures Dante even. Legions of grotesques sweep under his hand; for has not nature, too, her grotesques—the rent rock, the distorting light of evening on lonely roads, the unveiled structure of man in the embryo or the skeleton?

All these swarming fancies unite in the Medusa of the Uffizi. Vasari's story of an earlier Medusa, painted on a wooden shield, is perhaps an invention; and yet, properly told, has more of the air of truth about it than anything else in the whole legend. For its real subject is not the serious work of a man, but the experiment of a child. The lizards and glow-worms and other strange small creatures which haunt an Italian vineyard bring before one the whole picture of a child's life in a Tuscan dwelling, half castle, half farm; and are as true to nature as the pretended astonishment of the father for whom the boy has prepared a surprise. It was not in play that he painted that other Medusa, the one great picture which he left behind him in Florence. The subject has been treated in various ways; Leonardo alone cuts to its centre; he alone realizes it as the head of a corpse, exercising its power through all the circumstances of death. What we may call the fascination of corruption penetrates in every touch its exquisitely-finished beauty. About the dainty lines of the cheek a rabbit creeps unheeded. The delicate snakes seem literally strangling each other in terrified struggle to escape from the Medusa brain. The hue which violent death always brings with it is in the features—features singularly massive and grand, as we catch them inverted, in a dexterous foreshortening, sloping upwards, almost sliding down upon us, crown foremost, like a great calm stone against which the wave of serpents breaks. But it is a subject that may well be left to the beautiful verses of Shelley.

The science of that age was all divination, clairvoyance, unsubjected to our exact modern formulas, seeking in an instant of vision to concentrate a thousand experiences. Later writers, thinking only of the well-ordered treatise on painting which a Frenchman, Raffaelle du Fresne, a hundred years after, compiled from Leonardo's bewildered manuscripts, written strangely, as his manner was, from right to left, have imagined a rigid order in his inquiries. But such rigid order was little in accordance with the restlessness of his character; and if we think of him as the mere reasoner who subjects design to anatomy, and composition to mathematical rules, we shall hardly have of him that impression which those about him received from him. Poring over his crucibles, making experiments with colour, trying by a strange variation of the alchemist's dream to discover the secret, not of an elixir to make man's natural life immortal, but rather of giving immortality to the subtlest and most delicate effects of painting, he seemed to them rather the sorcerer or the magician, possessed of curious secrets and a hidden knowledge, living in a world of which he alone possessed the key. What his philosophy seems to have been most like is that of Paracelsus or Cardan; and much of the spirit of the older alchemy still hangs about it, with its confidence in short cuts and odd by-ways to knowledge. To him philosophy was to be something giving strange swiftness and double sight, divining the sources of springs beneath the earth or of expression beneath the human countenance, clairvoyant of occult gifts in common or uncommon things, in the reed at the brook-side or the star which draws near to us but once in a century. How in this way the clear purpose was overclouded, the fine chaser's hand perplexed, we but dimly see; the mystery which at no point quite lifts from Leonardo's life is thickest here. But it is certain that at one period of his life he had almost ceased to be an artist.

The year 1483—year of the birth of Raphael and the thirty-first of Leonardo's life—is fixed as the date of his visit to Milan by the letter in which he recommends himself to Ludovico Sforza, and offers to tell him for a price strange secrets in the art of war. It was that Sforza who murdered his young nephew by slow poison, yet was so susceptible to religious impressions that he turned his worst passions into a kind of religious cultus, and who took for his device the mulberry tree—symbol, in its long delay and sudden yielding of flowers and fruit together, of a wisdom which economizes all forces for an opportunity of sudden and sure effect. The fame of Leonardo had gone before him, and he was to model a colossal statue of Francesco, the first duke. As for Leonardo himself, he came not as an artist at all, or careful of the fame of one;

but as a player on the harp—strange harp of silver of his own construction, shaped in some curious likeness to a horse's skull. The capricious spirit of Ludovico was susceptible to the charm of music, and Leonardo's nature had a kind of spell in it. Fascination is always the word descriptive of him. No portrait of his youth remains; but all tends to make us believe that up to this time some charm of voice and aspect, strong enough to balance the disadvantage of his birth, had played about him. His physical strength was great; it was said that he could bend a horseshoe like a coil of lead.

The Duomo, work of artists from beyond the Alps, so fantastic to a Florentine used to the mellow, unbroken surfaces of Giotto and Arnolfo, was then in all its freshness; and below, in the streets of Milan, moved a people as fantastic, changeful, and dreamlike. To Leonardo least of all men could there be anything poisonous in the exotic flowers of sentiment which grew there. It was a life of exquisite amusements—Leonardo became a celebrated designer of pageants—and brilliant sins; and it suited the quality of his genius, composed in almost equal parts of curiosity and the desire of beauty, to take things as they came.

Curiosity and the desire of beauty! They are the two elementary forces in Leonardo's genius; curiosity often in conflict with the desire of beauty, but generating, in union with it, a type of subtle and curious grace.

The movement of the thirteenth century was twofold: partly the Renaissance, partly also the coming of what is called the modern spirit, with its realism, its appeal to experience; it comprehended a return to antiquity, and a return to nature. Raphael represents the return to antiquity, and Leonardo the return to nature. In this return to nature he was seeking to satisfy a boundless curiosity by her perpetual surprises, a microscopic sense of finish by her finesse, or delicacy of operation, that *subtilitas naturae* which Bacon notices. So we find him often in intimate relations with men of science, with Fra Luca Paccioli the mathematician, and the anatomist Marc Antonio della Torre. His observations and experiments fill thirteen volumes of manuscript; and those who can judge describe him as anticipating long before, by rapid intuition, the later ideas of science. He explained the obscure light of the unilluminated part of the moon, knew that the sea had once covered the mountains which contain shells, and the gathering of the equatorial waters above the polar.

He who thus penetrated into the most secret parts of nature preferred always the more to the less remote, what, seeming exceptional, was an instance of law more refined, the construction about things of a peculiar atmosphere and mixed lights. He paints flowers with such curious felicity that different writers have attributed to him a fondness for particular flowers, as Clement the cyclamen, and Rio the jasmine; while at Venice there is a stray leaf from his portfolio dotted all over with studies of violets and the wild rose. In him first appears the taste for what is bizarre or *recherché* in landscape—hollow places full of the green shadow of bituminous rocks, ridged reefs of trap-rock which cut the water into quaint sheets of light—their exact antitype is in our own western seas—all solemn effects of moving water; you may follow it springing from its distant source among the rocks on the heath of the Madonna of the Balances, passing as a little fall into the treacherous calm of the Madonna of the Lake, next, as a goodly river below the cliffs of the Madonna of the Rocks, washing the white walls of its distant villages, stealing out in a network of divided streams in La Gioconda to the seashore of the Saint Anne—that delicate place, where the wind passes like the hand of some fine etcher over the surface, and the untorn shells lie thick upon the sand, and the tops of the rocks, to which the waves never rise, are green with grass grown fine as hair. It is the landscape, not of dreams or fancy, but of places far withdrawn, and hours selected from a thousand with a miracle of finesse. Through his strange veil of sight things reach him so; in no ordinary night or day, but as in faint light of eclipse, or in some brief interval of falling rain at daybreak, or through deep water.

And not into nature only; but he plunged also into human personality, and became above all a painter of portraits; faces of a modelling more skilful than has been seen before or since, embodied with a reality which almost amounts to illusion on dark air. To take a character as it was, and delicately sound its stops, suited one so curious in observation, curious in invention. So he painted the portraits of Ludovico's mistresses, Lucretia Crivelli and Cecilia Galerani the poetess, of Ludovico himself, and the Duchess Beatrice. The portrait of Cecilia Galerani is lost, but that of Lucretia Crivelli has been identified with La Belle Feronière of the Louvre, and Ludovico's pale, anxious face still remains in the Ambrosian. Opposite is the portrait of Beatrice d'Este, in whom

Leonardo seems to have caught some presentiment of early death, painting her precise and grave, full of the refinement of the dead, in sad earth-coloured raiment, set with pale stones.

Sometimes this curiosity came in conflict with the desire of beauty; it tended to make him go too far below that outside of things in which art begins and ends. This struggle between the reason and its ideas and the senses, the desire of beauty, is the key to Leonardo's life at Milan—his restlessness, his endless retouchings, his odd experiments with colour. How much must he leave unfinished, how much recommence! His problem was the transmutation of ideas into images. What he had attained so far had been the mastery of that earlier Florentine style, with its naïve and limited sensuousness. Now he was to entertain in this narrow medium those divinations of a a humanity too wide for it—that larger vision of the opening world which is only not too much for the great irregular art of Shakespeare; and everywhere the effort is visible in the work of his hands. This agitation, this perpetual delay, give him an air of weariness and ennui. To others he seems to be aiming at an impossible effect, to do something that art, that painting, can never do. Often the expression of physical beauty at this or that point seems strained and marred in the effort, as in those heavy German foreheads—too heavy and German for perfect beauty.

There was a touch of Germany in that genius which, as Goethe said, had 'müde sich gedacht', *thought itself weary*. What an anticipation of modern Germany, for instance, in that debate on the question whether sculpture or painting is the nobler art![1] But there is this difference between him and the German,. that, with all that curious science, the German would have thought nothing more was needed; and the name of Goethe himself reminds one how great for the artist may be the danger of overmuch science; how Goethe, who, in the *Elective Affinities* and the first part of *Faust*, does transmute ideas into images, who wrought many such transmutations, did not invariably find the spell-word, and in the second part of *Faust*, presents us with a mass of science which has no artistic character at all. But Leonardo will never work till the happy moment comes—that moment of *bien-être*, which to imaginative men is a moment of invention. On this moment he waits; other moments are but a preparation or after-taste of it. Few men distinguish between them as jealously as he did. Hence so many flaws even in the choicest work. But for Leonardo the distinction is absolute, and in the moment of *bien-être* the alchemy complete; the idea is stricken into colour and imagery; a cloudy mysticism is refined to a subdued and graceful mystery, and painting pleases the eye while it satisfies the soul.

This curious beauty is seen above all in his drawings, and in these chiefly in the abstract grace of the bounding lines. Let us take some of these drawings, and pause over them awhile; and, first, one of those at Florence—the heads of a woman and a little child, set side by side, but each in its own separate frame. First of all, there is something exquisitely tender in the reappearance in

[1] How princely, how characteristic of Leonardo, the answer, 'Quanto più un' arte porta seco fatica di corpo, tanto più è vile!'

the fuller curves of the child, of the sharper, more chastened lines of the worn and older face, which leaves no doubt that the heads are those of a little child and its mother, indicative of a feeling for maternity always characteristic of Leonardo; a feeling further indicated here by the half-humorous pathos of the diminutive rounded shoulders of the child. You may note a like tenderness in drawings of a young man, seated in a stooping posture, his face in his hands, as in sorrow; of a slave sitting in an uneasy sitting attitude in some brief interval of rest; of a small Madonna and Child, peeping sideways in half-reassured terror, as a mighty griffin with bat-like wings—one of Leonardo's finest *inventions*—descends suddenly from the air to snatch up a lion wandering near them. But note in these, as that which especially belongs to art, the contour of the young man's hair, the poise of the slave's arm above his head, and the curves of the head of the child, following the little skull within, thin and fine as some sea-shell worn by the wind.

Take again another head, still more full of sentiment, but of a different kind—a little red chalk drawing, which every one remembers who has seen the drawings at the Louvre. It is a face of doubtful sex, set in the shadow of its own hair, the cheek-line in high light against it, with something voluptuous and full in the eyelids and the lips. Another drawing might pass for the same face in childhood, with parched and feverish lips, but with much sweetness in the loose, short-waisted, childish dress, with necklace and bulla, and the daintily bound hair. We might take the thread of suggestion which these two drawings offer, thus set side by side, and following it through the drawings at Florence, Venice, and Milan, construct a sort of series, illustrating better than anything else Leonardo's type of womanly beauty. Daughters of Herodias, their fantastic head-dresses knotted and folded so strangely, to leave the dainty oval of the face disengaged, they are not of the Christian family, or of Raphael's. They are the clairvoyants, through whom, as through delicate instruments, one becomes aware of the subtler forces of nature, and the modes of their action, all that is magnetic in it, all those finer conditions wherein material things rise to that subtlety of operation which constitutes them spiritual, where only the finer nerve and the keener touch can follow; it is as if in certain revealing instances we actually saw them at their work on human flesh. Nervous, electric, faint always with some inexplicable faintness, they seem to be subject to exceptional conditions, to feel powers at work in the common air unfelt by others, to become, as it were, receptacles of them, and pass them on to us in a chain of secret influences.

But among the more youthful heads there is one at Florence which Love chooses for its own—the head of a young man, which may well be the likeness of Salaino, beloved of Leonardo for his curled and waving hair—*belli capelli ricci e inanellati*—and afterwards his favourite pupil and servant. Of all the interests in living men and women which may have filled his life at Milan, this attachment alone is recorded; and in return, Salaino identified himself so entirely with Leonardo, that the picture of St. Anne, in the Louvre, has been attributed to him. It illustrates Leonardo's usual choice of pupils—men of some natural charm of person or intercourse, like Salaino; or men of birth and princely habits of life, like Francesco Melzi—men with just enough genius to be capable of initiation into his secret, for which they were ready to efface their own individuality. Among them, retiring often to the villa of the Melzi at Canonica al Vaprio, he worked at his fugitive manuscripts and sketches, working for the present hour, and for a few only, perhaps chiefly for himself. Other artists have been as careless of present or future applause, in self-forgetfulness, or because they set moral or political ends above the ends of art; but in him this solitary culture of beauty seems to have hung upon a kind of self-love, and a carelessness in the work of art of all but art itself. Out of the secret places of a unique temperament he brought strange blossoms and fruits hitherto unknown; and for him the novel impression conveyed, the exquisite effect woven, counted as an end in itself—a perfect end.

And these pupils of his acquired his manner so thoroughly, that though the number of Leonardo's authentic works is very small indeed, there is a multitude of other men's pictures, through which we undoubtedly see him, and come very near to his genius. Sometimes, as in the little picture of the Madonna of the Balances, in which, from the bosom of his mother, Christ weighs the pebbles of the brook against the sins of men, we have a hand, rough enough by contrast, working on some fine hint or sketch of his. Sometimes, as in the subjects of the daughter of Herodias and the head of John the Baptist, the lost originals have been re-echoed and varied upon again and again by Luini and others. At other times the original remains, but has been a mere theme or motive, a type of which the accessories might be modified or changed; and these variations have but brought out the more the purpose or expression of the original. It is so with the so-called St. John the Baptist of the Louvre—one of the few naked figures Leonardo painted—whose delicate brown flesh and woman's hair no one would go out into the wilderness to seek, and whose treacherous smile would have us understand something far beyond the outward gesture or circumstance. But the long reed-like cross in the hand, which suggests John the Baptist, becomes faint in a copy at the Ambrosian, and disappears altogether in another in the Palazzo Rosso at Genoa. Returning from the last to the original, we are no longer surprised by St. John's strange likeness to the Bacchus, which hangs near it, which set Gautier thinking of Heine's notion of decayed gods, who, to maintain themselves, took employment in the new religion. We recognize one of those symbolical inventions in which the ostensible subject is used, not as matter for definite pictorial realization, but as the starting-point of a train of sentiment, subtle and vague as a piece of music. No one ever ruled over his subject more entirely than Leonardo, or bent it more dexterously to purely artistic ends. And so it comes to pass that though he handles sacred subjects continually, he is the most profane of painters; the given person or subject, Saint John in the Desert, or the Virgin on the Knees of Saint Anne, is often merely the pretext for a kind of work which carries one quite out of the range of its conventional associations.

About the Last Supper, its decay and restorations, a whole literature has risen up, Goethe's pensive sketch of its sad fortunes being far the best. The death in child-birth of the Duchess Beatrice, was followed in Ludovico by one of those paroxysms of religious feeling which in him were constitutional. The low, gloomy, Dominican church of Saint Mary of the Graces had been the favourite shrine of Beatrice. She had spent her last days there, full of sinister presentiments; at last it had been almost necessary to remove her from it by force. And now it was here that mass was said a hundred times a day for her repose; and a mania for restoring churches took possession of the duke. So on the damp wall of the refectory, oozing with mineral salts, Leonardo painted the Last Supper. A hundred anecdotes were told about it, his retouchings and delays. They show him refusing to work except at the moment of invention, scornful of whoever thought that art was a work of mere industry and rule, often coming the whole length of Milan to give a single touch. He painted it, not in fresco, where all must be impromptu, but in oils, the new method which he had been one of the first to welcome, because it allowed of so many after-thoughts, such a refined working cut of perfection. It turned out that on a plastered wall no process could have been less durable. Within fifty years it had fallen into decay. Protestants, who always found themselves much edified by a certain biblical turn in it, have multiplied all sorts of bad copies and engravings of it. And now we have to turn back to Leonardo's own studies,—above all, to one drawing of the central head at the Brera, which in a union of tenderness and severity in the face-lines, reminds one of the monumental work of Mino da Fiesole—to trace it as it was.

It was another effort to set a thing out of the range of its conventional associations. Strange, after all the misrepresentations of the Middle Age, was the effort to see it, not as the pale host of the altar, but as one taking leave of his friends. Five years after, the young Raphael, at Florence, painted it with sweet and solemn effect in the refectory of Saint Onofrio; but still with all the mystical unreality of the school of Perugino. Vasari pretends that the central head was never finished. Well; finished or unfinished, or owing part of its effect to a mellowing decay, this central head does but consummate the sentiment of the whole company—ghosts through which you see the wall, faint as the shadows of the leaves upon the wall on autumn afternoons; this figure is but the faintest, most spectral of them all. It is the image of what the history it symbolizes has been more and more ever since, paler and paler as it recedes from us. Criticism came with its appeal from mystical unrealities to originals, and restored no life-like reality but these transparent shadows—spirits which have not flesh and bones.

The Last Supper was finished in 1497; in 1498 the French entered Milan, and whether or not the Gascon bowmen used it as a mark for their arrows,[1] the model of the Sforza certainly did not survive. Ludovico became a prisoner, and the remaining years of Leonardo's life are more or less years of wandering. From his brilliant life at court he

[1] M. Arsène Houssaye comes to save the credit of his countrymen.

had saved nothing, and he returned to Florence a poor man. Perhaps necessity kept his spirit excited: the next four years are one prolonged rapture or ecstasy of invention. He painted the pictures of the Louvre, his most authentic works, which came there straight from the cabinet of Francis I at Fontainebleau. One picture of his, the Saint Anne—not the Saint Anne of the Louvre, but a mere cartoon now in London—revived for a moment a sort of appreciation more common in an earlier time, when good pictures had still seemed miraculous; and for two days a crowd of people of all qualities passed in naïve excitement through the chamber where it hung, and gave him a taste of Cimabue's triumph. But his work was less with the saints than with the living women of Florence; for he moved still in the polished society that he loved, and in the salons of Florence, left perhaps a little subject to light thoughts by the death of Savonarola (the latest gossip is of an undraped Monna Lisa, found in some out-of-the-way corner of the late Orleans collection), he met Ginevra di Benci, and Lisa, the young third wife of Francesco del Giocondo. As we have seen him using incidents of the sacred legend, not for their own sake, or as mere subjects for pictorial realization, but as a symbolical language for fancies all his own, so now he found a vent for his thoughts in taking one of these languid women, and raising her as Leda or Pomona, Modesty or Vanity, to the seventh heaven of symbolical expression.

La Gioconda is, in the truest sense, Leonardo's masterpiece—the revealing instance of his mode of thought and work. In suggestiveness, only the Melancholia of Dürer is comparable to it;

and no crude symbolism disturbs the effect of its subdued and graceful mystery. We all know the face and hands of the figure, set in its marble chair, in that cirque of fantastic rocks, as in some faint light under sea. Perhaps of all ancient pictures time has chilled it least.[1] As often happens with works in which invention seems to reach its limit, there is an element in it given to, not invented by, the master. In that inestimable folio of drawings, once in the possession of Vasari, were certain designs by Verrocchio—faces of such impressive beauty that Leonardo in his boyhood copied them many times. It is hard not to connect with these designs of the elder by-past master, as with its germinal principle, the unfathomable smile, always with a touch of something sinister in it, which plays over all Leonardo's work. Besides the picture is a portrait. From childhood we see this image defining itself on the fabric of his dreams; and but for express historical testimony, we might fancy that this was but his ideal lady, embodied and beheld at last. What was the relationship of a living Florentine to this creature of his thought? By what strange affinities had she and the dream grown thus apart, yet so closely together? Present from the first incorporeal in Leonardo's thought, dimly traced in the designs of Verrocchio, she is found present at last in Il Giocondo's house. That there is much of mere portraiture in the picture is attested by the legend that by artificial means, the presence of mimes and flute-players, that subtle expression was protracted on the face. Again, was it in four years and by renewed labour

[1] Yet for Vasari there was some further magic of crimson in the lips and cheeks, lost for us.

never really completed, or in four months, as by stroke of magic, that the image was projected?

The presence that thus so strangely rose beside the waters is expressive of what in the ways of a thousand years man had come to desire. Hers is the head upon which all 'the ends of the world are come', and the eyelids are a little weary. It is a beauty wrought out from within upon the flesh—the deposit, little cell by cell, of strange thoughts and fantastic reveries and exquisite passions. Set it for a moment beside one of those white Greek goddesses or beautiful women of antiquity, and how would they be troubled by this beauty, into which the soul with all its maladies has passed? All the thoughts and experiences of the world have etched and moulded there in that which they have of power to refine and make expressive the outward form—the animalism of Greece, the lust of Rome, the reverie of the Middle Age with its spiritual ambition and imaginative loves, the return of the Pagan world, the sins of the Borgias. She is older than the rocks which she sits; like the vampire, she has been dead, many times, and learned the secrets of the grave; and has been a diver in deep seas, and keeps their fallen day about her; and trafficked for strange webs with Eastern merchants; and, as Leda, was the mother of Helen of Troy, and, as Saint Anne, the mother of Mary; and all this has been to her but as the sound of lyres and flutes, and lives only in the delicacy with which it has moulded the changing lineaments and tinged the eyelids and the hands. The fancy of a perpetual life, sweeping together ten thousand experiences, is an old one; and modern thought has conceived the idea of humanity as wrought upon by, and summing up in itself, all modes of thought and life. Certainly, Lady Lisa might stand as the embodiment of the old fancy, the symbol of the modern idea.

During these years at Florence Leonardo's history is the history of his art; he himself is lost in the bright cloud of it. The outward history begins again in 1502, with a wild journey through central Italy, which he makes as the chief engineer of Caesar Borgia. The biographer, putting together the stray jottings of his manuscripts, may follow him through every day of it, up the strange tower of Sienna, which looks towards Rome, elastic like a bent bow, down to the seashore at Piombino, each place appearing as fitfully as in a fever dream.

One other great work was left for him to do—a work all trace of which soon vanished—the Battle of the Standard, in which he had for his rival Michelangelo. The citizens of Florence, desiring to decorate the walls of the great council chambers, had offered the work for competition, and any subject might be chosen from the Florentine wars of the fifteenth century. Michelangelo chose for his cartoon an incident of the war with Pisa, in which the Florentine soldiers, bathing in the Arno, are surprised by the sound of trumpets, and run to arms. His design has reached us only in an old engraving, which perhaps would help us less than what we remember of the backgound of his Holy Family in the Uffizi to imagine in what superhuman form, such as might have beguiled the heart of an earlier world, those figures may have riser from the water. Leonardo chose an incident from the battle of Anghiari, in which two parties of soldiers fight for a standard. Like Michelangelo's, his cartoon is lost, and has come to us only in sketches and a fragment of Rubens. Through the accounts given we may discern some lust of terrible things in it, so that even the horses tore each other with their teeth; and yet one fragment of it, in a drawing of his at Florence, is far different—a waving field of lovely armour, the chased edgings running like lines of sunlight from side to side. Michelangelo was twenty-seven years old; Leonardo more than fifty; and Raphael, then nineteen years old, visiting Florence for the first time, came and watched them as they worked.

We catch a glimpse of him again at Rome in 1514, surrounded by his mirrors and vials and furnaces, making strange toys that seemed alive of wax and quicksilver. The hesitation which had haunted him all through life, and made him like one under a spell, was on him now with double force. No one had ever carried political indifferentism farther; it had always been his philosophy to 'fly before the storm'; he is out with the Sforzas and in with the Sforzas as the tide of fortune turns. Yet now he was suspected by the anti-Gallican, Medicean society at Rome, of French leanings. It paralysed him to find himself among enemies; and he turned wholly to France, which had long courted him.

France was going to be an Italy more Italian than Italy itself. Francis I, like Louis XII before him, was attracted by the finesse of Leonardo's work. La Gioconda was already in his cabinet, and he offered Leonardo the little Château de Clou, with its vineyards and meadows, in the soft valley of the Masse—not too far from the great outer sea.

M. Arsène Houssaye has succeeded in giving a pensive local colour to this part of his subject, with which, as a Frenchman, he could best deal. 'A Monsieur Lyonard, peinteur du Roy pour Amboyse,' so the letter of Francis I is headed. It opens a prospect—one of the most attractive in the history of art—where, under a strange mixture of lights Italian art dies away as a French exotic. M. Houssaye does but touch it lightly, and it would carry us beyond the present essay if we allowed ourselves to be seduced by its interest.

Two questions remain, after all busy antiquarianism, concerning Leonardo's death—the question of his religion, and the question whether Francis I was present at the time. They are of about equally little importance in the estimate of Leonardo's genius. The directions in his will about the thirty masses and the great candles for the church of St. Florentin are things of course—their real purpose being immediate and practical; and on no theory of religion could such hurried candle-burning be of much consequence. We forget them in speculating how one who had been always so desirous of beauty, but desired it always in such precise and definite forms, as hands or flowers or hair, looked forward now into the vague land, and experienced the last curiosity.

JOHN ADDINGTON SYMONDS

1840–1893

PERSONAL STYLE

A SURVEY of language, however superficial, makes it evident that when we speak of style, we have to take into account those qualities of national character which are embodied in national speech. If two men could be born of precisely the same physical, mental, and moral nature, at precisely the same moment of history, and under precisely the same social conditions ; and if these men learned different languages in the cradle, and used those languages in after life, they would be unable to deliver exactly the same message to the world through literature. The dominant qualities of each mother-tongue would impose definite limitations on their power of expressing thoughts, however similar or identical those thoughts might be.

We cannot conceive two men born with the same physical, mental, and moral nature, at the same moment, under precisely the same conditions, and using the same language. They would be identical; and everything they uttered would be clothed with exactly the same words. The absurdity of this conception brings home to us the second aspect of style. Style is not merely a sign of those national qualities which are generic to established languages, and which constitute the so-called genius of a race. It is also the sign of personal qualities, specific to individuals, which constitute the genius of a man. Whatever a man utters from his heart and head is the index of his character. The more remarkable a person is, the more strongly he is differentiated from the average of human beings, the more salient will be the characteristic notes of his expression. But even the commonest people have, each of them, a specific style. The marks of difference become microscopical as we descend from Dante or Shakespeare to the drudges of the clerk's desk in one of our great cities. Yet these marks exist, and are no less significant of individuality than the variations between leaf and leaf upon the lime-trees of an avenue.

It may be asked whether the manner of expression peculiar to any person is a complete index to his character—whether, in other words, there is 'an art to find the mind's construction' in the style. Not altogether and exhaustively. Not all the actions and the utterances of an individual betray the secret of his personality. You may live with men and women through years, by day, by night, yet you will never know the whole about them. No human being knows the whole about himself.

The deliberate attitude adopted by a literary writer implies circumspection; invites suppression, reservation, selection; is compatible with affectation, dissimulation, hypocrisy. So much cannot be claimed for critical analysis as that we should pretend to reproduce a man's soul after close examination of his work. What we may assert with confidence is that the qualities of style are intimately connected with the qualities and limitations of the writer, and teach us much about him.

He wrote thus and thus, because he was this or this. In the exercise of style it is impossible for any one to transcend his inborn and acquired faculties of ideation, imagination, sense-perception, verbal expression—just as it is impossible in the exercise of strength for an athlete to transcend the limits of his physical structure, powers of innervation, dexterity, and courage.[1] The work of art produced by a writer is therefore of necessity complexioned and determined by the inborn and acquired faculties of the individual. This is what we mean by the hackneyed epigram: 'Le style c'est l'homme.'

II

Certain broad distinctions of moral and emotional temperament may undoubtedly be detected in literary style. A tendency toward exaggeration, toward self-revelation, toward emphasis upon the one side; a tendency to reserve, to diminished tone in colouring, to parsimony of rhetorical resource upon the other; these indicate expansiveness or reticence in the writer. Victor Hugo differs by the breadth of the whole heavens from Leopardi. One man is ironical by nature, another sentimental. Sterne and Heine have a common gift of humour; but the quality of humour in each case is conditioned by sympathetic or by caustic undercurrents of emotion. Sincerity and affectation, gaiety and melancholy, piety and scepticism, austerity and sensuality penetrate style so subtly and unmistakably that a candid person cannot pose as the mere slave of convention, a boon companion

[1] See Émile Hennequin, *La Critique Scientifique*, pp. 64–7, for a full and luminous exposition of these points.

cannot pass muster for an anchorite, the founder of a religious sect cannot play the part of an agnostic. In dramatic work the artist creates characters alien from his own personality, and exhibits people widely different from himself acting and talking as they ought to do. This he achieves by sympathy and intuition. Yet all except the very greatest fail to render adequately what they have not felt and been. In playwrights of the second order, like our Fletcher, or of the third order, like our Byron, the individual who writes the tragedy and shapes the characters is always apparent under every mask he chooses to assume. And even the style of the greatest, their manner of presenting the varieties of human nature, betrays individual peculiarities. Aeschylus sees men and women differently from Sophocles, Corneille from Racine, Shakespeare from Goethe.

In like manner the broad distinctions of mental temperament may be traced in style. The abstract thinker differs from the concrete thinker in his choice of terms; the analytical from the synthetic; the ratiocinative from the intuitive; the logical from the imaginative; the scientific from the poetical. One man thinks in images, another in formal propositions. One is diffuse, and gets his thought out by reiterated statement. Another makes epigrams, and finds some difficulty in expanding their sense or throwing light upon them by illustrations. One arrives at conclusions by the way of argument. Another clothes assertion with the tropes and metaphors of rhetoric.

The same is true of physical and aesthetical qualities. They are felt inevitably in style. The sedentary student does not use the same figures of speech as come naturally to the muscular and active lover of field sports. According as the sense for colour, or for sound, or for light, or for form shall preponderate in a writer's constitution, his language will abound in references to the world, viewed under conditions of colour, sound, light, or form. He will insensibly dwell upon those aspects of things which stimulate his sensibility and haunt his memory. Thus, too, predilections for sea or mountains, for city-life or rural occupations, for flowers, precious stones, scents, birds, animals, insects, different kinds of food, torrid or temperate climates, leave their mark on literary style.

Acquired faculties and habits find their expression in style no less than inborn qualities. Education, based upon humanism or scientific studies; contact with powerful personalities at an impressible period of youth; enthusiasm aroused for this or that great masterpiece of literature; social environment; high or low birth; professional training for the bar, the church, medicine, or commerce; life in the army, at sea, upon a farm, and so forth, tinge the mind and give a more or less perceptible colour to language.

The use of words itself yields, upon analysis, valuable results illustrative of the various temperaments of authors. A man's vocabulary marks him out as of this sort or that sort—his preference for certain syntactical forms, for short sentences or for periods, for direct or inverted propositions, for plain or figurative statement, for brief or amplified illustrations. Some compose sentences, but do not build paragraphs—like Emerson; some write chapters, but cannot construct a book. Nor is punctuation to be disregarded, inasmuch as stops enable us to measure a writer's sense of time-values, and the importance he attaches to several degrees of rest and pause.

III

It is impossible to do more than indicate some of the leading points which illustrate the meaning of the saying that style is the man ; any one can test them and apply them for himself. We not only feel that Walter Scott *did not* write like Thackeray, but we also know that he *could not* write like Thackeray, and vice versa. This impossibility of one man producing work in exactly the same manner as another makes all deliberate attempts at imitation assume the form of parody or caricature. The sacrifice of individuality involved in scrupulous addiction to one great master of Latin prose, Cicero, condemned the best stylists of the Renaissance—men like Muretus—to lifeless and eventually worthless production. Meanwhile the exact psychology is wanting which would render our intuitions regarding the indissoluble link between style and personal character irrefutable.[1]

Literary style is more a matter of sentiment, emotion, involuntary habits of feeling and observing, constitutional sympathy with the world and men, tendencies of curiosity and liking, than of the pure intellect. The style of scientific works,

[1] While I was engaged in writing this essay, a young French author, now, alas! dead, sent me a book which may be considered as an important contribution to the psychology of style. It is entitled, *La Critique Scientifique*, par Émile Hennequin. Paris: Perrin et Ce, 1888.

affording little scope for the exercise of these psychological elements, throws less light upon their authors' temperament than does the style of poems, novels, essays, books of travel, descriptive criticism. In the former case all that need be aimed at is lucid exposition of fact and vigorous reasoning. In the latter the fact to be stated, the truth to be arrived at, being of a more complex nature, involves a process akin to that of the figurative arts. The stylist has here to produce the desired effect by suggestions of infinite subtlety, and to present impressions made upon his sensibility.

Autobiographies, epistolary correspondence, notes of table-talk, are of the highest value in determining the correlation between a writer's self and his style. We not only derive a mass of information about Goethe's life from Eckermann, but we also discover from those conversations in how true a sense the style of Goethe's works grew out of his temperament and experience. Gibbon and Rousseau, Alfieri and Goldoni, Samuel Johnson in his *Life* by Boswell, John Stuart Mill in his autobiographical essay, Petrarch in his *Secretum* and fragment of personal confessions, have placed similar keys within our reach for unlocking the secret of their several manners.

The rare cases in which men of genius have excelled in more than one branch of art are no less instructive. Michelangelo the sonnet-writer helps us to understand Michelangelo the sculptor. Rossetti the painter throws light on Rossetti the poet; William Blake the lyrist upon William Blake the draughtsman. We find, on comparing the double series of work offered by such eminent and exceptionally gifted individuals, that their styles in literature and plastic art possess common qualities, which mark the men and issue from their personalities. Michelangelo in the sonnets is as abstract, as ideal, as form-loving, as indifferent to the charm of brilliant colour, as neglectful of external nature as Michelangelo in his statues and the frescoes of the Sistine Chapel. Rossetti's pictures, with their wealth of colour, their elaborate execution, their sharp incisive vision, their deep imaginative mysticism and powerful perfume of intellectual sensuousness, present a close analogue to his ballads, sonnets, and descriptive poems. With these and similar instances in our mind, we are prepared to hear that Victor Hugo designed pictures in the style of Gustave Doré ; nor would it surprise us to discover that Gustave Doré had left odes or fiction in the manner of Victor Hugo.

The problems suggested by style as a sign and index of personality may be approached from many points of view. I have not aimed at exhaustiveness even of suggestion in my treatment of the topic ; and while saying much which will appear perhaps trivial and obvious, have omitted some of the subtler and more interesting aspects of the matter. A systematic criticism of personal style would require a volume, and would demand physiological and psychological knowledge which is rarely found in combination with an extensive study of literatures and arts.

RICHARD JEFFERIES

1848–1887

THE JULY GRASS

A July fly went sideways over the long grass. His wings made a burr about him like a net, beating so fast they wrapped him round with a cloud. Every now and then, as he flew over the trees of grass, a taller one than common stopped him, and there he clung, and then the eye had time to see the scarlet spots—the loveliest colour—on his wings. The wind swung the bennet and loosened his hold, and away he went again over the grasses, and not one jot did he care if they were *Poa* or *Festuca*, or *Bromus* or *Hordeum*, or any other name. Names were nothing to him; all he had to do was to whirl his scarlet spots about in the brilliant sun, rest when he liked, and go on again. I wonder whether it is a joy to have bright scarlet spots, and to be clad in the purple and gold of life; is the colour felt by the creature that wears it? The rose, restful of a dewy morn before the sunbeams have topped the garden wall, must feel a joy in its own fragrance, and know the exquisite hue of its stained petals. The rose sleeps in its beauty.

The fly whirls his scarlet-spotted wings about and splashes himself with sunlight, like the children on the sands. He thinks not of the grass and sun; he does not heed them at all—and that is why he is so happy—any more than the barefoot children ask why the sea is there, or why it does not quite dry up when it ebbs. He is unconscious; he lives without thinking about living; and if the sunshine were a hundred hours long, still it would not be long enough. No, never enough of sun and sliding shadows that come like a hand over the table to lovingly reach our shoulder, never enough of the grass that smells sweet as a flower, not if we could live years and years equal in number to the tides that have ebbed and flowed counting backwards four years to every day and night, backward still till we found out which came first, the night or the day. The scarlet-dotted fly knows nothing of the names of the grasses that grow here where the sward nears the sea, and thinking of him I have decided not to wilfully seek to learn any more of their names either. My big grass book I have left at home, and the dust is settling on the gold of the binding. I have picked a handful this morning of which I know nothing. I will sit here on the turf and the scarlet-dotted flies shall pass over me, as if I too were but a grass. I will not think, I will be unconscious, I will live.

Listen! that was the low sound of a summer wavelet striking the uncovered rock over there beneath in the green sea. All things that are beautiful are found by chance, like everything that is good. Here by me is a praying-rug, just wide enough to kneel on, of the richest gold inwoven with crimson. All the Sultans of the East never had such beauty as that to kneel on. It is, indeed, too beautiful to kneel on, for the life in these golden flowers must not be broken down even for that purpose. They must not be defaced, not a stem bent; it is more reverent not to kneel on them, for this carpet prays itself. I will sit by it and let it pray for me. It is so common, the bird's-foot lotus, it grows everywhere; yet if I purposely searched for days I should not have found a plot like this, so rich, so golden, so glowing with sunshine. You might pass it by in one stride, yet it is worthy to be thought of for a week and remembered for a year. Slender grasses, branched round about with slenderer boughs, each tipped with pollen and rising in tiers cone-shaped—too delicate to grow tall—cluster at the base of the mound. They dare not grow tall or the wind would snap them. A great grass, stout and thick, rises three feet by the hedge, with a head another foot nearly, very green and strong and bold, lifting itself right up to you; you must say, 'What a fine grass!' Grasses whose awns succeed each other alternately; grasses whose tops seem flattened; others drooping over the shorter blades beneath; some that you can only find by parting the heavier growth around them; hundreds and hundreds, thousands and thousands. The kingly poppies on the dry summit of the mound take no heed of these, the populace, their subjects so numerous they cannot be numbered. A barren race they are, the proud poppies, lords of the July field, taking no deep root, but raising up a brilliant blazon of scarlet heraldry out of nothing. They are useless, they are bitter, they are allied to sleep and poison and everlasting night; yet they are forgiven because they are not commonplace. Nothing, no abundance of them, can ever make the poppies commonplace. There is genius in them, the genius of colour, and they are saved. Even when they take the room of the corn we must admire them. The mighty multitude of nations, the millions and millions of the grass stretching away in intertangled ranks, through pasture and mead from shore to shore, have no kinship with these their lords. The ruler is always a foreigner. From England to China the native born is no king; the poppies are the Normans of the field. One of these on the mound is very beautiful, a width of petal, a clear silkiness of colour three shades higher than the rest—it is almost dark with scarlet. I wish I could do something more than gaze at all this scarlet and gold and crimson and green, something more than see it, not exactly to drink it or inhale it, but in some way to make it part of me that I might live it.

The July grasses must be looked for in corners and out-of-the-way places, and not in the broad acres—the scythe has taken them there. By the wayside on the banks of the lane, near the gateway—look, too, in uninteresting places behind incomplete buildings on the mounds cast up from abandoned foundations where speculation has been and gone. There weeds that would not have found resting-place elsewhere grow unchecked, and uncommon species and unusually large growths appear. Like everything else that is looked for, they are found under unlikely conditions. At the back of ponds, just inside the enclosure of woods, angles of cornfields, old quarries, that is where to find grasses, or by the sea in the brackish marsh. Some of the finest of them grow by the mere roadside; you may look for others up the lanes in the deep ruts, look too inside the hollow trees by the stream. In a morning you may easily garner together a great sheaf of this harvest. Cut the larger stems aslant, like the reeds imitated deep in old green glass. You must consider as you gather them the height and slenderness of the stems, the droop and degree of curve, the shape and colour of the panicle, the dusting of the pollen, the motion and sway in the wind. The sheaf you may take home with you, but the wind that was among it stays without.

ROBERT LOUIS STEVENSON

1850–1894

A PLEA FOR GAS LAMPS

CITIES given, the problem was to light them. How to conduct individual citizens about the burgess-warren, when once heaven had withdrawn its leading luminary? or—since we live in a scientific age—when once our spinning planet has turned its back upon the sun? The moon, from time to time, was doubtless very helpful; the stars had a cheery look among the chimney-pots; and a cresset here and there, on church or citadel, produced a fine pictorial effect, and, in places where the ground lay unevenly, held out the right hand of conduct to the benighted. But sun, moon, and stars abstracted or concealed, the night-faring inhabitant had to fall back—we speak on the authority of old prints—upon stable lanthorns, two stories in height. Many holes, drilled in the conical turret-roof of this vagabond Pharos, let up spouts of dazzlement into the bearer's eyes; and as he paced forth in the ghostly darkness, carrying his own sun by a ring about his finger, day and night swung to and fro and up and down about his footsteps. Blackness haunted his path; he was beleaguered by goblins as he went; and, curfew being struck, he found no light but that he travelled in throughout the township.

Closely following on this epoch of migratory lanthorns in a world of extinction, came the era of oil-lights, hard to kindle, easy to extinguish, pale and wavering in the hour of their endurance. Rudely puffed the winds of heaven; roguishly clomb up the all-destructive urchin; and, lo! in a moment night re-established her void empire, and the cit groped along the wall, suppered but bedless, occult from guidance, and sorrily wading in the kennels. As if gamesome winds and gamesome youths were not sufficient, it was the habit to sling these feeble luminaries from house to house above the fairway. There, on invisible cordage, let them swing! And suppose some crane-necked general to go speeding by on a tall-charger, spurring the destiny of nations, red-hot in expedition, there would indubitably be some effusion of military blood, and oaths, and a certain crash of glass; and while the chieftain rode forward with a purple coxcomb, the street would be left to original darkness, unpiloted, unvoyageable, a province of the desert night.

The conservative, looking before and after, draws from each contemplation the matter for content. Out of the age of gas lamps he glances back slightingly at the mirk and glimmer in which his ancestors wandered; his heart waxes jocund at the contrast; nor do his lips refrain from a stave, in the highest style of poetry, lauding progress and the golden mean. When gas first spread along a city, mapping it forth about evenfall for the eye of observant birds, a new age had begun for sociality and corporate pleasure-seeking, and begun with proper circumstance, becoming its own birthright. The work of Prometheus had advanced by another stride. Mankind and its supper parties were no longer at the mercy of a few miles of sea-fog; sundown no longer emptied the promenade; and the day was lengthened out to every man's fancy. The city-folk had stars of their own; biddable, domesticated stars.

It is true that these were not so steady, nor yet so clear, as their originals; nor indeed was their lustre so elegant as that of the best wax candles. But then the gas stars, being nearer at hand, were more practically efficacious than Jupiter himself. It is true, again, that they did not unfold their rays with the appropriate spontaneity of the planets, coming out along the firmament one after another, as the need arises. But the lamplighters took to their heels every evening, and ran with a good heart. It was pretty to see man thus emulating the punctuality of heaven's orbs; and though perfection was not absolutely reached, and now and then an individual may have been knocked on the head by the ladder of the flying functionary, yet people commended his zeal in a proverb, and taught their children to say, 'God bless the lamplighter!' And since his passage was a piece of the day's programme, the children were well pleased to repeat the benediction, not, of course, in so many words, which would have been improper, but in some chaste circumlocution, suitable for infant lips.

God bless him, indeed! For the term of his twilight diligence is near at hand; and for not much longer shall we watch him speeding up the street and, at measured intervals, knocking another luminous hole into the dusk. The Greeks would have made a noble myth of such an one; how he distributed starlight, and, as soon as the need was over, re-collected it; and the little bull's-eye, which was his instrument, and held enough fire to kindle a whole parish, would have been fitly commemorated in the legend. Now, like all heroic tasks, his labours draw towards apotheosis, and in the light of victory himself shall disappear. For another advance has been effected. Our tame stars are to come out in future, not one by one, but all in a body and at once. A sedate electrician somewhere in a back office touches a spring—and behold! from one end to another of the city, from east to west, from the Alexandra to the Crystal Palace, there is light! *Fiat Lux*, says the sedate electrician. What a spectacle, on some clear, dark nightfall, from the edge of Hampstead Hill, when in a moment, in the twinkling of an eye, the design of the monstrous city flashes into vision—a glittering hieroglyph many square miles in extent; and when, to borrow and debase an image, all the evening street-lamps burst together into song! Such is the spectacle of the future, preluded the other day by the experiment in Pall Mall. Star-rise by electricity, the most romantic flight of civilization; the compensatory benefit for an innumerable array of factories and bankers' clerks. To the artistic spirit exercised about Thirlmere, here is a crumb of consolation; consolatory, at least, to such of them as look out upon the world through seeing eyes, and contentedly accept beauty where it comes.

But the conservative, while lauding progress, is ever timid of innovation; his is the hand upheld to counsel pause; his is the signal advising slow advance. The word *electricity* now sounds the note of danger. In Paris, at the mouth of the Passage des Princes, in the place before the Opera portico, and in the Rue Drouot at the *Figaro* office, a new sort of urban star now shines out nightly, horrible, unearthly, obnoxious to the human eye ; a lamp for a nightmare ! Such a light as this should shine only on murders and public crime, or along the corridors of lunatic asylums, a horror to heighten horror. To look at it only once is to fall in love with gas, which gives a warm domestic radiance fit to eat by. Mankind, you would have thought, might have remained content with what Prometheus stole for them and not gone fishing the profound heaven with kites to catch and domesticate the wildfire of the storm. Yet here we have the levin brand at our doors, and it is proposed that we should henceforward take our walks abroad in the glare of permanent lightning. A man need not be very superstitious if he scruple to follow his pleasures by the light of the Terror that Flieth, nor very epicurean if he prefer to see the face of beauty more becomingly displayed. That ugly blinding glare may not improperly advertise the home of slanderous *Figaro*, which is a back-shop to the infernal regions ; but where soft joys prevail, where people are convoked to pleasure and the philosopher looks on smiling and silent, where love and laughter and deifying wine abound, there, at least, let the old mild lustre shine upon the ways of man.

THE ENGLISH ADMIRALS

'Whether it be wise in men to do such actions or no, I am sure it is so in States to honour them.'—Sir William Temple.

There is one story of the wars of Rome which I have always very much envied for England. Germanicus was going down at the head of the legions into a dangerous river—on the opposite bank the woods were full of Germans—when there flew out seven great eagles which seemed to marshal the Romans on their way; they did not pause or waver, but disappeared into the forest where the enemy lay concealed. 'Forward!' cried Germanicus, with a fine rhetorical inspiration, 'Forward! and follow the Roman birds.' It would be a very heavy spirit that did not give a leap at such a signal, and a very timorous one that continued to have any doubt of success. To appropriate the eagles as fellow countrymen was to make imaginary allies of the forces of nature; the Roman Empire and its military fortunes, and along with these the prospects of those individual Roman legionaries now fording a river in Germany, looked altogether greater and more hopeful. It is a kind of illusion easy to produce. A particular shape of cloud, the appearance of a particular star, the holiday of some particular saint, anything in short to remind the combatants of patriotic legends or old successes, may be enough to change the issue of a pitched battle; for it gives to the one party a feeling that Right and the larger interests are with them.

If an Englishman wishes to have such a feeling, it must be about the sea. The lion is nothing to us; he has not been taken to the hearts of the people, and naturalized as an English emblem. We know right well that a lion would fall foul of us as grimly as he would of a Frenchman or a Moldavian Jew, and we do not carry him before us in the smoke of battle. But the sea is our approach and bulwark; it has been the scene of our greatest triumphs and dangers; and we are accustomed in lyrical strains to claim it as our own. The prostrating experiences of foreigners between Calais and Dover have always an agreeable side to English prepossessions. A man from Bedfordshire, who does not know one end of the ship from the other until she begins to move, swaggers among such persons with a sense of hereditary nautical experience. To suppose yourself endowed with natural parts for the sea because you are the countryman of Blake and mighty Nelson, is perhaps just as unwarrantable as to imagine Scotch extraction a sufficient guarantee that you will look well in a kilt. But the feeling is there, and seated beyond the reach of argument. We should consider ourselves unworthy of our descent if we did not share the arrogance of our progenitors, and please ourselves with the pretension that the sea is English. Even where it is looked upon by the guns and battlements of another nation we regard it as a kind of English cemetery, where the bones of our seafaring fathers take their rest until the last trumpet; for I suppose no other nation has lost as many ships, or sent as many brave fellows to the bottom.

There is nowhere such a background for heroism as the noble, terrifying, and picturesque conditions of some of our sea fights. Hawke's battle in the tempest, and Aboukir at the moment when the French Admiral blew up, reach the limit of what is imposing to the imagination. And our naval annals owe some of their interest to the fantastic and beautiful appearance of old warships and the romance that invests the sea and everything seagoing in the eyes of English lads on a half-holiday at the coast. Nay, and what we know of the misery between decks enhances the bravery of what was done by giving it something for contrast. We like to know that these bold and honest fellows contrived to live, and to keep bold and honest, among absurd and vile surroundings. No reader can forget the description of the *Thunder* in *Roderick Random*: the disorderly tyranny; the cruelty and dirt of officers and men; deck after deck, each with some new object of offence; the hospital, where the hammocks were huddled together with but fourteen inches space for each; the cockpit, far under water, where, 'in an intolerable stench,' the spectacled steward kept the accounts of the different messes; and the canvas enclosure, six feet square, in which Morgan made flip and salmagundi, smoked his pipe, sang his Welsh songs, and swore his queer Welsh imprecations. There are portions of this business on board the *Thunder* over which the reader passes lightly and hurriedly, like a traveller in a malarious country. It is easy enough to understand the opinion of Dr. Johnson: 'Why, sir,' he said, 'no man will be a sailor who has contrivance enough to get himself into a jail.' You would fancy any one's spirit would die out under such an accumulation of darkness, noisomeness, and injustice, above all when he had not come there of his own free will, but under the cutlasses and bludgeons of the press-gang. But perhaps a watch on deck in the sharp sea air put a man on his mettle again; a battle must have been a capital relief; and prize-money, bloodily earned and grossly squandered, opened the doors of the prison for a twinkling. Somehow or other, at least, this worst of possible lives could not overlie the spirit and gaiety of our sailors; they did their duty as though they had some interest in the fortune of that country which so cruelly oppressed them, they served their guns merrily when it came to fighting, and they had the readiest ear for a bold, honourable sentiment, of any class of men the world ever produced.

Most men of high destinies have high-sounding names. Pym and Habakkuk may do pretty well, but they must not think to cope with the Cromwells and Isaiahs. And you could not find a better case in point than that of the English Admirals. Drake and Rooke and Hawke are picked names for men of execution. Frobisher, Rodney, Boscawen, Foul-Weather, Jack Byron, are all good to catch the eye in a page of a naval history. Cloudesley Shovel is a mouthful of quaint and sounding syllables. Benbow has a bull-dog quality that suits the man's character, and it takes us back to those English archers who were his true comrades for plainness, tenacity, and pluck. Raleigh is spirited and martial, and signifies an act of bold conduct in the field. It is impossible to judge of Blake or Nelson, no names current among men being worthy of such heroes. But still it is odd enough, and very appropriate in this connexion, that the latter was greatly taken with his Sicilian title. 'The signification, perhaps, pleased him,' says Southey; 'Duke of Thunder was what in Dahomey would have been called a *strong name*; it was to a sailor's taste, and certainly to no man could it be more applicable.' Admiral in itself is one of the most satisfactory of distinctions; it has a noble sound and a very proud history; and Columbus thought so highly of it, that he enjoined his heirs to sign themselves by that title as long as the house should last.

But it is the spirit of the men, and not their names, that I wish to speak about in this paper. That spirit is truly English; they, and not Tennyson's cotton-spinners or Mr. D'Arcy Thompson's Abstract Bagman, are the true and typical Englishmen. There may be more *head* of bagmen in the country, but human beings are reckoned by number only in political constitutions. And the Admirals are typical in the full force of the word. They are splendid examples of virtue, indeed, but of a virtue in which most Englishmen can claim a moderate share; and what we admire in their lives is a sort of apotheosis of ourselves. Almost everybody in our land, except humanitarians and a few persons whose youth has been depressed by exceptionally aesthetic surroundings, can understand and sympathize with an Admiral or a prize-fighter. I do not wish to bracket Benbow and Tom Cribb; but, depend upon it, they are practically bracketed for admiration in the minds of many frequenters of ale-houses. If you told them about Germanicus and the eagles, or Regulus going back to Carthage, they would very likely fall asleep; but tell them about Harry Pearce and Jem Belcher, or about Nelson and the Nile, and they put down their pipes to listen. I have by me a copy of *Boxiana*, on the fly-leaves of which a youthful member of the fancy kept a chronicle of remarkable events and an obituary of great men. Here we find piously chronicled the demise of jockeys, watermen, and pugilists—Johnny Moore, of the Liverpool Prize Ring; Tom Spring, aged fifty-six; 'Pierce Egan, senior, writer of *Boxiana* and other sporting works'—and among all these, the Duke of Wellington! If Benbow had lived in the time of this annalist, do you suppose his name would not have been added to the glorious roll? In short, we do not all feel warmly towards Wesley or Laud, we cannot all take pleasure in *Paradise Lost*; but there are certain common sentiments and touches of nature by which the whole nation is made to feel kinship. A little while ago everybody, from Hazlitt and John Wilson down to the imbecile creature who scribbled his register on the fly-leaves of *Boxiana*, felt a more or less shamefaced satisfaction in the exploits of prize-fighters. And the exploits of the Admirals are popular to the same degree, and tell in all ranks of society. Their sayings and doings stir English blood like the sound of a trumpet; and if the Indian Empire, the trade of London, and all the outward and visible ensigns of our greatness should pass away, we should still leave behind us a durable monument of what we were in these sayings and doings of the English Admirals.

Duncan, lying off the Texel with his own flagship, the *Venerable*, and only one other vessel, heard that the whole Dutch fleet was putting to sea. He told Captain Hotham to anchor alongside of him in the narrowest part of the channel, and fight his vessel till she sank. 'I have taken the depth of the water,' added he, 'and when the *Venerable* goes down, my flag will still fly.' And you observe this is no naked Viking in a prehistoric period; but a Scotch member of Parliament, with a smattering of the classics, a telescope, a cocked hat of great size, and flannel underclothing. In the same spirit, Nelson went into Aboukir with six colours flying; so that even if five were shot away, it should not be imagined he had struck. He too must needs wear his four stars outside his Admiral's frock, to be a butt for sharpshooters. 'In honour I gained them,' he said to objectors, adding with sublime illogicality, 'in honour I will die with them.' Captain Douglas of the *Royal Oak*, when the Dutch fired his vessel in the Thames, sent his men ashore, but was burned along with her himself rather than desert his post without orders. Just then, perhaps the Merry Monarch was chasing a moth round the supper-table with the ladies of his court. When Raleigh sailed into Cadiz, and all the forts and ships opened fire on him at once, he scorned to shoot a gun, and made answer with a flourish of insulting trumpets. I like this bravado better than the wisest dispositions to ensure victory; it comes from the heart and goes to it. God has made nobler heroes, but He never made a finer gentleman than Walter Raleigh. And as our Admirals were full of heroic superstitions, and had a strutting and vainglorious style of fight, so they discovered a startling eagerness for battle, and courted war like a mistress. When the news came to Essex before Cadiz that the attack had been decided, he threw his hat into the sea. It is in this way that a schoolboy hears of a half-holiday; but this was a bearded man of great possessions who had just been allowed to risk his life. Benbow could not lie still in his bunk after he had lost his leg; he must be on deck in a basket to direct and animate the fight. I said they loved war like a mistress; yet I think there are not many mistresses we should continue to woo under similar circumstances. Trowbridge went ashore with the *Culloden*, and was able to take no part in the battle of the Nile. 'The merits of that ship and her gallant captain,' wrote Nelson to the Admiralty, 'are too well known to benefit by anything I could say. Her misfortune was great in getting aground, *while her more fortunate companions were in the full tide of happiness.*' This is a notable expression, and depicts the whole great-hearted, big-spoken stock of the English Admirals to a hair. It was to be 'in the full tide of happiness' for Nelson to destroy five thousand five hundred and twenty-five of his fellow creatures, and have his own scalp torn open by a piece of langridge shot. Hear him again at Copenhagen: 'A shot through the mainmast knocked the splinters about; and he observed to one of his officers with a smile, "It is warm work, and this may be the last to any of us at any moment"; and then, stopping short at the gangway, added, with emotion, "*But, mark you—I would not be elsewhere for thousands.*"'

I must tell one more story, which has lately been made familiar to us all, and that in one of the noblest ballads in the English language. I had written my tame prose abstract, I shall beg the reader to believe, when I had no notion that the sacred bard designed an immortality for Greenville. Sir Richard Greenville was Vice-Admiral to Lord Thomas Howard, and lay off the Azores with the English squadron in 1591. He was a noted tyrant to his crew: a dark, bullying fellow apparently; and it is related of him that he would chew and swallow wine-glasses, by way of convivial levity, till the blood ran out of his mouth. When the Spanish fleet of fifty sail came within sight of the English, his ship, the *Revenge*, was the last to weigh anchor, and was so far circumvented by the Spaniards, that there were but two courses open—either to turn her back upon the enemy or sail through one of his squadrons. The first alternative Greenville dismissed as dishonourable to himself, his country, and her Majesty's ship. Accordingly, he chose the latter, and steered into the Spanish armament. Several vessels he forced to luff and fall under his lee; until, about three o'clock of the afternoon, a great ship of three decks of ordnance took the wind out of his sails, and immediately boarded. Thenceforward, and all night long, the *Revenge* held her own single-handed against the Spaniards. As one ship was beaten off, another took its place. She endured, according to Raleigh's computation, 'eight hundred shot of great artillery, besides many assaults and entries.' By morning the powder was spent, the pikes all broken, not a stick was standing, 'nothing left overhead either for flight or defence'; six feet of water in the hold; almost all the men hurt; and Greenville himself in a dying condition. To bring them to this pass, a fleet of fifty sail had been mauling them for fifteen hours, the *Admiral of the Hulks* and the *Ascension* of Seville had both gone down alongside, and two other vessels had taken refuge on shore in a sinking state. In Hawke's words, they had 'taken a great deal of drubbing'. The captain and crew thought they had done about enough; but Greenville was not of this opinion; he gave orders to the master gunner, whom he knew to be a fellow after his own stamp, to scuttle the *Revenge* where she lay. The others, who were not mortally wounded like the Admiral, interfered with some decision, locked the master gunner in his cabin, after having deprived him of his sword, for he manifested an intention to kill himself if he were not to sink the ship; and sent to the Spaniards to demand terms. These were granted. The second or third day after, Greenville died of his wounds aboard the Spanish flagship, leaving his contempt upon the 'traitors and dogs' who had not chosen to do as he did, and engage fifty vessels, well found and fully manned, with six inferior craft ravaged by sickness and short of stores. He at least, he said, had done his duty as he was bound to do, and looked for everlasting fame.

Some one said to me the other day that they considered this story to be of a pestilent example. I am not inclined to imagine we shall ever be put into any practical difficulty from a superfluity of Greenvilles. And besides, I demur to the opinion. The worth of such actions is not a thing to be decided in a quaver of sensibility or a flush of righteous common sense. The man who wished to make the ballads of his country, coveted a small matter compared to what Richard Greenville accomplished. I wonder how many people have been inspired by this mad story, and how many battles have been actually won for England in the spirit thus engendered. It is only with a measure of habitual foolhardiness that you can be sure, in the common run of men, of courage on a reasonable occasion. An army or a fleet, if it is not led by quixotic fancies, will not be led far by terror of the Provost-Marshal. Even German warfare, in addition to maps and telegraphs, is not above employing the *Wacht am Rhein.* Nor is it only in the profession of arms that such stories may do good to a man. In this desperate and gleeful fighting, whether it is Greenville or Benbow,

Hawke or Nelson, who flies his colours in the ship, we see men brought to the test and giving proof of what we call heroic feeling. Prosperous humanitarians tell me, in my club smoking-room, that they are a prey to prodigious heroic feelings, and that it costs them more nobility of soul to do nothing in particular, than would carry on all the wars, by sea or land, of bellicose humanity. It may very well be so, and yet not touch the point in question. For what I desire is to see some of this nobility brought face to face with me in an inspiriting achievement. A man may talk smoothly over a cigar in my club smoking-room from now to the Day of Judgement, without adding anything to mankind's treasury of illustrious and encouraging examples. It is not over the virtues of a curate-and-tea-party novel, that people are abashed into high resolutions. It may be because their hearts are crass, but to stir them properly they must have men entering into glory with some pomp and circumstance. And that is why these stories of our sea-captains, printed, so to speak, in capitals, and full of bracing moral influence, are more valuable to England than any material benefit in all the books of political economy between Westminster and Birmingham. Greenville chewing wine-glasses at table makes no very pleasant figure, any more than a thousand other artists when they are viewed in the body, or met in private life; but his work of art, his finished tragedy, is an eloquent performance; and I contend it ought not only to enliven men of the sword as they go into battle, but send back merchant clerks with more heart and spirit to their book-keeping by double entry.

There is another question which seems bound up in this; and that is Temple's problem: whether it was wise of Douglas to burn with the *Royal Oak*? and by implication, what it was that made him do so? Many will tell you it was the desire of fame.

'To what do Caesar and Alexander owe the infinite grandeur of their renown, but to fortune? How many men has she extinguished in the beginning of their progress, of whom we have no knowledge; who brought as much courage to the work as they, if their adverse hap had not cut them off in the first sally of their arms? Amongst so many and so great dangers, I do not remember to have anywhere read that Caesar was ever wounded; a thousand have fallen in less dangers than the least of these he went through. A great many brave actions must be expected to be performed without witness, for one that comes to some notice. A man is not always at the top of a breach, or at the head of an army in the sight of his general, as upon a platform. He is often surprised between the hedge and the ditch; he must run the hazard of his life against a hen roost; he must dislodge four rascally musketeers out of a barn; he must prick out single from his party, as necessity arises, and meet adventures alone.'

Thus far Montaigne, in a characteristic essay on *Glory*. Where death is certain, as in the cases of Douglas or Greenville, it seems all one from a personal point of view. The man who lost his life against a hen roost is in the same pickle with him who lost his life against a fortified place of the first order. Whether he has missed a peerage or only the corporal's stripes, it is all one if he has missed them and is quietly in the grave. It was by a hazard that we learned the conduct of the four marines of the *Wager*. There was no room for these brave fellows in the boat, and they were left behind upon the island to a certain death. They were soldiers, they said, and knew well enough it was their business to die; and as their comrades pulled away they stood upon the beach, gave three cheers, and cried 'God bless the king!' Now, one or two of those who were in the boat escaped, against all likelihood, to tell the story. That was a great thing for us; but surely it cannot, by any possible twisting of human speech, be construed into anything great for the marines. You may suppose, if you like, that they died hoping their behaviour would not be forgotten; or you may suppose they thought nothing on the subject, which is much more likely. What can be the signification of the word 'fame' to a private of marines, who cannot read and knows nothing of past history beyond the reminiscences of his grandmother? But whichever supposition you make, the fact is unchanged. They died while the question still hung in the balance; and I suppose their bones were already white, before the winds and the waves and the humour of Indian chiefs and Spanish governors had decided whether they were to be unknown and useless martyrs or honoured heroes. Indeed, I believe this is the lesson: if it is for fame that men do brave actions, they are only silly fellows after all.

It is at best but a pettifogging, pickthank business to decompose actions into little personal motives, and explain heroism away. The Abstract Bagman will grow like an Admiral at heart, not by ungrateful carping, but in a heat of admiration. But there is another theory of the personal motive in these fine sayings and doings, which I believe to be true and wholesome. People usually do things, and suffer martyrdoms, because they have an inclination that way. The best artist is not the man who fixes his eye on posterity, but the one who loves the practice of his art. And instead of having a taste for being successful merchants and retiring at thirty, some people have a taste for high and what we call heroic forms of excitement. If the Admirals courted war like a mistress; if, as the drum beat to quarters, the sailors came gaily out of the forecastle,—it is because a fight is a period of multiplied and intense experiences, and, by Nelson's computation, worth 'thousands' to any one who has a heart under his jacket. If the marines of the *Wager* gave three cheers and cried 'God bless the king', it was because they liked to do things nobly for their own satisfaction. They were giving their lives, there was no help for that; and they made it a point of self-respect to give them handsomely. And there were never four happier marines in God's world than these four at that moment. If it was worth thousands to be at the Baltic, I wish a Benthamite arithmetician would calculate how much it was worth to be one of these four marines; or how much their story is worth to each of us who read it. And mark you, undemonstrative men would have spoiled the situation. The finest action is the better for a piece of purple. If the soldiers of the *Birkenhead* had not gone down in line, or these marines of the *Wager* had walked away simply into the island, like plenty of other brave fellows in the like circumstances, my Benthamite arithmetician would assign a far lower value to the two stories. We have to desire a grand air in our heroes; and such a knowledge of the human stage as shall make them put the dots on their own i's, and leave us in no suspense as to when they mean to be heroic. And hence, we should congratulate ourselves upon the fact that our Admirals were not only great-hearted but big-spoken.

The heroes themselves say, as often as not, that fame is their object; but I do not think that is much to the purpose. People generally say what they have been taught to say; that was the catchword they were given in youth to express the aims of their way of life; and men who are gaining great battles are not likely to take much trouble in reviewing their sentiments and the words in which they were told to express them. Almost every person, if you will believe himself, holds a quite different theory of life from the one on which he is patently acting. And the fact is, fame may be a forethought and an afterthought, but it is too abstract an idea to move people greatly in moments of swift and momentous decision. It is from something more immediate, some determination of blood to the head, some trick of the fancy, that the breach is stormed or the bold word spoken. I am sure a fellow shooting an ugly weir in a canoe has exactly as much thought about fame as most commanders going into battle; and yet the action, fall out how it will, is not one of those the muse delights to celebrate. Indeed it is difficult to see why the fellow does a thing so nameless and yet so formidable to look at, unless on the theory that he likes it.

I suspect that is why; and I suspect it is at least ten per cent of why Lord Beaconsfield and Mr. Gladstone have debated so much in the House of Commons, and why Burnaby rode to Khiva the other day, and why the Admirals courted war like a mistress.

FRANCIS THOMPSON

1859–1907

THE WAY OF IMPERFECTION

Ovid, with the possible exception of Catullus, is the most modern-minded of Latin poets. It is therefore with delight that we first encounter his dictum, so essentially modern, so opposed to the aesthetic feeling of the ancient world, *decentiorem esse faciem in qua aliquis naevus esset.* It was a dictum borne out by his own practice, a practice at heart essentially romantic rather than classic; and there can therefore be little wonder that the saying was scouted by his contemporaries as an eccentricity of genius. The dominant cult of classicism was the worship of perfection, and the Goth was its iconoclast. Then at length literature reposed in the beneficent and quickening shadow of imperfection, which gave us for consummate product Shakespeare, in whom greatness and imperfection reached their height. Since him, however, there has been a gradual decline from imperfection. Milton, at his most typical, was far too perfect; Pope was ruined by his quest for the quality; and if Dryden partially escaped, it was because of the rich faultiness with which Nature had endowed him. The stand made by the poets of the early part of this century was only temporarily successful; and now, we suppose, no thoughtful person can contemplate without alarm the hold which the renascent principle has gained over the contemporary mind. Unless some voice be raised in timely protest, we feel that English art (in its widest sense) must soon dwindle to the extinction of unendurable excellence.

The elementary truth of Ovid's maxim it is scarcely requisite to uphold. We have yet to see the perfect faces that are one half so attractive as the imperfect faces. Can any reader tolerate the novelistic heroine with the Greek features and the exquisitely chiselled nose? The hero invariably marries her instead of the other young lady (whose nose is perhaps a trifle *retroussé*), in every respect more charming, who misses him simply through this essential note of a heroine.

Would, however, that the thing stopped here. This vicious taste for perfection is the fruitful parent of unnumbered evils. It is difficult to calculate the ravages caused by the insane passion. We will say this—that a man who once indulges in it never knows where he may end. At first, perhaps, he will content himself with spiritual perfection; but the fatal craving, once established, demands continually fresh gratification. He presently begins to find fault with Nature, and to desire an unimpeachably artistic house; insensibly he forms an addiction to the sonnet, and thence glides into the research of orbed perfection in his jokes; by degrees he even comes to admire the paintings of M. Bouguereau, and so to the final abomination of the camellia and the double dahlia. We would not be thought to denounce *ex cathedra* the wish for religious perfection. Abstractly it is harmless enough; but we should be careful how we allow ourselves even these innocent gratifications, they are often the first step on a course of unconscious declension which we shall regret all our after-lives. It is this which sometimes causes secular poets after a time to write distinctly inferior religious verse; under the impression, apparently, that secular poetry is an error of youth which must be expiated in maturity, and that only by direct consecration to religion can their art give glory to God. As if the flower could not give glory to God, until it abnegated its fragrance; as if the clouds of sunset could not give glory to God, until they had been passed through a bleaching-vat; as if the bird could not give glory to God, until it selected its airs from the diocesan hymnal! Over the whole contemporary mind is the trail of this serpent perfection. It even affects the realm of colour, where it begets cloying, enervating harmonies, destitute of those stimulating contrasts by which the great colourists threw into relief the general agreement of their hues. It leads in poetry to the love of miniature finish, and *that* in turn (because minute finish is most completely attainable in short poems) leads to the tyranny of sonnet, ballade, rondeau, triolet, and their kin. The principle leads again to aestheticism, which is simply the aspiration for a hot-house seclusion of beauty in a world which Nature has tempered by bracing gusts of ugliness. And yet again, by a peculiar refinement of perversity, it leads to the desire for perfect wives; though wherefore a man should desire a perfect wife it is indeed difficult to conceive—Why, he has to live with her! Now does any one seriously long to companion a 'Treatise on Spiritual Perfection' bound in cloth—with the additional privilege of paying for the rebinding?

Returning to literature, however, let us consider more particularly the iniquity of this cult in generating the hero and heroine; who spring merely from the ambition to draw perfect characters—an ambition fatal to lifelike rendering. The most nobly conceived character in assuming *vraisemblance* takes up a certain quantity of imperfection; it is its water of crystallization: expel this, and far from securing, as the artist fondly deems, a more perfect crystal, the character falls to powder. We by no means desire those improbable incongruities which, frequent enough in actual life, should in art be confined to comedy. But even incongruities may find their place in serious art, if they be artistic incongruities, not too glaring or suggestive of unlikelihood; incongruities which are felt by the reader to have a whimsical hidden keeping with the congruities of the character, which enhance the consent of the general qualities by an artistically modulated dissent; which just lend, and no more than lend, the ratifying seal of Nature to the dominating regularities of characterization. From the neglect of all this have come the hero and the heroine; and of these two the heroine is the worse. In most cases she is not a woman at all, but a male dream of a woman.

Among all prevalent types of heroine, *the* worst is one apparently founded on Pope's famous dictum,

> Most women have no characters at all—

a dictum which we should denounce with scorn, if so acute an observer as De Quincey did not stagger us by defending it. He defends it to attack Pope. Pope (says De Quincey) did not see that what he advances as a reproach against women constitutes the very beauty of them. It is the absence of any definite character which enables their character to be moulded by others ; and it is this soft plasticity which renders them such charming companions as wives. It may be so. And it may be paradisaical bliss to have a wife whom you can cut out on a paper pattern. Personally, we should prefer to keep a dog ; it would be less expensive. But possibly all these things are so ; and we address our remarks to De Quincey, therefore, with diffidence. Nor do we mean them to have more than a generic application : we are by no means of that influential class who think that the Almighty creates men, but makes women—as they make sausages. Still, we are inclined to fancy that you take outward pliability and the absence of imperiousness for lack of essential character. Now to execute your determination by command you must have a position of command ; the lever requires a fulcrum. Without this position you must either maintain an isolated, futile obstinacy, or be content to sway not by bending, but by manipulating, the will of others. It is, we think, the pleasanter way, and we are not sure that it is the less effectual way. Partly by nature, partly by the accumulative influence of heredity, partly perhaps by training, it is the way which instinctively commends itself to most women. But because in the majority of cases they accommodate themselves to male character and eschew direct opposition, it by no means follows, if our view be correct, that they forgo their own character. You might as well accuse the late Lord Beaconsfield of being wanting in character, because instead of hurling his ideas against an unstormable opposition he tactfully and patiently insinuated them. We should be inclined to say that the feminine characteristic which De Quincey considered plasticity was rather elasticity. Now the most elastic substance in Nature is probably ivory. What are the odds, you subtle, paradoxical, delightful ghost of delicate thought, what *are* the odds on your moulding a billiard ball? Watching the other day an insect which betrayed a scientific curiosity with regard to our lower extremities, we signified to it our inhospitable disposition by poking it with a stick. Never did we see such a plastic insect. Curling up into a little black-brown pellet, it lay so motionless that we thought it dead; but in a few moments it slowly uncurled, and after a period of cautious delay resumed its advance. Four times was this repeated, and on each occasion the advance was resumed as if never resisted. Then patience gave way. The insect was sent rolling into a little hole, where it lay curled up as before. For twenty minutes by the clock it remained still as death. Death, indeed, we thought had this time certainly overtaken it, and with a passing regret for our thoughtlessness we forgot the tiny being in thought. Tenderer were its recollections of us. When we awoke to consciousness it had resumed its crawling. If this be plasticity, then many women *are* plastic—very plastic.

An embodiment—or enshadowment—of the villainous saying which De Quincey thus approves, is that favourite creation of fiction which finds its most recognizable (because extremest) expression in Patient Grizzel and the Nut-brown Maid. Does any one believe in Patient Grizzel? Still more, does any one believe in the Nut-brown Maid? Their descendants infest literature, from Spenser to Dickens and Tennyson, from Una to Enid; made tolerable in the poem only by their ideal surroundings. The dream of 'a perfect woman nobly planned' underlies the thing; albeit Wordsworth goes on to show that his 'perfect woman' had her little failings. Shakespeare was not afraid to touch with such failings his finest heroines; he knew that these defects serve only to enhance the large nobilities of character, as the tender imperfections and wayward wilfulnesses of individual rose-petals enhance the prevalent symmetry of the rose. His most consummate woman, Imogen, possesses her little naturalizing traits. Take the situation where she is confronted with her husband's order for her murder. What the Patient Grizzel heroine would have done we all know. She would have behaved with unimpeachable resignation, and prepared for death with a pathos ordered according to the best canons of art. What does this glorious Imogen do? Why (and we publicly thank Heaven for it), after the first paroxysm of weeping, which makes the blank verse sob, she bursts into a fit of thoroughly feminine and altogether charming jealousy. A perfect woman indeed, for she is imperfect! Imogen, however, it may be urged, is not a Patient Grizzel. Take, then, Desdemona, who is. That is to say, Desdemona represents the type in nature which Patient Grizzel misrepresents. Mark now the difference in treatment. Shakespeare knew that these gentle, affectionate, yielding, all-submissive and all-suffering dispositions are founded on weakness, and accordingly he gave Desdemona the defects of her qualities. He would have no perfection in *his* characters. Rather than face the anger of the man whom she so passionately loves, Desdemona will lie—a slight lie, but one to which the ideal distortion of her would never be allowed to yield. Yet the weakness but makes Shakespeare's lady more credible, more piteous, perhaps even more lovable, because more human. And Shakespeare's knowledge is borne out by the experience of those best qualified to speak. Woman is not, as a Shakespearian maxim belied by Shakespearian practice asserts, 'a dish for the gods an the devil dress her not.' She is a dish for men, and if she be imperfect the devil has little to do with it. Indeed we are sorry that Shakespeare stooped to this kind of thing. He might have left it to inferior men.

From the later developments of contemporary fiction the faultless hero and heroine have, we admit, relievingly disappeared. So much good has been wrought by the craze for 'human documents'. But alas! the disease expelled, who will expel the medicine? And the hydra perfection merely shoots up a new head. It is now a desire for the perfect reproduction of Nature, uninterfered with by the writer's ideals or sympathies; so that we have novelists who stand coldly aloof from their characters, and exhibit them with passionless countenance.[1] We all admire the representations which result: 'How beautifully drawn! How exactly like Nature!' Yes, beautifully drawn; but they do not live. They resemble

[1] We will not shield ourselves under generalities. We refer especially to Mr. Henry James.

the mask in 'Phaedrus'—a cunning semblance, *at animam non habet.* The attitude of the novelist is fatal to artistic illusion: his personages do not move us because they do not move him. Partridge believed in the ghost because 'the little man on the stage was more frightened than I'; and in novel-reading we are all Partridges, we only believe in the novelist's creations when he shows us that he believes in them himself. Finally, this pestilence attacks in literature the form no less than the essence, the integuments even more than the vitals. Hence arises the dominant belief that mannerism is vicious; and accordingly critics have erected the ideal of a style stripped of everything special or peculiar, a style which should be to thought what light is to the sun. Now this pure white light of style is as impossible as undesirable; it *must* be splintered into colour by the refracting media of the individual mind, and humanity will always prefer the colour. Theoretically we ought to have no mannerisms; practically we cannot help having them, and without them style would be flavourless—'faultily faultless, icily regular, splendidly null.' No man will drink distilled water; it is entirely pure and entirely insipid. The object of writing is to communicate individuality, the object of style to adequately embody that individuality; and since in every individuality worth anything there are characteristic peculiarities, these must needs be reproduced in the embodiment. So reproduced we call them mannerisms. They correspond to those little unconscious tricks of voice, manner, gesture in a friend which are to us the friend himself, and which we would not forgo. Conscious tricks of habit, it is true, a person must avoid, because they become exaggerations; similarly, conscious mannerisms must be pruned, lest *they* become exaggerations. It is affected to imitate another's tricks of demeanour: similarly, it is affected to imitate another's mannerisms. We should avoid as far as possible in conversation passing conventionalities of speech, because they are brainless; similarly, we should avoid as far as possible in writing the mannerisms of our age, because they corrupt originality. But in essence, mannerisms—individual mannerisms, are a season of style, and happily unavoidable. It is, for instance, stated in the lately completed *Encyclopaedia Britannica* that De Quincey is not a manneristic writer; and so put the assertion has much truth. Yet he is full of mannerisms, mannerisms which every student lovingly knows, and without which the essayist would not be our very own De Quincey.

We say, therefore: Be on your guard against this seductive principle of perfection. Order yourselves to a wise conformity with that Nature who cannot for the life of her create a brain without making one half of it weaker than the other half, or even a fool without a flaw in his folly; who cannot set a nose straight on a man's face, and whose geometrical drawing would be tittered at by half the young ladies of South Kensington. Consider who is the standing modern oracle of perfection, and what resulted from *his* interpretation of it. 'Trifles make perfection, and perfection is no trifle.' No; it is half a pound of muscle to the square inch—and *that* is no trifle. One satisfactory reflection we have in concluding. Wherever else the reader may be grieved by perfection, this article, at least, is sacred from the accursed thing.

Now, how much of all this do we mean ?

Hearken, O reader, to an apologue. Once on a time there was a hypochondriac, who—though his digestion was excellent—believed that his delicate system required a most winnowed choice of viands. His physician, in order to humour him, prescribed a light and carefully varied diet. But the hypochondriac was not satisfied.

'I want to know, doctor,' he said, 'how much of this food really contributes to the building up of my system, and how much is waste material ?'

'That,' observed the sage physician, 'I cannot possibly tell you without recondite analysis and nice calculation.'

'Then,' said the hypochondriac, in a rage, 'I will not eat your food. You are an impostor, sir, and a charlatan, and I believe now your friends who told me that you were a homoeopath in disguise.'

'My dear sir,' replied the unmoved physician, 'if you will eat nothing but what is entire nutriment, you will soon need to consult, not a doctor, but a chameleon. To what purpose are your digestive organs, unless to secrete what is nutritious, and excrete what is innutritious ?'

And the moral is—no. On second thoughts our readers shall have a pleasure denied to them in their outraged childhood. They shall draw the moral themselves. He that hath understanding, let him understand.

MARY COLERIDGE

1861–1907

TRAVELLERS' TALES

THAT the spring is the season for wandering, who that has ever understood the signs of the times will doubt? The winter is housekeeping time—housekeeping time in town, if possible—with fires and lamps and books. The summer is garden time, among the roses and strawberries. The autumn is too sad to think about at all. But the spring is the time to wander. 'Try something new!' says the old earth, and puts out all her new flowers and leaves to tempt us, and to fill us with strange melancholy, that is more than half longing—a kind of home-sickness for distant lands. The very air tells us, in soft balmy whispers, how the myrtles and orange trees are blossoming over the sea; the swallows come again, from far, far away, 'und ich, ich schnüre den Sack und wandere.'

> Once more the Heavenly Power
> Makes all things new.

The old earth has something of the tenderness and beauty of a young mother.

There are few things more delightful than travelling, to those who really enjoy it. But people are born travellers, as they are born poets, painters, and musicians. 'Thursday's bairn hath far to go,' says the old rhyme, and Thursday's bairn, and Thursday's bairn only, enjoys it. Some men might go from the world's beginning north (I do not know why, but I am quite sure the world began north) to the world's end south, and never get out of England the whole time. For unless you travel in the spirit as well as in the body, you get but a little way; and there are people (*Prue and I* for example) who, scarcely stirring from their own fireside, have yet gone further than many a ''mercial' that knows *Bradshaw* by heart. Even an undeveloped genius for travelling will do wonders. What did not the hero and heroine of *Their Wedding Journey* accomplish, by the mere determination to treat their native land as if it were a foreign country?

What fine fellows are the great explorers, from Columbus to Greeley! With what magnificent chivalry do they go forth to fight the sun, the sea, the snow, that they may win new lands, new light for the world! My lady Science hath her martyrs among them, not saints indeed, but men as grand, as brave, and as enduring. The traveller is certainly not a martyr; yet doth he feel a little sting of the same spirit within him, and his small discoveries are to him an America. For to travel anywhere intelligently is to discover for yourself, if not for any one else; and the Undiscovered Country lies not only in the heart of Africa, nor round about the Poles. Who, for instance, discovered Yorkshire before Charlotte Brontë?

There are people who ought to be paid to travel, they do it so well. Miss Bird[1] is one of these.

[1] Now, however, this lady has a more than dangerous rival in the author of *A Social Departure*. The vivid, yet reposeful effect of certain aspects of Eastern colouring,—the freshness and the familiarity of certain aspects of Eastern life,—are described with still greater delicacy in a small, unpretending volume, recently published, called *Pilgrims in Palestine*.

She is such excellent company in Japan, that we could almost find it in our hearts, even at the end of her two fat volumes, to wish she had stayed there a month longer. Hers are no sentimental journeys; she does not burst into lyrics, and nobody ever tries to murder her; but she has good eyes, and she uses them. And then Miss Bird is such a charming name for a traveller! Fate clearly had something to do with it. Heresy though it be to say so, her travels are much better reading than Goethe's. The strange influence that Italy exercised over him is to be learnt from other sources; but if he fled to her like a lover, he described her like the coldest of connoisseurs. He—and George Eliot after him—seem to have been afflicted with a tendency to rival the best Guide Books in their possession, that is perfectly maddening. If it were not for *Kennst du das Land*, and for the pictures of Florence in *Romola*, they certainly might have been paid to stay at home. One sighs to think what poor Frau von Stein had to wade through, every time that she got a letter. Heine, on the other hand, was an ideal traveller. Perhaps the nightingales sing a thought too often, and the moonlight is now and then excessive, but still his is the magic music, and whither he goes we follow him, as the children followed the Pied Piper of Hamelin. Some people, in whom one would have suspected the latent traveller, disappoint one terribly. Of this number is Hawthorne, whose notebooks are redeemed from the utter flatness of Goethe's and George Eliot's only by those occasional odd touches that make everything that he wrote characteristic. What does he think of in the Louvre? He does not seem to care for one of the great pictures. He passes 'Mona Lisa' by—'Mona Lisa,' whom he alone of all men, since Leonardo, could have understood. Instead, he fancies grimly, what a scene there would be, if all the dead came back to claim his or her own relic —the dagger, the bracelet, the brooch,—from its particular glass case.

French, Germans, Americans see things with very different eyes. Kinglake is the most English of travellers. The chivalry, the detestation of humbug, the quiet, practical, foolhardy courage of a typical English gentleman, are all represented in *Eothen*. Who that has ever read that wonderful book, can forget the whirl of feeling about the Virgin Mary,—the passing of the other Englishman on camel-back, in the desert, without a word,—the wilful risk of life, merely for the excitement of staying in a plague-stricken city? These things are, in their way, national. Perhaps only the English can understand them. Laurence Oliphant, at his best, gives one the same delightful sensations.

'There is a sense, of course, in which all true books are books of travel.' So writes the traveller, whom, of all others, he that goes forth with eyes eager to see, would choose for his companion. Modestine was a happy animal, if she had but known it. *Treasure Island* is a good book, but some people would give ten *Treasure Islands* for one *Inland Voyage*. It seems almost a pity, that any one who can describe real life thoroughly well should ever do anything else. There are so many who can fly—a little; so few who know how to walk, or how to manage a boat in print. Here is at last a writer of fiction, whose journeying is something more than an inferior episode in his novels.

He is himself his own best hero ; we would rather know what he thinks and feels, we would rather hear what grieved, amused, endangered him, than anything else that he can tell us. Dickens, who could make a hero, tragic or comic, out of any one, had not this faculty, or had it not in perfection. In the Italian notes, for instance, we cannot but feel that he would rather be telling, and we would much rather be hearing, a story. Either he bored himself, or else he did not pay us the compliment of being quite frank with us, and put on spectacles, when he wanted to see things for the public. So, too, Scott's diary, deeply interesting when he speaks of himself in private, becomes positively dull when he takes a voyage—I suppose, because he then wrote consciously for others.

Stevenson is very matter-of-fact about his mental experiences. Apparently—

> He thinks it something less than vain,
> What has been done, to do again.

All roads, it is said, lead to Rome ; but Robert Louis's do not. He goes to odd little out-of-the-way places, and he goes in queer ways of his own, that are not in the least dangerous or extraordinary, but only very amusing. He takes a donkey or a canoe. The deliberate cheerfulness with which he surmounts every difficulty rises unconsciously to the level of courage, and the reader is surprised and altogether delighted to find that, while he thought he was merely laughing, he is really admiring. And then Stevenson has plucked out the heart of the matter. 'To travel hopefully,' says he, 'is better than to arrive.'

ALPHABETICAL LIST OF AUTHORS